SOLDIER
SECRETARY

SOLDIER SECRETARY

Warnings from the Battlefield & the Pentagon about
AMERICA'S MOST DANGEROUS ENEMIES

CHRISTOPHER C. MILLER

with Ted Royer

CENTER
STREET

Nashville • New York

Center Street
Hachette Book Group
1290 Avenue of the Americas, New York, NY 10104
centerstreet.com
twitter.com/CenterStreet

First Edition: February 2023

Center Street is a division of Hachette Book Group, Inc.

The Center Street name and logo are trademarks of Hachette Book Group, Inc.

The publisher is not responsible for websites (or their content) that are not owned by the publisher.

The Hachette Speakers Bureau provides a wide range of authors for speaking events. To find out more, go to www.hachettespeakersbureau.com or call (866) 376-6591.

Library of Congress Cataloging-in-Publication Data
Names: Miller, Christopher C., 1965- author. | Royer, Ted, author.
Title: Soldier Secretary : warnings from the battlefield & the Pentagon about America's most dangerous enemies / Christopher C. Miller, with Ted Royer.
Other titles: Warnings from the battlefield & the Pentagon about America's most dangerous enemies
Description: First edition. | Nashville : Center Street, 2023.
Identifiers: LCCN 2022042116 | ISBN 9781546002444 (hardcover) | ISBN 9781546002468 (ebook)
Subjects: LCSH: Miller, Christopher C., 1965- | United States. Department of Defense—Officials and employees—Biography. | United States—Military policy—History—21st century. | National security—United States—History—21st century. | United States—Politics and government—2017-2021. | Afghan War, 2001-2021—Personal narratives, American. | United States. Army. Officers—Biography. | United States. Army. Special Forces—Biography.
Classification: LCC E897.4.M55 A3 2023 | DDC 355.6092 [B]—dc23/eng/20220902
LC record available at https://lccn.loc.gov/2022042116

ISBNs: 978-1-5460-0244-4 (hardcover), 978-1-5460-0246-8 (ebook)

Printed in the United States of America

LSC-C

Printing 1, 2022

WITH GRATITUDE AND HUMILITY TO:

My family

The Special Forces regiment (the Green Berets)

Those that didn't come home from our wars

Our servicemembers still on their journey back

The families and loved ones that gave their treasure in the pursuit of peace during my time as the leader of the United States Department of Defense:

Captain Seth Vandekamp (U.S. Army)

Chief Warrant Officer 3 Dallas Garza (U.S. Army)

Chief Warrant Officer 2 Marwan Ghabour (U.S. Army)

Staff Sergeant Kyle McKee (U.S. Army)

Sergeant Jeremy Sherman (U.S. Army)

Sergeant Major Michaela Tichá (Czech Army)

Lieutenant Colonel Sébastien Botta (French Army)

De Oppresso Liber

—CHRIS MILLER

For John and Dillon and the heroes of Generation X.

—TED ROYER

CONTENTS

Introduction
ix

CHAPTER ONE
On the Outside Looking In
1

CHAPTER TWO
Management vs. Labor
25

CHAPTER THREE
"Huge Times for Huge Men"
45

CHAPTER FOUR
Beyond Thunderdome
65

CHAPTER FIVE
"I Can't Believe We're Really Doing This"
87

CHAPTER SIX
The Price We Pay
111

Contents

CHAPTER SEVEN

The Deadliest Enemy

137

CHAPTER EIGHT

Jackpot

157

CHAPTER NINE

The Soldier Secretary

181

CHAPTER TEN

"The Capitol Has Fallen"

205

CHAPTER ELEVEN

A New Way Forward for America

227

ACKNOWLEDGMENTS

253

INDEX

257

INTRODUCTION

At 3:44 p.m. on January 6, 2021, I was sitting at my desk in the Pentagon holding a phone six inches away from my ear, trying my best to make sense of the incoherent shrieking blasting out of the receiver. House Speaker Nancy Pelosi was on the line, and she was in a state of total nuclear meltdown.

To be fair, the other members of Congressional leadership on the call weren't exactly composed, either. Every time Pelosi paused to catch her breath, Senator Mitch McConnell, Senator Chuck Schumer, and Congressman Steny Hoyer took turns hyperventilating into the phone.

Two hours earlier, a crowd of Trump supporters had unlawfully entered the Capitol. Congressional leadership had been swept away to a secure location at a pre–Civil War era Army installation less than two miles away. As Acting Secretary of Defense, I was across the river at the Pentagon, speaking to them by phone and watching the mayhem play out on my TV screen.

Pelosi demanded that I send troops to the Capitol *now*. The irony wasn't lost on me. Prior to that very moment, the Speaker and her Democrat colleagues had spent months decrying the use of National Guard troops to quell left-wing riots following the death of George Floyd that caused countless deaths and billions of dollars in property damage nationwide.[1] But as soon as it was her ass on the line, Pelosi had been miraculously born again as a passionate, if less than altruistic, champion of law and order.

When I could finally wedge a comment in, I pointed out that I had already ordered the complete mobilization of the District of Columbia National Guard and that forces were on their way to the Capitol as soon as they were properly equipped and synchronized with the Capitol Police.

At this point in time, I had been President Donald Trump's Acting Secretary of Defense for approximately two months. I had known when I took the job that it was going to be wild. But I never could have imagined anything like this—getting reamed out by a histrionic Nancy Pelosi and Mitch McConnell as they implored me to send troops to forcibly expel a rowdy band of MAGA supporters, infiltrated by a handful of provocateurs,[2,3] who were traipsing

---

[1] David Welna, "Don't Send U.S. Military to Protests, Hill Democrats Warn Trump," NPR, June 2, 2020, https://www.npr.org/2020/06/02/868338367/dont-send-u-s-military-to-protests-hill-democrats-warn-trump.

[2] Larry Celona, "Two Known Antifa Members Posed as Pro-Trump to Infiltrate Capitol Riot: Sources," *New York Post*, January 7, 2021, https://nypost.com/2021/01/07/known-antifa-members-posed-as-pro-trump-to-infiltrate-capitol-riot-sources/.

[3] Alan Feuer and Adam Goldman, "Among Those Who Marched into the Capitol on Jan. 6: An F.B.I. Informant," *New York Times*, September 25, 2021, https://www.nytimes.com/2021/09/25/us/politics/capitol-riot-fbi-informant.html.

through the halls of the Capitol, taking selfies, and generally making a mockery of the entire institution.

As a lifelong soldier who had spent nearly 24 years in Special Forces, I'd been in my share of shitstorms. I had been among the first Green Berets on the ground in Afghanistan after 9/11. I'd dodged bullets, grenades, missiles, and mortars in Iraq. I'd captured genocidal war criminals in Bosnia with the CIA. I'd hunted down the world's most dangerous terrorists as director of the National Counterterrorism Center. But I had never seen anyone—not even the greenest, pimple-faced 19-year-old Army private—panic like our nation's elder statesmen did on January 6 and in the months that followed.

For the American people, and for our enemies watching overseas, the events of that day undeniably laid bare the true character of our ruling class. Here were the most powerful men and women in the world—the leaders of the legislative branch of the mightiest nation in history—cowering like frightened children for all the world to see.

Do I blame a bunch of geriatrics for acting like a bunch of geriatrics? Of course not. But do I judge them for it? You're damned right I do. Most of all, I resent that we are ruled by a bunch of geriatrics that ruthlessly and selfishly maintain their hold on power and refuse to develop the next generation of leaders.

In the military, stress becomes hardwired into your cerebral cortex. It's always there, and you either learn to live with it, or you don't live. And you sure as hell don't run away when you've got a job to do.

That's what I learned from my dad and uncles as a kid growing up in Iowa. They survived the Depression, fought in World War II and Korea, then raised their kids to be patriots in the maelstrom of the Vietnam era. All of the adults I grew up around were tough as nails, and they taught us to be just as tough.

At family get-togethers, the typical topic of conversation was ass-kicking. I would routinely overhear crazy stories about my dad's service in Korea, or an uncle rolling 55-gallon barrels of gasoline into caves to burn out the Japanese.

Their conversations absolutely petrified me—yet I was enthralled. To this day, some small part of me wonders whether I joined the Army out of a desire to live life like they did—on the edge, in the crosshairs, serving the nation they loved on one death-defying adventure after another. I've collected a few of my own crazy stories over the years, which I'll happily share in the pages to come.

Unlike the typical book written by retired military men, this is not a book of recycled policy prescriptions or repackaged "lessons in leadership." This is the story of one soldier's rise from a private in the Army Reserve to the highest office at the Pentagon. It's about the heroes I fought alongside in Iraq and Afghanistan who didn't live to tell their tales, and the sacrifices my generation has made on behalf of our nation. It's about the rank-and-file troops I humbly served as Acting Secretary of Defense, who bestowed on me an affectionate nickname: the "Soldier Secretary." This book is also about our country, and how our military, our institutions, and our leaders failed to change in the decades following September 11, 2001—and how we *must* change in the future if America is to survive.

The battles I've fought at home and abroad have left me profoundly worried for our nation's future. Yet I am not without hope. I believe we can save America from the self-anointed experts who have led our country into one disastrous war after another. All it takes is a little common sense, and common sense is one thing our elites have yet to take from the American people.

In the pages that follow, I won't make myself out to be some kind of flawless superhero who always did the right thing. I made plenty of mistakes, as both a soldier and a public servant, and I'll do my best to give you an honest picture of people and events as I saw them.

I'm not looking to gain the plaudits of a national security establishment that has spent the last two decades losing wars in the Middle East. I'm not looking for fame or fortune or a lucrative deal as a talking head on cable news. Other than my family and a handful of friends, I don't give two shits about what anybody thinks of me.

I profoundly dislike talking about myself, and I am the first to acknowledge that anything I accomplished was because of others. I have always viewed myself as just a guy doing his job and trying his best to serve his family, nation, and God with dignity, empathy, and honor.

I have written my experiences and thoughts simply to help the American people make sense of this brief, but likely important, period of American history that we find ourselves living through, and perhaps, to help us find our way forward. And, just maybe, some 14-year-old kid in the Middle West like I once was will be inspired to serve and contribute to this incredible experiment that is the United States of America.

SOLDIER SECRETARY

CHAPTER ONE

ON THE OUTSIDE
LOOKING IN

The Vietnam War was the background noise of my childhood in Delaware and Iowa. Every night, the TV was an endless stream of stories about battles and killing and death and protest. The draft was still going on, and I just assumed I would join the Army and go to war. I used to lie awake in bed at night trying to figure out how to get out of it.

But when your dad and uncles are a bunch of hard-assed combat veterans in the 1970s, learning to be a man means facing your fears and overcoming them, so that's what I had to do. In my circle of rambunctious teenaged friends, the code we lived by was "Manliness or death." An *interesting* life—not a long or comfortable life—that was what mattered.

When I was 14, Iranian revolutionaries overthrew the Shah, stormed the American embassy in Tehran, and took our diplomats hostage. The story captivated the nation for months, and my group of friends in particular. This wasn't supposed to happen to Americans—our people were the ones who liberated the oppressed, not the ones who begged to be rescued. Finally, President Jimmy Carter authorized a rescue mission. It was a disaster. I felt personally humiliated. On April 25, 1980—one day after the failed rescue attempt—I decided to join the Army.

As soon as I graduated from high school, I walked into the post office and went upstairs to see the Army recruiter.

I figured you just showed up and signed a form, then they shipped you off to some kind of troop replacement depot where you got a uniform and started marching around and shit. Bing, bang, boom.

The recruiter glanced at my paperwork and tossed it back. "Need your parent's approval." Oops. As a 17-year-old, I could volunteer to kill people as long as my parents were cool with it. No biggie. I returned the next day with a signed permission slip.

My recruiter picked me up early Sunday morning and delivered me to the bus station. I always walked briskly past the bus station because that's where strange people congregated and weird stuff happened. Only vagrants and hippies and hobos rode Greyhound buses, in my mind. And now I was one of them. I had packed a lovely Case brand fixed blade knife that I had purchased from the True Value hardware store, where I worked part time, just in case.

I assumed I'd be dropped off at a barracks and greeted by a shouting drill sergeant as we scurried off the bus. Instead, I was shuttled to a Marriott hotel in Des Moines and issued my first roommate. He was why I packed my Case knife. He was in his 20s, *clearly* enjoyed using drugs, and didn't seem mentally stable—definitely the kind of guy who rode Greyhounds. I lay awake clutching my knife the entire night. But hey—at least I was finally seeing the world and meeting interesting people!

The next day, we went to Camp Dodge. I got my physical and took the Armed Services Vocational Aptitude Battery (ASVAB)—basically, the military version of an IQ test—then reported to my career counselor, who asked me what I wanted to do in the Army.

"I just want to be in the Army," I said. Everything I knew about the Army was distilled from the stories recounted by my dad and uncles, all of whom were combat soldiers. I had no idea there were other jobs available.

"Yeah, I got that, but what do you want to *do* in the Army?" asked the befuddled sergeant. "You have a super high ASVAB score. You can do anything you want—intelligence, communications, engineers?"

"I want to carry a gun," I said. "Go on patrols. You know, be a soldier."

The sergeant realized that Christmas had come early: Here was an above average yet totally clueless recruit that he could jam into whatever quota hole was dogging him that month. And that month, like every month, the most difficult quota to fill was for the Infantry.

Nobody volunteered for the Infantry. To many career soldiers or those who join to gain a marketable skill, the Infantry is the worst job in the Army. You're always outside, dirty, and tired, and if war breaks out, there's a good chance you'll end up dead. I knew none of this at the time. I didn't even know there was an alternative.

"Miller, I can't make any promises, but I'll see what I can do. Go sit in the waiting area." He was the quintessential used-car salesman wearing down his prey. Six hours later, I was the last recruit in the building when he called me back into his office with "some really great news."

He told me that a kid from Minnesota had broken his leg and couldn't go to Fort Benning for Basic Training. I could take this newly available slot, but only if I signed the enlistment contract *right now*—it was a limited time offer! If he had asked me to hand over $19.95 for the privilege, I would have gladly done so.

I paused as I put pen to paper—"Hey, I want to be a paratrooper too. Can I do that?"

"Sure thing, Miller," he replied with a grin. "Just ask them when you get to Fort Benning." And I believed him.

I had a bit of a problem though—I had to get rid of my Case knife. After busting my ass to pay for such a pretty blade, I sure as hell wasn't going to let Uncle Sam confiscate it. I sauntered outside and surveyed Camp Dodge. I found some loose earth near a lone tree, and buried it wrapped in a pilfered black garbage bag. Years later, I went back and recovered it, still in perfect condition.

A few days later, I arrived at Fort Benning, Georgia, and was greeted by a swirling swarm of screaming banshees. I remember hearing once that psychologists determined that one's personality is set by the age of 14, and the only way to change it is through a "significant emotional experience." In 1983, when I attended Basic Training between my senior year of high school and freshman year of college, it definitely succeeded in providing that significant emotional experience.

The days of beating recruits senseless had passed, but the drill instructors were still allowed to inflict enormous physical and emotional stress. No one forgets their first 24 hours of Basic Training. It is a kaleidoscope of pain, suffering, exhaustion, and fear. It was designed to weed out the weak and to instill physical and mental toughness in those who remained. But the stress was calibrated carefully to avoid a mass exodus—it was the rite of passage required to form a new value system.

It was during Basic Training that I first realized I had an above-average capacity for pain, thanks to random luck in the genetic lottery and the example set by my Mother, the most physically and mentally toughest person I know. Apparently, I also possessed above-average smarts—relatively speaking. I've never considered myself the smartest guy in the room, except during Basic Training.

The regimen hadn't changed much since World War II. A task was presented with the conditions and standards announced. For instance, "During this block of instruction you will learn to employ the M47 Dragon Anti-tank Missile. You will perform this task in battlefield conditions in under five minutes." Screwups were met with increasing levels of physical discipline—primarily push-ups—to allow the recruit the opportunity to "refocus" before receiving remedial training.

Like the rest of my generation, I'd been an unknowing lab rat for the experimental educational approaches born in the 1960s, with self-paced learning and an unhealthy obsession with self-esteem. At the time, the Army's approach seemed antiquated and barbaric to me. In hindsight, I now realize it was brilliant. If you plopped an M47 Dragon Anti-tank Missile in front of me today, I could put it into opera-tion. This is what the Army does best. Everything our public schools have forgotten, the Army remembers.

Even though it was against the law by the early 1980s, some judges still gave delinquent young men the choice of joining the Army or going to jail. It was viewed as a win for everybody—the community got rid of a troublemaker, the Army gained another warm body, and the "volunteer" got a healthy dose of discipline and a chance to become a con-tributing member of society.

My bunkmate, a sinewy, hollow-eyed Tennessean who reminded me of a character in *Deliverance* and seemed prone to psychopathic behavior, was one of many such cases. He had decorated his bony knuckles with a delightful jailhouse tattoo: *F U C K* on the four fingers of his right hand; *Y O U !* on his left. On the off chance that was too subtle for you, he'd fold down his lower lip to reveal the same message. I had no idea there were so many uses for those crappy dis-posable ink pens!

Needless to say, Private Fuck You! and I did not become best friends, but we did learn to rely on one another. No recruit was capable of meeting the two-minute standard for making our bunks. After multiple failed individual attempts, our disgusted drill sergeant informed us that we were complete dumb shits and the only way to succeed was by using the buddy system. Private Fuck You! and I became partners to avoid the disgrace of failure. That's another thing the Army does well—it has a way of tearing down barriers between people, including the barriers you'd rather leave up.

I had always been an average student in school—I did the minimum required to avoid an ass-chewing. But compared to my bunkmate and many others in my cohort, I was a genius. If you paid attention and did a bit of homework (which was required anyway), you could excel and earn rewards like additional specialized training, advanced promotion with higher pay, and extra time off. The Army's incentive system was the ultimate meritocracy: If you got the job done, you were rewarded. It didn't matter if you were a middle-class kid from Iowa or an illegally paroled ex-con. All that mattered was performing, and it was extremely effective motivation.

I finally figured out that I might have an affinity for this military thing on one brutally hot afternoon in July 1983, four weeks into the eight-week ordeal of Basic Infantry Training. We had marched out to a sandy training area nestled in the pine wasteland and were greeted by a sergeant standing on an elevated platform. We knew he wasn't a drill instructor because he wasn't wearing a Smokey the Bear hat. Rather, he was a subject matter expert who was responsible for teaching us a yet to be described martial task.

The sergeant was thin, gangly, and well over six feet tall, with the kind of sinewy leanness that denotes a metabolism working overtime due to severe hyperactivity. I couldn't tell his ethnicity—he seemed to be everything and nothing at once. But his defining and most distracting feature was the pencil-thin mustache that crept perfectly along his upper lip. It wiggled and danced as he chain-smoked Kools,

spellbinding you as he strode confidently across the platform like Genghis Khan surveying his cavalry.

As we sat at his feet, raptly waiting to gather the crumbs
of wisdom that fell from his table, Sergeant Pencil-Stache
proceeded to unleash the most blasphemous, outrageously
profane, scatological tirade I had ever heard. We learned
intimate details about every sexual encounter he ever had.
We learned about the differences in genitalia of every ethnicity, and what our mothers enjoyed in the bedroom. He
clearly reveled in having a captive audience.

After some time, he finally revealed that we were going
to learn how to put on our protective masks. He talked us
through the process in painstaking detail, though it was
actually quite simple. When you heard someone shout
"Gas, gas, gas" or the sound of banging metal, you completed a 10-step process that culminated in moving out of
the area with your protective mask securely attached.

We practiced until the sun began to drop, when our drill
instructors blessedly reappeared and ordered us to march
back to the barracks. Once we were breathing heavily and
the sweat was flowing freely, a billowing gray cloud began
to envelop us. Someone yelled, "Gas, gas, gas" and we all
scrambled to complete Steps 1 through 10.

With my mask quickly secured, I could see phantom-
like figures scurrying and scattering in every direction until
I was alone. I crested a hill and was met by several drill
instructors who pulled me off the road and announced,
"All clear." Over the next 15 minutes, 138 recruits staggered up the hill in various degrees of distress. Their eyes
were red and swollen and full of panic. Their sinus cavities
had voided, and snot sloshed across their faces. Some were

vomiting profusely. Others had abandoned their weapons, and many had lost their helmets.

We had just been subjected to our first simulated gas attack. Only two of us out of 140 had kept our cool and passed the test. Maybe, I thought, this was something I could be good at. And if not, it would probably still make for an interesting story.

When I entered Ranger School in 1988, it was the equivalent of the Navy's Top Gun, but without the screaming F-14 Tomcats, Tom Cruise, or the ambiguously gay locker room machismo.

Ranger School was eight weeks of starvation, sleep deprivation, torture, and abuse unlike anything I had experienced. Only one in three students completed on the first try. It was merciless. I had absolutely no idea if I would pass the test, and to this day, I'm still surprised that I did.

Any time I feel like I suck or have let down the people I care about, I reach deep into my closet and pull out a midnight black sweatshirt that I've had for years. It hasn't pilled or shrunk or faded. I put it on, and I instantly feel stronger and more confident. It has one word emblazoned on the front in gold: RANGER.

I absolutely thrived in Ranger School. Finally, I was doing the type of stuff I joined the Army to do.

Many of our instructors had served as Infantrymen in Vietnam. They were distinguished by the unit patch they wore on their right sleeve. But more distinctively, they wore the Combat Infantryman Badge (CIB) over their right breast pocket.

In the panoply of military awards, decorations, and

accoutrements, none rated higher in our young minds than the CIB. It was nothing more than a four-inch-long musket surrounded by a wreath, but to us, it was everything. It announced that you had engaged in close combat with an armed opponent. The CIB gave the wearer instant credibility. When they spoke, we hung on their every word.

The CIB was created during World War II when the generals realized that without some form of recognition for the "poor, bloody infantryman" who carried the burden of the war and suffered horrendous casualties as a result, the Army risked a collapse of morale. Infantry units were eviscerated fighting in Western Europe. It was common for units that landed at Normandy on D-Day to consist of 90 percent replacements several months later. The answer was to follow Napoleon's maxim and give them a piece of ribbon. Earning that piece of ribbon—leading men into combat—was the singular focus of our existence.

I had heard my father's and my uncles' criticism of those who panicked or froze or hid in battle—their stories were forever ingrained in my mind. The endless stream of movies and TV shows about the Vietnam War always had a character that couldn't hack it. My greatest fear, a fear that kept me awake at night, was that I would fail in the trial of combat—or worse, that I would never get my chance.

I was determined to find out as soon as possible whether I was made of the same stuff as my dad and uncles. In 1987, the only place you could find the answer to a question like that was in South Korea—specifically, the Demilitarized

Zone (DMZ) that divided the communist North from the democratic South after the 1953 armistice. My dad fought in Korea. I studied Korean in college and spent time learning about the culture and history. I was determined to go to Korea. I just had to find a way to get there.

In the Army's infinite wisdom, I had been assigned to Germany. For most aspiring career soldiers, Germany was the premiere assignment. The Cold War was still raging, and staring down the Red Army was a great résumé builder. But Infantry in Germany were mechanized, which meant they drove around in lightly armored vehicles to support the tanks that were the arm of decision. Fat and lazy dudes loved mechanized infantry because they always had heat, a dry place to sleep, and never had to walk. I *despised* those fat pogues. And anyway, Europe was never going to see any real action. The stakes were too high, and everyone had too much to lose. But the North Koreans might be crazy enough to roll the dice.

In 1987, the Army was still operating on the General Motors industrial philosophy of the 1950s—a production line system cranking out identical parts that could be inserted into any product at minimal cost and effort. I quickly surmised that, as a widget, all I needed to do was find an officer in my class who would trade me Korea for Germany. The military machine would swap our numbers and the balance sheet would be unaffected. As luck would have it, an ROTC classmate had a degree in German history and an assignment in Korea. It didn't take much convincing. I shipped off to the Second Infantry Division in Korea on Memorial Day in 1988.

SOLDIER SECRETARY

* * *

I was assigned to the 1st Battalion, 506th Parachute Infantry Regiment—nicknamed the "Currahees" after the Native American peoples who once populated Georgia and highlighted in Stephen Ambrose's *Band of Brothers*. We were stationed at Camp Greaves on the sliver of land between the Imjin River and the DMZ in Korea, making us the most forward-deployed Infantry battalion in the free world.

Our motto was "Be Ready to Fight Tonight," and we were. Every bridge was rigged with explosives for rapid destruction. Most hills were bisected with trench lines. Our machine gun positions were studded with range cards, which showed the distance to various points of the terrain to ease target acquisition of the charging North Korean hordes. For me, it was paradise.

I learned I would be the night watch officer in the Tactical Operations Center—the field command and control node for the battalion commander. Early on, I got my bearings from Second Lieutenant Russ Howe of New Jersey, the day watch officer who preceded my arrival by four weeks.

Howe regaled me with gossip about our battalion commander, Lieutenant Colonel Mitchell "Mick" Zais. Zais was military royalty. His father, Melvin, fought in World War II and was lauded as the ideal Army officer: tough and skilled in combat, but also erudite and intellectual. He retired as a four-star general, the highest rank in the Army.

Zais the Elder was well-known as the commander of the storied 101st Airborne Division during the infamous Battle of Hamburger Hill in Vietnam. Over the course of a week, the 101st Airborne Division waged a brutal frontal assault on heavily fortified enemy positions, finally capturing the strategically worthless mountain after suffering appalling casualties, only to abandon it weeks later. The epic fight is rightfully remembered as a testament to the toughness of the United States Infantry. But it also illustrates the futility and stupidity of the American strategy of attrition in Vietnam, as well as the inability of our leaders to change course once the strategy had clearly failed.

One night, Howe told me something I hadn't heard about Zais the Elder. Mutiny is as old as armed conflict, but in Vietnam the practice of soldiers murdering their officers for actual or perceived incompetence became widespread enough to gain the appellation "fragging," after the use of fragmentation grenades for such purposes. Howe told me that soldiers collected a pot of money to be awarded to the one who killed Zais for his conduct at Hamburger Hill.

Fearing the worst, the authorities promoted Zais to three-star general and shuttled him off to a higher command to save him from imminent danger. I had no idea if the story was apocryphal, exaggerated, or true, but it marked the birth of my awareness, which has only grown in the intervening years, that many leaders at the highest echelons of power have reached their lofty stations by failing upward.

Zais the Younger was neither hated nor loved. After graduating from West Point, he did six months as a platoon leader in Vietnam, the minimum amount of time required to receive credit for a combat tour, and then was moved to a staff officer position. Some noted that he wore no Silver Star, an award for heroism that adorned the uniforms of platoon leaders that had seen intense combat. After

Vietnam, Zais followed the path of many up-and-comers by getting his master's degree and teaching at West Point.

Lieutenant Colonel Zais's academic bent followed him to Korea, and he loved giving writing assignments to his junior officers. Zais would give you an article or book excerpt, and you were required to provide a two-page review the next day.

It didn't take long to figure out that Zais always agreed with the thesis of each reading assignment, and the least painful approach was to agree with the author, give an example of how Lieutenant Colonel Zais exemplified the characteristics embodied in the reading, and move on.

I never did that. My peers reveled in the sea of red ink that blanketed my critiques of well-worn military doctrines, theories, and strategies. It became something of a game to see how much I could infuriate my battalion commander—but I was also simply writing what I believed to be true.

But when we weren't pissing away time on high school homework assignments, there was plenty of real work to be done. For three months in the brutally cold winter, we were the unit responsible for patrolling the U.S. section of the 180-mile DMZ and manning two combat outposts to prevent North Korean infiltration. We stared at the Potemkin Village to the north in amazement at the lengths the regime went to provide a facade of strength, power, and prosperity. We went on combat patrols that were planned in microscopic detail and carried live ammunition—the only soldiers in the world to do so at the time.

That yearlong tour in Korea sticks with me. One year in Korea was the equivalent of three years based in the United States. We worked six days a week, spent a huge amount of time in the field, and there were no families or distractions.

I still keep up with a bunch of the lieutenants I served with. I never served in a better unit. We were all alone up there north of the Imjin. We knew that if the shit hit the fan, no one was coming to get us. We'd have to rely on each other, fighting in the most desperate operation of all—"Die in Place." We'd do it. Together.

And then the Berlin Wall came down. In the blink of an eye, the Cold War was over. America stood atop the world as the lone Superpower. All our enemies were vanquished. History, we were told, had ended.

Euphoria swept across the country, and indeed most of the Western world. I was happy too, of course—who wouldn't be?

But if I'm honest, there was another part of me—the soldier part, the part that wanted to prove himself—that was disappointed. More than anything else, I just wanted to know if I had what it took to be a real combat soldier. With the Cold War over, how could I ever discover what I was truly made of?

Yet peace had come at the perfect time in my personal life. While serving in Korea, I had gotten engaged to a woman named Kate back home. Kate and I had been dating for three years. I met her in the common kitchen area of my junior-year dorm at George Washington University. Her self-confidence and poise, as well as her ravishing good looks, enthralled me. I began arranging excuses to bump into her regularly. We became friends. Her upbringing in

West Hartford, Connecticut, life experiences, outspoken-ness, and razor-sharp intellect captivated me. She was the most amazing and beautiful person I had ever met. Over the months, as we got to know each other, I broke down her resistance and we began dating. Our relationship survived the separations inherent to the itinerant Army life I chose, and she agreed to go all in during a visit to Korea for my mid-tour leave in 1988. I asked her to marry me (after getting her mom's approval) in my Quonset hut room at Camp Greaves on the DMZ. Her stunned reply was, "This is serious." We were married about a year later. The end of the Cold War was a blessing, because it meant I wouldn't be living in the field at the start of my married life.

Traditionally, officers returning from Korea got to pick their next assignment. Naturally, that tradition ended while I was in Korea. General Maxwell Thurman, an Army legend known for solving major problems by relentlessly driving his subordinates, had taken over the Army's Training and Doctrine Command (TRADOC).

TRADOC was responsible for all Army training, and Thurman quickly recognized that he had a dearth of talent. Unlike the U.S. Marine Corps, which assigned only its best officers to initial entry training units, the Army relied on third-rate officers that couldn't cut it in the operational formations. Thurman knew the only way to improve Army training was to first improve the trainers. Thus, he ordered all lieutenants returning from Korea be assigned to Basic Training units. The lot I drew was the Air Defense Artillery (ADA) School at Fort Bliss, near El Paso, Texas.

But I was an Infantry Officer. I *loathed* ADA even more than the mechanized infantry. If you were assigned to air defense, you sat around twiddling your thumbs waiting to fire missiles at waves of enemy aircraft that never materialized. I'd lose my mind from boredom.

I had good reason to think so. Back in 1986, I'd spent four weeks as an ROTC (Reserve Officer Training Corps) intern lieutenant with an ADA unit at Fort Bliss. It was a complete shit show. I had shown up to the battery headquarters to the scene of a uniformed woman chasing a terrified man in civilian clothes down the hallway; she was screaming obscenities and threatening to murder him. He was her Platoon Leader, and he'd been banging her best friend. Every day there was full of chaos and drama.

I only had one other option: the 3rd United States Infantry Regiment (The Old Guard) at Fort Myer, Virginia. All I knew about The Old Guard was that it was a ceremonial unit that buries the fallen at Arlington National Cemetery and guards the Tomb of the Unknown Soldier. As it turned out, Mitchell "Mick" Zais's brother was about to take command of The Old Guard, and my old battalion commander was downright thrilled to arrange my assignment there. In hindsight, I can't help but wonder if this was his revenge for my being a consistent pain in his ass.

I clearly had no idea what I was getting myself into. I was standing in the basement of a warehouse, pushing two grocery carts down a long line of counters. Every few feet, someone would hand me another stack of clothing to put in my cart: green uniforms, dress blue uniforms, a saber, shoes, and hats with patent leather bills. It was the finest quality, made of wool and natural fibers instead of the polyester crap I had worn up to that point. It was interesting, but perplexing—why did I need all this stuff?

The further I went, the stranger it got. Now I was being handed an assortment of what looked like continental-era uniforms—a long blue coat, frilly white shirt, tricornered hat, leather belts of various colors and lengths, old-fashioned black leather shoes, knee-high socks, and off-white wool tights.

The guy behind the counter smiled at the confusion on my face. "Alpha Company—Commander in Chief's Guard—right?" he asked. "Yeah, Alpha Company," I replied.

"You'll need this too," he said, holding out not one, but two white powdered wigs.

I stood there paralyzed with fear, struggling to make sense of what was happening, like a shell-shocked soldier depicted in a bad war movie. Then the horrible truth swept over me: I'm in the company that dresses up in period costumes and marches around with muskets in parades. I'm a historical reenactor. An embarrassment. A joke. A fucking toy soldier.

I took the wigs and stumbled with my gear toward the door.

"Hey, don't forget to grab a couple of hairnets for your wigs on the way out!"

Every aspect of my job was humiliating. Status in The Old Guard was based on appearance, showmanship, and the ability to stand motionless for long periods of time without passing out. Having a loud voice was crucial, so you could impress observers with your crisp and audible commands on the parade field.

Even the leadership elements were embarrassing. You had to inspect your men to ensure they were wearing their hairnets properly—otherwise, the ponytail on their wigs might come undone during a ceremony. You also had to make sure everyone was wearing underwear. At evening ceremonies with the sun setting behind you, your tights would become translucent, and the younger guys thought it was funny to show off their junk.

Since I was 6'4" and slim, I was selected for service as the Cordon platoon leader in the company that conducted the highest visibility ceremonies. The only requirement to be in the Cordon Platoon was to look somewhat physically impressive. We served as the photo backdrop for VIP visits to the White House. I would be the first military officer the VIP would see when driving onto the White House grounds or entering the building. The route would be lined with a member from each service spaced in a visually appealing and militarily precise manner.

My mission—the sole reason for my existence—was to raise the tip of my saber in salute to the approaching dignitary, and then drop it at the exact moment the VIP's vehicle or outstretched foot drew even with me.

I am not making this up. Mission success for 1st Lieutenant Christopher C. Miller, 2nd Platoon, E Company, 3rd United States Infantry Regiment (The Old Guard) was dropping my saber at the precise moment the VIP bisected the right angle in which I stood. And then I was done. Mission accomplished.

SOLDIER SECRETARY

I couldn't believe how far I had fallen professionally in just a matter of months. I'd gone from crossing the Han River in amphibious landing craft and conducting combat patrols hoping to shoot North Korean infiltrators to being a background extra in some low-budget made-for-TV movie.

More than the fat-ass in the mechanized infantry, more than the air defense artillery guy sitting around playing solitaire, the person I despised most in the U.S. Army was me. At least the other guys were actual soldiers. I was a Christmas decoration—a nutcracker that collected dust on a mantle for a few weeks every winter. It did not fill my heart with Christmas cheer.

For State Dinners at the White House—the big soirees where very serious people discuss very important topics while sipping champagne—I'd typically be the senior military officer from The Old Guard. The higher ranks, understandably, didn't want to stand around for the four-plus hours from the entry ceremony to the VIP's departure.

Winter events were especially brutal and reminded me of freezing my ass off back in the DMZ. We had no warming tent and couldn't return to our bus because it was parked too far away.

Instead, we huddled outside the ornate frosted windows in our ridiculous costumes, shivering like a band of vagrants while inside the fire roared, toasts were made, and world leaders laughed and made the decisions that would chart the course of days to come.

There was no martial virtue in being a toy soldier. I was in hell and on my knees praying for a savior.

But I never thought it would be Saddam Hussein. In one of history's most epic strategic miscalculations, Mr. Hussein decided that the end of the Cold War was an auspicious time to recoup some of the costs of his destructive and expensive decade-long war with Iran. It was just Kuwait, a tiny appendage that no one cared about. Quickly grabbing his neighbor's oil fields would be a fait accompli, and no one would be the wiser.

What Saddam didn't realize was that the end of the Cold War created new pressures on America's large standing military and the defense contractors that relied on it. Some politicians were talking about delivering a "peace dividend" to the American people by rapidly reducing the number of active-duty troops. To the military-industrial complex, and most especially to the neoconservative movement ascendant in the first Bush Administration, this was a disaster to be avoided at all costs.

President George H. W. Bush and National Security Advisor Brent Scowcroft couldn't have asked for a better alignment of interests and constituencies to advance their vision of a new world order. This was the first test—would the world be divided by tribal concerns, or would the community of nations join together to overturn Saddam's blatant act of aggression?

And it was going to be a big war. Colin Powell put 250,000 GIs into the region and then doubled it. What was Saddam thinking? His timing couldn't have been worse. Over the preceding half century, the United States had spent hundreds of billions of dollars to create the most lethal fighting force in the history of the world—and now it had nothing to do.

The actuarial tables predicted significant casualties. This was going to be a real war, not some contingency operation like Grenada or Panama. After so many years of waiting, it looked like I'd finally get my chance to fight.

But soon the word came down that no one in The Old Guard was going overseas. Our mission would be to bury those Killed-in-Action. Our services were needed at home.

I immediately requested reassignment to the Middle East, but without my colonel's approval, I wasn't going anywhere. After several attempts, I was called to the regimental headquarters for an audience with the deputy commander, Lieutenant Colonel John Shortal.

Shortal had been my Battalion Executive Officer at the 1/506th in Korea. I idolized him. He was the Patton-like counterbalance to our effeminate battalion commander. Shortal had a PhD in history and taught at West Point. He'd written a book on General Robert Eichelberger, an obscure figure who served under the megalomaniacal Douglas MacArthur in the World War II Pacific theater. Now he was back in the field.

Shortal was a real ass-kicker. He camouflaged his intellect behind a stream of profanity and invective that would have horrified the nuns at his parochial school in New Jersey. His genius was that he always let you in on the joke. He'd tear into you with a volcanic tirade highlighting the enormous shame and embarrassment your dereliction of duty had brought on the United States Army, then punctuate it with a wink or friendly pat on the shoulder.

"Hey, Chris, I'm with you. I'm trying to get over there too. I'll sign it," Shortal said. What more could you ask for? Shortal saved me from eternal embarrassment and shame. I was finally on my way.

Thankfully—for our nation, if not for me—the war concluded after 100 hours of ground combat.

I still hadn't tested my mettle, and I was beginning to consider myself a failure as an Infantryman. I knew that our nation typically engaged in serious warfare once a generation. I'd missed my generation's war and needed to come up with an alternate plan if I was going to continue serving in the Army. I'd read about Army Special Forces as a kid—maybe I could give it a try. If it didn't work out, I could always be a cop back in Iowa City.

CHAPTER TWO

MANAGEMENT VS. LABOR

Compared to the horrors of Ranger School, Special Forces training was a breeze. I was assigned to the 5th Special Forces Group (5th SFG) upon completion of training in 1993, and I spent three years at Fort Campbell in Kentucky learning how to be a Green Beret.

The 5th SFG was comprised of a bunch of blue-collar, working-class Green Berets that disdained panache and flair—they were tough, focused, and always got the job done. I immediately felt right at home.

The character of the 5th SFG was shaped in part by the environment in which it operated, which was the desert of the Middle East. Working in very reserved Muslim societies, we couldn't go out drinking, dancing, or chasing women— all common pastimes for the groups stationed in Europe and other cosmopolitan environs. With nothing else to do, we trained religiously, perfecting our bodies, minds, and craft.

One of my first deployments was to Kuwait, where the 5th SFG had maintained a company-sized presence of six 12-soldier A Teams since the end of the 1991 Gulf War. We trained and advised the Kuwaiti Army and were prepared to fight with them if Iraq invaded again.

The Kuwaiti Army was essentially a part-time force that knocked off at 1100 daily. A typical day was a game of soccer in the morning, an hour of classroom instruction on a subject of mutual interest (such as land navigation, communications, or medical treatment), and an hour of tea.

Some team members were disenchanted with the lack of commitment and professionalism of our counterparts. I didn't care. It was their country, and if that was the effort they wanted to put into defending it, so be it. For me, the beauty of the situation was that you had unlimited training opportunities. Ammunition was plentiful, aircraft were available, and you were in the biggest desert training area in the world—all you had to do was drive out the gate and you could do whatever you wanted. There were no family distractions or pointless garrison chores. All we did was train. It was glorious.

But we had issues on the team. The younger guys, myself included, felt the older ones weren't taking things seriously. In retrospect, I realize the older guys were all combat veterans who had been on the team for 10 years. They knew what was required and didn't want to waste time on nonessential tasks. But that realization came later. At the time, I viewed the team as slothful and unfocused.

I had been the Detachment Commander—the senior officer—of the 12-soldier Operational Detachment Alpha (ODA) 573 for 10 months. I was the Team Leader responsible for everything that did or didn't happen on the A Team. The challenge of being a new commander on a Special Forces A Team in that era was that you were the youngest, most inexperienced team member. Unlike the conventional Army where you typically were better trained and a few years older than most of your subordinates, in the Green Berets, a commander might be in his late 20s while his subordinates are infinitely more experienced and pushing 40.

Most of my team members sported the Combat Infantryman Badge. I had never been in combat, yet I was the one who was supposed to remind everyone that we needed to focus and sacrifice and endlessly train to prepare for combat. It was like being a professional football coach having never played the game. And in Special Forces, you can't impose your will through intimidation or by pulling rank. Success requires building trust slowly and deliberately. Every action is analyzed and parsed for meaning and potential. You are the one who ultimately controls their safety, future, and life, and they want to know your character, intellect, weaknesses, and strengths.

In many ways, Special Forces is also borderline anti-authority. It's been said that the only thing that distinguishes an A Team from a biker gang is discipline and a veneer of legitimacy. Special Forces are essentially the alternative high school for the Army. Those drawn to its ranks typically have a great deal of discipline and passion, and they are smarter than the average soldier. They study military manuals and hit the gym while other soldiers go out drinking. They loathe artificially imposed hierarchies and frivolous displays of bravado and ceremony. Competence and commitment, not punditry and pedantism, are the attributes that matter.

Soldiers are drawn to Special Forces (SFs) because it provides a culture that embraces the same rugged individualism that is disdained, quite necessarily, by the conventional Army. And that's the genius of Army Special Forces—for those who feel stifled in the conventional Army, it provides a place they can thrive.

An A Team wants a commander that makes good decisions, listens to their concerns, and will have their back when higher headquarters is out hunting for an ass to chew. Martinets can be successful in the conventional Army, but they aren't tolerated on an A Team. Officers who carry themselves with an air of superiority based on their education or experience will often find their personal effects piled in the hallway outside their team room—an unspoken but unmistakable sign that they have lost the confidence of their men. This bottom-up evaluation and culling process makes sense—you can't lead men if they won't follow—but it would never be tolerated in the conventional Army.

The challenge for new SF commanders is to earn the respect of your team so that they will, in fact, follow you into battle. But there is a fine line between being the Team Leader and being the Team Mascot. Some new A Team commanders, in their efforts to win acceptance, focus too much on being *part* of the team rather than *leading* the team. They strive to be "one of the guys" rather than a boss that sets and enforces high standards and ruthlessly pursues improvements.

This is the trap I fell into as a young commander. By the time we got to Kuwait, the members of ODA 573 considered me their Team Mascot. I had done nothing to distinguish myself as their leader, and our A Team was unremarkable as a result.

*   *   *

I needed to toughen up the team, and I needed to toughen up as their leader. I knew that changing the status quo would require a shock to the system. To bring the team together, I needed to manufacture a crisis that we could overcome as a team. So in secret, I developed a training mission, briefing only the Company Commander, Al Knox. I scripted the whole thing down to the minute. It was going to be hard, and it was going to feel real, because no one would know it was a training exercise. I was going to find out who was who.

At 3:30 p.m. on the designated afternoon, the company headquarters called and directed our communications man to be prepared to receive secure message traffic in five minutes. I was intentionally out for a run because I wanted to see how the team would react without me present. The encrypted message directed the team to execute our escape and evasion (E&E) plan—without vehicles.

Detailed E&E planning is a pillar of Special Forces, which typically operate in politically fragile environments where the situation can deteriorate rapidly. For instance, the government could decide that it no longer wanted to partner with the United States, or like Afghanistan in 2021, it could be overthrown by hostile elements. In the Special Forces vernacular, such an event is categorized as "losing rapport." Prior to going on a mission, the warrant officer, who is the second-in-command of the team, studies the environment and develops an intricately detailed plan for how the team will escape the area. The precise route, rest locations, and hide sites are all mapped out. Signals noting the team's location and condition are prepared for display to aircraft and satellites in case all radio communication is lost.

In the best-case scenario, the team moves a short distance and is picked up by a helicopter or small plane. But the E&E plan is designed to cover the worst-case scenario and includes routes to the nearest friendly country. Every member of the A Team is supposed to memorize every aspect of the E&E plan. In reality, most of them are too busy preparing for the actual mission to give the E&E plan anything more than a cursory glance. This was the case with my A Team, and I knew it.

I always took E&E planning very seriously. Some people are terrified of drowning or burning to death; my night terrors involve dying of thirst in the desert. I had heard the stories of the Strategic Reconnaissance teams discovered by Iraqi forces behind enemy lines during Operation Desert Storm. Solid E&E plans had turned certain disasters into narrow escapes, but those events still scared the hell out of me.

Being in the Kuwaiti desert—my first time in the region—confirmed my suspicion that there was no place to hide. If you got your vehicles shot out from under you, as routinely happened with the British Long Range Desert Group and Special Air Service in North Africa during World War II, you needed to have a plan to move overland to a recovery location. But every time we discussed an E&E plan, I felt like my men were humoring me. Our briefings would be punctuated with a few quiet sighs and discreet eye rolls. "We'll never do dismounted E&E in Kuwait," they must have thought. "We own the country."

I returned to our headquarters about 30 minutes after

the alert came in. The place was a beehive of activity, but I could tell most team members suspected this was some bullshit exercise. I had to up my game. I called higher headquarters and had a terse conversation with the company commander. I paced back and forth with pursed lips and furrowed brow, doing my best to seem genuinely concerned to the men I knew were watching my every move. I hung up the phone and announced that this was not a drill and that we needed to discreetly leave the camp, move to the location designated in our E&E plan, and establish secure communications to receive further instructions. My third-rate acting seemed to help, but they weren't yet fully sold.

Then a sergeant walked up to me with an armful of explosives and informed me that he was ready to blow up all of our vehicles to prevent them from falling into enemy hands. Giving him the green light would definitely convince the team that this wasn't a drill, but needlessly destroying a million dollars' worth of equipment for a training exercise is the kind of thing the Army typically frowns on. I bullshitted my way out of the predicament. "Mark, do we really want to destroy all of our vehicles? Won't that alert the Kuwaitis that something is going on? And what if we have to come back and mount up?" Instead, I ordered him to disable the vehicles by removing a few small engine parts and burying them nearby in an ammo can.

As we concluded our preparations, I upped the ante by giving the order to break out the live ammunition and prepare a basic load of 210 rounds for each rifle. Everyone stopped in their tracks, and I could see their lingering doubts dissipating further from their sweaty faces. In peacetime, you are prohibited from carrying live ammunition, except on a rifle range. I didn't have approval to authorize my team to carry live ammo, but it was a stupid rule, and I knew that dramatically ignoring it at this moment would help sell my deception.

At last light we moved through the camp's gate, chambered a round into our M16 rifles, and tried to disappear into the desert. I say we "tried" to disappear, because it was impossible while carrying our 140-pound backpacks (called rucksacks in homage to our German ancestors) stuffed with food, water, ammunition, radios, batteries, signaling devices, and light sleeping bags. This was the load dictated in the E&E plan that specified down to the toothbrush what each person carried. I suspected the weight would crush us—and, in fact, that was one of the things I wanted to learn from the exercise.

After 15 minutes, we conducted a "SiLLS" stop, the first halt during a patrol when everyone stops, looks, listens, and smells for several minutes to adjust our senses to the environment. After lying quietly for several minutes, adjustments are made to equipment and clothing while the leaders convene in the center of the perimeter to review the map and plan next steps. The consensus was still that the whole exercise was bullshit contrived by the company commander to show off to the visiting battalion commander. But at least I had convinced them that I wasn't part of the conspiracy.

When those initial tasks were completed, we hoisted our rucksacks onto our backs and began moving to the designated location to set up radio contact with higher headquarters. The distance was about five kilometers. A human being in decent physical condition can walk one kilometer at a normal pace in the desert in about 15 minutes. With 140 pounds on your back, it takes about an hour.

It's difficult to describe just how soul-crushing such a burden becomes. We began our journey at a moderate pace in a dispersed wedge formation to guarantee that all sectors around us were observed. In the movies, patrols always move stealthily and in perfect formation. We lasted about an hour. By the second hour, we had morphed into a long column of stumbling soldiers soaked with sweat and cursing under their breath. By the third hour, discipline had broken down and many on the team were loudly cursing higher headquarters.

I worried we might be on the verge of a mutiny, but I kept quiet. And then, completely unplanned, a flight of U.S. Air Force jets streaked low overhead toward Iraq. As if on cue, they hit their afterburners, lighting up the night sky like the Fourth of July. We had not seen such a large group of planes during our deployment. Something must be happening, the men declared. The bitching stopped.

We reached the designated location around midnight. The moon provided a bit of illumination and a welcome degree of clarity—it's positively miserable trying to set up a radio in the pitch dark. An A Team has two radio men, each of whom has mastered the full spectrum of radio technology. They are often the smartest guys on the team, by necessity, because their job is most essential to the survival of a Special Forces team operating alone.

When deployed, an A Team makes two "comms shots" per day with higher headquarters, during which they might ask for instructions, provide a situation report, or request resupply. The 15-minute time windows are strictly observed. Frequencies were changed regularly for security purposes, requiring customized antennas cut to specific lengths. Code words were established. Specific locations for making comms shots were chosen to provide a degree of concealment from visual and technical observation. And all of this had to be memorized prior to departure. Radio men studied the frequency charts, distances between radio stations, and weather forecasts with Talmudic intensity.

All of us were cross-trained in communications, but in truth, we were completely at the mercy of the comms men. They knew everything there was to know about wave propagation theory, antenna theory, and meteorology. As far as we knew, *FM* stood for "Fucking Magic." The pressure on the radio magicians was intense. When they pressed the transmit key and whispered the recipient's call sign into the microphone, our ears attained bionic listening power, scouring the air like a satellite dish for the reply from higher headquarters. If nothing was heard after several tries, stress levels began to rise quickly.

Connections would be checked, batteries replaced, calculations reviewed, and the process repeated. It was not uncommon to miss a comms window altogether. Everyone understood the difficulties, but a missed window was still a sledgehammer to team morale. Work priorities shifted to charging batteries with a demonic hand crank system, designing additional antennas, securing higher ground for broadcast, or doing whatever the hell the comms specialists needed done.

Everything now rode on making the second comms window. If you missed again, higher headquarters would immediately start a series of actions to try to find you.

Worse, they notified *their* higher headquarters, and you never want that type of attention. The radio guys would lamely offer that clouds or sunspots or some other wizardry were creating too much interference. Exchanges grew terse and unfriendly: "I don't give a fuck about sunspots—are you kidding me? *Sunspots*?! You two better get this shit straightened out ASAP!"

It was horribly unfair, but that was the nature of the business. The crazy thing was that communications problems oftentimes *were* the result of atmospheric conditions or solar activity. But it didn't matter—if you missed your comms windows and were listed as missing, you were a shit Team Leader. You were in charge of training the team members, planning the operation, and rehearsing and developing responses to every conceivable contingency. If you didn't make comms, you were a failure, pure and simple.

Fortunately, our first comms shot was a success. The comms officer at higher headquarters read from the script I had provided, relaying a fake report from the Embassy in Kuwait City that there had been a military coup, possibly led by a "fifth column" of Iraqis. All Teams were ordered to initiate their E&E plan and get away from their Kuwaiti Army partners to avoid confusion and possible violence. We were instructed to move overland to a hide site, where we would await extraction.

This time, the team took the bait hook, line, and sinker. We broke out our maps and hunkered under a poncho to shield our flashlights from any prying eyes that may have been watching. Our hide site was near an escarpment several hundred feet above a six-lane highway, which separated the lower desert of Kuwait City and the upper desert that led to the Iraqi border. It was the only significant terrain feature in Kuwait. Most Americans of a certain age remember it as the "Highway of Death" during Operation Desert Storm. Fleeing convoys of Iraqi military vehicles had been decimated by the most devastating display of American aerial firepower since World War II. Nearly 2,000 Iraqi vehicles had been destroyed in roughly 10 hours, leaving behind a traffic jam of smoldering wreckage that stretched to the horizon. The killing was so dramatic that then Chairman of the Joint Chiefs of Staff Colin Powell called off the attack for fear of being accused of unnecessary and wonton destruction in violation of the Law of Armed Conflict.

We pointed ourselves to the south and staggered in the direction of the glowing lights of Kuwait City on the horizon. The Army standard for moving cross-country is to walk for 50 minutes and rest for 10 minutes, with a goal of covering between three and four miles per hour. Of course, that is while carrying a 45-pound rucksack in a normal climate. We were carrying triple the weight, and the temperature was still above 80 degrees at midnight. Perhaps there are elite units that can move in a textbook formation under such conditions, but I've never seen one.

The weight becomes excruciating. Your shoulders burn and your knees buckle with every step. Your rucksack jams your pistol belt into your back, gouging bloody trenches into your skin. It feels as if cartilage is oozing from every joint, like toothpaste from a tube. Old injuries present themselves once again, darkening your thoughts with the worry that you may be inflicting permanent injury. As light-headedness inevitably sets in from the heat and exertion, a voice in your head begins to warn that you are becoming dangerously dehydrated and might collapse from heat exhaustion at any moment. Each Green Beret is fighting multiple demons on multiple fronts, all causing doubt and a tinge of fear, all designed to convince you to stop, to rest, to give up. Your world shrinks to the ground in front of you—only the terrain beneath your next step exists, and the sound of your labored breathing. I called it "Going to my House of Pain."

Soon you see the wisdom in clichés handed down by generations of drill sergeants, like "You are only as strong as your weakest link." Who would be the first man to drop? As the hours pass, the time spent moving contracts, and the time spent resting expands until the ratio is inverted, and you are walking for barely 10 minutes before collapsing and resting for 50. You lose sense of time and place and enter a fugue state, but as a leader you are required to maintain your senses. You have to know where you are, where you are going, and the state of everyone on the team. And above all, you have to keep them moving. You become the enemy within, the one forcing everyone to continue on what they increasingly believe is a death march. And in this case, they were right to think of me in this way, for I had the advantage of knowing the whole thing was a game, that we faced no real danger, that rescue was standing by in an emergency, and knowing this gave me the peace of mind to calmly observe everyone's behavior.

To the east, we saw truck lights, though there were no established roads on our maps. During a break, the few of us who were still coherent discussed the anomaly. One of our elders offered that they were probably fuel tankers transporting oil from the refineries to sell on the black market in Iraq, which was struggling under severe international sanctions. He suggested that he and a partner could ambush a truck, detain the driver, scoop up the team, and drive us to our hide site. I admired the artfulness of his suggestion. I obviously couldn't approve it, but dismissing it out of hand risked exposing the charade. Fortunately, the team war-gamed the option for a while and decided it wasn't necessary yet but could be executed later.

At about 4:30 a.m. our Weakest Link collapsed on the desert floor and began sobbing. He looked like a dying cockroach, lying on his bulbous rucksack with his legs and arms grasping for some unseen support in the air. He was delusional and repeating that he couldn't go on. There isn't a doctrinal solution for such a situation. Do you leave him with a partner and a radio and continue with the main body? Do you call for a medical evacuation? Do you declare the training exercise over and go home?

I decided to establish a 360-degree perimeter around the Weakest Link and see what my men came up with. Soon, the two youngest and least-experienced members of the team offered to recon the area and see if they could find a place to hunker down until morning.

They planned their route, and we reviewed our contingency plans that we had memorized with the mnemonic *GO TWA*, after the now-defunct airline. G—where the patrol is going; O—others going with the patrol leader; T—time of return; W—what to do if they return and the main body isn't there, or what the main body will do if the patrol doesn't return; and A—actions the main body will take if the patrol gets in a firefight and vice versa. These were the lessons learned at great expense by previous generations of soldiers, and we abided by this routine religiously.

After only a few minutes the two-soldier patrol returned. They had discovered that we were less than a hundred meters from our designated hide site. In the days before GPS, we had no way of knowing we were that close to our objective. The false horizon created by the lights of Kuwait City had skewed our depth perception. Another couple of minutes of walking was all that was required. I felt bad for the Weakest Link. He had exposed weakness to the team when all he had to do was hold on for another few steps. It was humiliating.

We established a circular perimeter and I volunteered to take the first watch. Although I wasn't experiencing the stress of the unknown like the others, I was equally physically exhausted and fell asleep—the pinnacle of failure when on guard—but no one was awake to note my abysmal shortcoming. At sunrise, we were jolted awake by the arrival of three huge Ford F-350s with Kuwaiti Border Patrol markings. Their leader stepped down from his truck as his subordinates, all armed, took up a loose formation around him.

I was determined to keep up the not-a-drill facade until the very end. Our standard operating procedure if such an event turned hostile was that the team interlocutor would drop flat on his stomach, triggering the team to attack. I prayed to God that I didn't inadvertently stumble.

I exchanged pleasantries with the border patrol officer before explaining in a hushed voice that we were U.S. Army personnel on a desert hike. They were concerned we hadn't properly coordinated with the Kuwaiti Ministry of the Interior, and they were always on the lookout for Iraqi infiltrators. I apologized and thanked them for their professionalism as they loaded their trucks.

I turned and noticed that everyone on the team had discretely directed their rifles toward the border guards, quietly moved the selector switch from "safe" to "three-round burst," and put their fingers on the triggers. As the trucks drove off, the team erupted in euphoric shit-talking: "Sir, we were ready to smoke them!"

I was shocked at how far I had gone in my efforts to toughen up the team. I could have caused an international incident. I would have been wholly responsible: I had never asked for permission to carry live ammunition, much less to move "locked-and-loaded." And what a masterful clandestine cross-desert movement—we were easily detected by a handful of border patrol yokels. I felt like an idiot.

We made our next comms window at 0900 and were directed to move to the nearby road for pickup. Once back at Camp Doha, near Kuwait City, we were escorted into a small briefing room. This was the standard practice when returning from a mission—before you could eat, shower, or sleep, military intelligence and operations personnel conducted an extensive debriefing. The team would explain the events from beginning to end and the debriefers asked a series of questions about enemy locations, activity, terrain, weather, and illumination. From these disparate tidbits, intelligence analysts would update their files and assessments.

After 90 minutes of debriefing, we were joined by the Company Commander, Al Knox. He was genuinely loved by the men and was recognized as a competent, good-hearted commander who loved nothing more than being a Green Beret. If he never got promoted but could stay in

Special Forces, he would have been the happiest guy in the world. Knox gave a few perfunctory comments and then revealed that the entire ordeal had been a training exercise. The men erupted: "I fucking *knew* it!" "What did I tell you?"

And then came the moment of truth; the men asked: Who had designed such an infernal exercise? Who was the engineer of their suffering, and for many, embarrassment? Knox just looked at me and smiled. "It was me," I confessed. And then the room fell silent.

I walked alone to the mess hall, my mind swirling with dark thoughts. I was an embarrassment. I was a horrible commander and officer. I had totally destroyed the team I was responsible for building and protecting. I had humiliated my men, unnecessarily exposed physical and psychological weaknesses in others, and damn near caused an international incident. I felt lower than whale shit. I was worse than a loser—I was a *dangerous* loser.

I got some food and sat down. The rest of ODA 573 staggered in, still wearing their sweat-stained uniforms and exhausted expressions, their sunken eyes glaring at me. One by one, they walked past me and sat in a group at the table farthest from me. I was being publicly shunned in front of the rest of the company. People were whispering and stealing furtive glances. I crammed down some calories and ditched as soon as I could.

As I left, a Datsun pickup pulled alongside me. The window rolled down and my battalion commander, Chip Paxton, ordered me to get in. I mentally prepared myself for an ass-chewing. Instead, he asked how I was doing. "Not so good, Sir. I think I destroyed my A Team."

Paxton was a beloved commander and one of the most experienced Green Beret officers in the Regiment, having started out as an enlisted Infantryman in Vietnam. We had spent a lot of time together back at Fort Campbell. We frequently went running on Saturdays, and he would pass on lessons on leadership in his Socratic style, asking me questions about this topic or that before imparting the wisdom gained over a lifetime in the Army.

Paxton talked a lot about an officer's role in Special Forces, and he was the one who introduced me to the concept of "Team Leader" versus "Team Mascot." His mental model was simple: Officers are management; sergeants are labor. I didn't like his construct when I first heard it. It felt horribly out of date, like a throwback to the 1960s. This wasn't a U.S. Steel plant, where management wore shirts and ties, and labor wore hard hats. This was the Green Berets, where respect was earned, and hierarchy was based on performance.

But now, slumped next to him at one of the darkest moments of my military career, it finally clicked. Paxton simply said, "You're management; they're labor. Good job. Get out."

At dinner that evening, I ran into a friend who was a sergeant from another A Team. He grabbed me as I walked by and asked if I had really made my team cross the desert on an E&E exercise. I thought he might offer a few words of sympathy for my stupidity. Instead, to my unalloyed surprise, he exclaimed, "Man, that's so cool! I wish my commander would do that." Several officers offered their praise as well, and I noticed a steady flow of sergeants talking and laughing with the rest of ODA 573 at a distant table.

After dinner, we headed back to our outpost. The team's mood had improved, and there was a light-heartedness I hadn't anticipated. They were ribbing each other about things someone had said or done during the exercise, bantering and talking shit the way soldiers do after a victory. Their peers on other A Teams had been heaping accolades on them for what they had accomplished. They had achieved something distinct and meaningful and in the tradition of the Special Forces Regiment. They had earned a reputation as a tough team that trained hard and didn't screw around.

We got loaded into the truck. They sat in back. In the past, I'd always sat with them as a demonstration of my egalitarian leadership style. That evening, I sat in front with the driver. I was their Team Leader.

CHAPTER THREE

"HUGE TIMES FOR HUGE MEN"

The next two years would be the most developmentally important of my military career, thanks to a buddy who randomly popped his head into my office one day and asked me to join him at a recruitment briefing. "It's the guys from Virginia," he said excitedly. I had no idea what he meant. Since returning home from Kuwait, I had been relegated to a nightmare assignment: serving as a battalion staff officer responsible for supply to "broaden my understanding" of Special Forces. After a few weeks of managing inventory and staring at spreadsheets, I would have done anything to get back into the field.

I walked into the cafeteria where a few dozen other Green Berets were gathered, and a guy in civilian clothes announced that he would be interviewing candidates for attendance at an assessment and selection course. He offered no details about his unit, its mission, or what we would be doing. That was it. Briefing over.

I headed for the door, wishing I could reclaim the 15 minutes I had just wasted, when the briefer handed me an application. It was unlike anything I had seen in the military. The questions piqued my curiosity: "If you had the choice between going for a long run or playing flag football, what would you choose?" "Are you more comfortable working alone or with a group?" "What publications do you read regularly?"

On a whim, I completed the application and a brief interview. A few weeks later, I received an envelope with bizarre orders to attend a two-month assessment course at a Las Vegas hotel. The orders were from a unit I didn't recognize that was established in the 1980s.

Unlike the Green Berets, Navy SEALs, and other well-known Special Forces units, this was a black ops group that married intelligence-gathering operations with unconventional warfare. Basically, whenever it was too dangerous for U.S. intelligence agencies like the CIA to put boots on the ground, they sent in this unit first to gather intelligence and blaze a path for strike teams to follow. It was part cloak-and-dagger, part Rambo. It sounded unbelievably cool.

After the two-month assessment course, I was selected for the yearlong training program required for entry into the operational unit. The standards were brutal. I had never been in such an uncompromising meritocracy in my life— not even the Green Berets. Even after you were accepted to the unit, every day was a test. If you passed, you kept your job. If you didn't meet the standard, you were gone.

No exceptions. This is the type of organization I had always aspired to be part of.

Over the next three years, I honed every skill to an intensity that I never imagined was possible—medical, demolitions, surveillance and reconnaissance, communications, weapons, planning, free-fall parachuting, driving, and shooting. We were part of a renaissance in Advanced Special Operations, using the arcane skills and techniques perfected by Cold War spooks that had been largely extinguished from the Special Forces Regiment following bureaucratic turf wars within the Intelligence Community.

(Redacted by U.S. government)

In the late 1990s there wasn't much going on for my unit. The only place that could be categorized as "operational" was Bosnia, which was still recovering from a barbaric civil

war between Muslims and Orthodox Christians following the breakup of Yugoslavia. Both sides had committed
atrocities and genocide. My new unit maintained a constant presence there, monitoring the miasma of threats to
the Dayton Accords, which the Clinton Administration had
brokered to end the bloodshed. We were there as manhunt-
ers, keeping a watchful eye on the competing factions and
tracking down those indicted for war crimes.

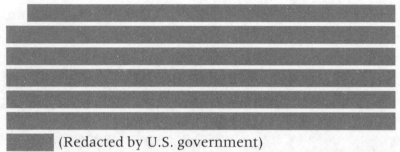

(Redacted by U.S. government)

We'd do whatever it took to get leads on targets. Once
we found them, we'd follow them for months and map out
their entire lives—where they lived, where they worked,
how they traveled, what they drank, who they loved, who
they hated, who they slept with, and what their weaknesses
were. When the time was right, a team would capture the
targets and take them to stand trial.

We worked with other members of the Intelligence
Community and applied new technologies enabled by
the burgeoning use of the internet and cellular phones
and advances in digital imaging. It was in many ways
a laboratory where the cost of failure was very low—if
your operations were compromised the only risk was
embarrassment—not incarceration or death.

I am brutally pale and, at the time, had a full head
and beard of shockingly orange hair. In the Middle East,

my genetics were a flashing neon sign that screamed "American!" But in Bosnia, I could pass as a local. It was refreshing to finally be able to move through an urban area unnoticed.

It was ridiculous how much autonomy we had, and it was completely atypical of the rest of the Army. We had unlimited amounts of money and minimal oversight. It was the definition of "big boy rules"—senior leaders provided us enormous trust, and if you violated it, you were purged in a heartbeat.

One thing you quickly master in such an environment is how to assess a different kind of risk. Unlike conventional warfare, the greatest threat wasn't a foreign army amassed on the field of battle; it was that society itself might collapse at any moment, and you would be dragged under in its wake. You didn't estimate the number of enemy soldiers hiding in the hills; you assessed how likely it was that this mob of citizens would start a revolution.

During one seemingly simple operation, I walked through the entertainment district of a small town near the Bosnia-Croatia border. I was checking on one of our targets to make sure he was at his favorite watering hole. A crowd began forming, protesting the presence of United Nations military forces. It quickly devolved into chaos, with rioters setting the UN motor pool on fire and breaking out any pane of glass they could get a rock through.

My mind instantly raced back to one of the defining events of recent Special Operations history—the vicious murder of two SOF operators in the streets of Mogadishu in 1993. I was now being pushed helplessly along by the roiling mob like a sailboat in a hurricane. Fearing that I would be identified as a foreign agent, I quickly removed my earpiece, leaving me out of radio contact and totally isolated from my team.

I also worried one of the bodies pressed against me would make contact with my concealed pistol and alert the crowd to my presence or try to grab it. I was all alone, with no support, being sucked out to sea by an uncontrollable riptide, struggling to keep my head above water. The only thing I could do was keep moving with as much confidence as I could muster, like I was a man of authority who belonged there. Hopefully, I could exploit most people's deference to the aura of authority and move through the area before being recognized as an imposter. It worked. I navigated through the town to my pickup point without further incident.

Every day in Bosnia provided another opportunity to hone new skills in a real-world situation. We developed the manhunting tactics, techniques, and technologies that would soon become commonplace for Special Operations Forces. We also developed close friendships with other Special Operations units and members of the Intelligence community and earned each other's trust and confidence. We were typically in our early to mid-30s with 10 years of service. We didn't know it at the time, but the skills we developed and the friendships we formed in Bosnia were about to be put to very good use.

After three hard years, my tour with my unit concluded. I was surprised and relieved to depart the area with my career and reputation still intact. It was an unforgiving and exacting assignment that oftentimes consumed unit leaders and I was looking forward to having a year to contemplate my recent experiences while learning about strategy and policy at the Naval War College in Newport, Rhode Island. Staff College is a yearlong master's degree program to prepare officers for higher level assignments. It was the most fertile and remarkable year of my military career. While I was there, Kate gave birth to our third and final child, which further enhanced the life-altering experience.

On July 4th, 2000, I pulled into our new house in Clarksville, Tennessee. It was the first home we ever owned, having always lived in military or rental properties. I was excited to return to take command of the Green Beret company I had served in as a Captain. By the turn of the millennium, I had miraculously been promoted to Major and was serving as Company Commander in the 5th Special Forces Group (Airborne) at Fort Campbell, Kentucky. Kate and I settled back in with our friends and colleagues with our newborn son and two elementary school-age daughters.

Kate and I had developed a lovely early evening ritual. Each night as I arrived at our house, we would have cocktails, giving us a few minutes to catch up and discuss the events of the day. The kids, then ages seven, five, and one, would be amused by the television.

Kate could measure the depth of my despair by the number of empty beer bottles on the table. Most nights, I only had one. But on Monday, September 10, 2001, I had pounded back three by the time I blurted out, "These are small times for small people." After 14 years as an Army Officer, I had decided to resign my commission and move on.

To any outside observer, I was enjoying a successful career. But that's not why I joined the Army; I signed up to go to combat. Maybe that sounds barbaric to civilized ears, but that's how soldiers think. If you're a banker, you want to close a billion-dollar deal. If you're a cop, you want to take down the mob. If you're a soldier, you want to fight— and win—the toughest battles against the fiercest enemies.

No matter what I did, I always felt like I was stuck on the sidelines. I missed out on Operation Just Cause—the 1989 operation to depose the former CIA-asset-turned-corrupt president of Panama, Manuel Noriega—because I was deployed to Korea. When the first Gulf War kicked off three years later, I was assigned to The Old Guard in Washington, DC, and the war ended before my transfer request to Saudi Arabia was approved.

I had tried. I had failed. Now I was trapped in the peace-time army, and it was suffocating. The Cold War had been over for less than a decade, but without the Soviet competition forcing the military to stay at peak performance, atrophy and complacency quickly set in. The military became consumed with bureaucratic micromanagement.

To get ahead in this system, I'd have to suppress every instinct and abandon my entire worldview. Worst of all, I'd have to pretend to care about petty chickenshit no one in their right mind should care about.

I knew myself well enough to know that if I stayed, I was going to self-destruct. I couldn't imagine myself being an honest and honorable leader in an organization I had come to abhor.

The hackneyed cliché repeated by every young soldier—"I'm going to stay in the Army until I'm not having fun"—bounced around my beer-soaked brain. I was definitely not having fun. I went to bed that night knowing it was time to leave.

The next time I saw my wife was about 11:30 p.m. on September 11, 2001. She was sitting alone in the dark watching cable news, the light from the television flickering off her teary, bloodshot eyes. My first words to her were, "These are huge times for huge men."

I didn't—and don't—claim to be one of those huge men. But my plan to leave the Army—indeed, the course of my entire life—was about to change dramatically.

"Jesus Christ, are you okay?" the goggle-clad, shirtless Marine shouted over the shrieking engines of the MC-130 transport plane.

It was December 5, 2001. Seconds earlier, I had taken my first step onto Afghan soil—straight into a foot-deep pothole. I felt something crack in my right leg, just above my ankle, and flipped ass over teakettle.

Now I was lying on my back in the middle of an airstrip in the wastelands of southern Afghanistan, staring up at the sky. Or rather, I was staring at where I thought the sky would be if the plane's engines weren't kicking up a human-made dust storm that would have impressed Tom Joad from *The Grapes of Wrath*.

Here I was, on the most important day of my professional life—my Super Bowl Sunday after a career spent on the sidelines of battle—and I broke my ankle before the opening kickoff. Of course, I didn't know how bad the break was until I got back to Kentucky four months later. For now, all I knew was that I was experiencing the most excruciating pain of my life, my mission was now going to be exponentially more difficult, every waking moment of the foreseeable future was going to suck immeasurably, and there wasn't a damn thing I could do about it.

For a moment, I gazed at the gaping maw of the transport plane, fantasizing about crawling on board and slinking away back to Uzbekistan, where we had been hours earlier. I was legitimately injured. No one would judge me. I could realistically save face. I imagined myself relaxing in a comfortable hospital bed, smiling as a pretty nurse pumped my veins full of opiates, the searing pain in my lower leg melting away as I drifted peacefully off to sleep. The whole thing probably played out in my mind in a nanosecond, but it seemed like I was in suspended animation.

"You all right, man?" the young Marine repeated as his face entered my field of view, jerking me back to reality. He was covered from head to toe with sand the consistency of talcum powder. I extended my arm for help up, but instead of grabbing it, the Marine leapt to attention and began profusely apologizing for failing to call me "Sir." I assume he saw the gold leaf on my collar that identified me as a Major, and his programming dictated that he should leave me lying in the dirt while he went through the prescribed motions of showing deference and respect. The cold heart of his Drill Instructor would have warmed with sadistic pride to see the effectiveness of his brainwashing. I might have laughed if I wasn't in so much pain. "I don't care, kid, just help me up."

We were standing on an airstrip in the middle of the desert where Middle Eastern sheiks used to land their private jets to play with their hunting falcons. It was absolutely desolate—I can't imagine the Taliban Immigration and Naturalization Service hassled them much. Special Operations Forces had christened it "Objective Rhino" when they parachuted onto it several months prior, and the Marines had since established a Forward Operating Base.

Objective Rhino was supposed to be an uneventful pitstop on our journey from Uzbekistan to Afghanistan. All we had to do was transfer our gear from the MC-130 transport plane to some MH-53 helicopters that would take us the rest of the way to Kandahar, the last stronghold of Afghan leader Mullah Omar's regime.

It didn't take Nostradamus to predict that the coming months were not going to be the height of comfort and enjoyment, especially with a broken leg. More importantly, there was a good chance I could end up very dead, leaving my beautiful bride and three young children $250,000 wealthier from my government life insurance policy, but without my sunny disposition and keen sense of humor. Even in the depths of my brutally self-sufficient, stoic, Oprah-hating psyche, I knew that by turning toward those helicopters, even if I came back, I wouldn't come back the same.

Once upright, I hobbled through the maelstrom to the helicopters where my team of 20 Green Berets were already loaded up and ready to go. Our mission was to reinforce a task force embedded with Hamid Karzai's guerilla army that had taken heavy casualties.

I crammed myself onto the jam-packed helicopter and nestled into a pile of gear at the ramp and rubbed my throbbing ankle. I had Motrin in my medical kit, but it was attached on my combat harness near the center of my back, and I couldn't contort myself to reach it. There was no point in asking for help—the helicopter's rotor was too loud. All I could remember from the endless hours of medical training over the years was, "Don't remove the boot—if you take off the boot, the ankle will swell and you won't be able to get it back on." "Screw it," I thought. "I'll deal with it later."

I knew right away that this wasn't a routine flight. The first clue was that no crew chief was yelling at us to buckle our seat belts, a cause célèbre of the bureaucratic nannies that dominated the peacetime military. The second clue was that there were no seats. You knew it was serious when the Air Force removed the seats that had been installed for pro-tection and safety during peacetime training. This was the first time I had ever been on a helicopter without seats in 18 years of military service—this was combat. Then there was the open rear ramp of the helo. Typically, the ramp would have been closed until just prior to landing, but keeping it open let us shoot out the back if we needed to.

Special Operation Forces (SOFs) pilots typically never fly during daylight to avoid enemy MANPADS (Man-Portable Air Defense Systems), which are commonly known as shoulder-fired rockets. I don't think there were any enemies with MANPADS out there, but we were all still operating with healthy Cold War paranoia that on every mountain and in every village were Soviet-trained air defense specialists waiting to launch their rockets. In reality, it was far more likely that a mujahideen would haphazardly fire one of the Stinger missiles the United States covertly supplied them for their war against the Soviets. Thankfully, we didn't see any of them either.

To minimize our exposure, the pilots flew insanely close to the ground and juked constantly just in case some smart-ass tried to take a shot at us. I kept hearing a strange cavitation sound as the helicopter blades clawed at the air. I would also feel a heaviness pushing me down as we skimmed up the knife-edge peak of a mountain, followed by sudden weightlessness as we immediately dove back down the other side. They were flying the helicopter at the absolute edge of the performance envelope.

An hour later, I limped off the helo onto an open plain near the village of Sayyd Alma Kalay. I could tell by the look on my comrades' faces that they were thinking the same thing I was: "Jesus H., we've gone back in time to the Stone Age."

We were the last handful of fighters that flew into Afghanistan before the war "ended"—or so we thought. Later, like the rest of America, we would find out that the successful invasion and conquest of Afghanistan would be retconned into merely the first phase of a permanent war. But for now, we were tasked with "unconventional warfare." It was like stepping ashore on Normandy beach at 23:59:59 on June 6, 1944: You get credit for "landing on D-Day" and can talk shit for the rest of your life, but you didn't do any of the heavy lifting. You just stepped over all the dead bodies and worried about getting sand in your boots. You felt like a complete poseur. But hey, those are the rules; I don't make them.

Rising above the village was a small hill littered by the detritus of war—bloody bandages, the smoldering hulls of pickup trucks, and military equipment. The carnage was the result of a friendly fire incident—an errant 2,000-pound Joint Direct Attack Munition, one of the largest munitions in the Air Force's inventory, had blown the place to hell. Three men from the Army Special Forces company I commanded as a 36-year-old Green Beret Major had been killed. Numerous Afghan fighters were also dead, and scores of Americans and Afghans had been wounded.

I lowered myself into the fighting position at the top of the hill. It was only once I was close to the ground that I could see what looked like raw hamburger meat scattered all around me. It took me a few seconds to realize that it was human flesh.

My path to that bomb-blasted hill began in 1993 when I tried out for Special Forces. My wife hated the idea, and she especially hated that I didn't tell her I was thinking about trying out—I just did it. I couldn't handle serving in the regular Army Infantry with the routine, the puffery, the martinets, and the mindless repetition justified as "instilling discipline." The tryout for Special Forces was a three-week freak show of mental tests, oddball scenarios, and straight-up gut checks requiring decision-making while exhausted and under extreme physical and mental duress. It really came down to not quitting—maybe not the most sophisticated process, but it was based on the British Special Air Service model and had survived the test of time.

War is never a beauty contest. When it gets really shitty (and inevitably it will get shitty—if it wasn't shitty, it wouldn't be war), mental and physical toughness can decide the outcome. If you were one of the 20 percent who passed the audition, you attended a yearlong training course that taught you to think independently, lead a small team behind enemy lines, develop cultural attentiveness, and learn a foreign language. Every day was a gut check. You never just showed up, put in eight hours, and glided home. You were evaluated either by your peers, instructors, or superiors. The strong survived, and the weak fell to the wayside.

Special Forces didn't let me down. I now thank God that our nation had such foresight to create a place for oddballs, ne'er-do-wells, borderline criminals, and those who want to serve but can't conform to the strictures of the regular Army. Special Forces provides young people the opportunity to become something more. If they withstand the mental and physical abuse, they will be entrusted with the most difficult, dangerous, and important missions. Quite simply, if it was easy or routine, someone else in the Army would do it. But at the time, I didn't really care about any of that. I was simply terrified of failing.

In late 2001 when my team and I landed in Afghanistan, we really didn't have shit for equipment. Nobody in the Army did. At the time, there was a schism in Special Forces leadership. One faction thought our raison d'être was to train ass-backward guerillas who would have shitty, antiquated gear—ergo, we should train and deploy with the same shitty, antiquated gear. The other faction believed we should have all the shiniest, newest kit to perform precision raids deep behind enemy lines á la *The Guns of Navarone*. It really didn't matter because in the 1990s there wasn't money to buy anything decent or to conduct high-tech training. So when my team and I landed in Afghanistan on December 5, 2001, we had a bunch of gear left over from Vietnam. Most of our radios, for example, were powered by rechargeable batteries that required lugging around a recharging contraption that you cranked by hand.

Since Special Forces were designed for parachuting behind enemy lines and forming guerilla bands to fight the Soviets as they rolled across Western Europe, logistics was always a primary focus. Everything you planned for was based on a mnemonic device—*PACE*—which required a plan for Primary, Alternate, Contingency, and Emergency methods. But since we were all beneficiaries of the endless munificence and bounty of the good old U.S. of A., we never really took the whole PACE thing seriously, especially for resupply. During planning it became a rote answer to your superior's questions concerning resupply: *Primary* is aerial resupply. *Alternate* is locally procured with our indigenous currency or gold Krugerrands. *Contingency* is recovery of caches stored prior to infiltration. *Emergency* is battlefield recovery (i.e., scavenging the battlefield for supplies).

But everyone knew that battlefield recovery is for poor, resource-starved, half-assed armies like the North Koreans. No American soldier, backed by trillions of taxpayer dollars, is going to have to rely on battlefield recovery, right?

My team and I went into Afghanistan with what is

known in the trade as a three-day pack. It's a light backpack with three days' worth of food, batteries, ammunition, medical supplies, socks (no other bulky clothes), and a lightweight polyester blanket called a poncho liner because it can be waterproofed with a poncho (but that's more weight/bulk, so no one ever takes a poncho—oh yeah, and we were going to the desert). I, however, detest the cold because I was raised in Iowa and spent my entire youth freezing my ass off. So I wedged a light sleeping bag into my rucksack, giving me the appearance of a vagrant. Everyone, and I mean EVERYONE, commented colorfully about the size of my rucksack and, under their breath (well, actually, it wasn't under their breath—I fucking heard them), about my seeming lack of manliness.

Our first night in Afghanistan we slept on the military crest of the hill—the area just below the top so that when you stood up you didn't silhouette yourself and get shot—peering through our night vision goggles toward the last known enemy activity. Our job was to provide early warning to the 20 or so exhausted and walking wounded Green Berets and Hamid Karzai—the warlord we were about to install as President of Afghanistan—in a schoolhouse and medical clinic to our rear.

One of the slogans repeated ad nauseam during the rebuilding of the Army in the 1980s was "train how you fight." For some reason, I really never questioned the validity of this trope. As a matter of fact, I didn't think of it as a trope but as revealed truth. One of the acid tests was staying awake when "pulling security"—aka lying on the ground or crouched in a foxhole while others slept. It was a matter of discipline to stay awake during training even when there were no enemies hunting you. But it didn't matter, because we had to "train how we were going to fight," and security was sacrosanct, which meant my dumbass fighting, and routinely failing, to stay awake while peering into the darkness fully knowing that there was no one out there.

During our first night in Afghanistan, I learned two things. First, at least in regard to pulling guard duty, "training how you are going to fight" is complete and utter nonsense: My ass was wide awake during my rotation on security. And second, I learned you should always take your sleeping bag, even when everyone makes fun of you. When I completed my two hours of guard duty with temperatures in the upper 20s, I jammed myself boots and all into my sleeping bag and drifted off to sleep to the lulling sounds of my esteemed comrades whimpering in agony. I'm a humble guy who goes out of his way to avoid making people feel bad, but, with the warming sun loosening up their frozen, stiff muscles, I might have said, "So, motherfuckers, who's the dumbass now?"

The next day, it didn't take us long to figure out that our three-day bags weren't going to cut it. One of our first tasks was to inventory all the equipment that the destroyed Special Forces A Team (officially referred to as "Operational Detachment Alpha [ODA] 574") had left behind when they were medically evacuated. Oddly, someone had piled it all in a Soviet-era communication truck. We went through their equipment and took whatever we needed.

This was the first "digital war," and looking through the digital photos of one of our killed comrades was haunting. One of my team members had been reassigned from

ODA 574 weeks prior, and his discomfort was palpable as we outfitted ourselves with the clothes and equipment his buddies left behind. I asked how he was doing. He snapped out of it and said, "They would have wanted us to take their stuff. They would have done it to us. That's how it works."

CHAPTER FOUR

BEYOND THUNDERDOME

W e stretched our cold and cramped limbs as the sun rose on our first full day in combat in Afghanistan on December 6, 2001. I had studied a little about Afghan culture and thought I knew the basics, but I realized I was in for a rude awakening when nature called that morning. As I searched for the latrine, the Afghans pointed to what looked like a wildfire lookout station you might find in a national park back home. It was a 20-foot-high wooden tower that consisted of a plank floor, railings on three sides, and one side completely open to the air, God, and anyone with functional eyeballs in their head.

This can't be real, I thought. Why would anyone go through the trouble of building a latrine tower? What was the purpose? The crap ends up on the ground anyway—why does it need to fly 20 feet through the air before splatting into its final destination? And was this a sick practical joke?

I didn't have the answer to any of those questions, and I still don't to this day. But I did know that the first Green Beret rule of building rapport with foreign forces is to avoid accidentally criticizing their culture and practices. I realized now that I had been staring at the tower for a good 30 seconds while the Afghans waved me along encouragingly. I had no choice but to accept their recommendation. I grabbed a couple of MRE packets of toilet paper, climbed the stairs, dropped my trousers, grabbed a hold of the handrail, extended my ass over the edge and took care of business. Far be it from me to criticize their latrine design and hygiene process. I needed to get this adventure started on the right foot, and if this was what it took, so be it. Only now do I realize that this event was an omen of even stranger things to come.

Our first order of business was expanding the small security perimeter around the health clinic and school building that housed soon-to-be President Hamid Karzai and our battalion headquarters. I quickly huddled with Captain Matt Peaks, who commanded the 12-soldier Special Forces A Team that flew in the day prior with the Company Headquarters I commanded. We decided to reposition on a slight ridgeline a couple of hundred yards away that was bisected by a two-lane dirt road. If any trouble arose, that's where it would come from.

We could see that the ridgeline wasn't currently occupied by any hostile forces, so we drove out in pickup trucks and set up along the high ground. We found the area pockmarked with shallow holes that had been used as fighting positions in some previous era of hostility, indicating that we weren't the first fighting force to see the utility of holding this key terrain. We interspersed with our Afghan allies and pondered our next move.

A little less than a mile to the south stood the remnants of a nineteenth-century British fort overlooking the Arghandab River. The Arghandab was the last physical barrier between us and Kandahar, the second largest city in Afghanistan and the spiritual capital of the Taliban, where the remnants of Mullah Omar's army and his al-Qaeda allies were holed up. Kandahar was about 15 miles south of the river. Its capture would end the war.

The fort remained in enemy hands. Several days earlier, ODA 574 had assaulted it but was forced to pull back after a Green Beret was shot and enemy activity made holding the outpost untenable. My new boss, Lieutenant Colonel Dave Fox, ordered us to retake the fort so we could control a critical bridge and have early warning of any enemy attack. I scanned the fort with my binoculars and didn't see any enemy activity. We didn't have access to aerial reconnaissance. I called over Matt Peaks and gave him his mission: to seize the fort and establish an outpost to control the bridge.

Like me, it was his first time in combat, but he had a decade of training. He gathered his men to formulate a plan. I didn't want to interfere, but I had developed my own backup plan just in case: to load up as many trucks as we could marshal and charge like hell ready to shoot up anything that posed a threat. A coup de main, if you will.

But as a company commander I wouldn't be part of the assault, so I always allowed the person leading the attack to think through the situation and develop their own plan.

The minutes dragged on as the sun rose higher in the sky. Finally, I couldn't help myself, and asked Peaks what he wanted to do.

Peaks had put together a beautiful plan for a deliberate attack with reconnaissance, preparatory fires, and intricate maneuver. He did exactly what I asked him to do, exactly the way he was trained. I just hadn't communicated effectively. I explained that we didn't have the time or resources for a hyperdetailed deliberate attack like the invasion of Normandy and instead needed to assault it expeditiously. His eyes widened with the realization that I was asking him to conduct a "movement to contact" mission. In other words, just head in that direction until you run into the enemy, then shoot him.

I knew he would take flak from some of his men. Movement to contact was an offensive maneuver as old as the Roman Legions, and many soldiers viewed it as outdated and needlessly dangerous because of our primacy in reconnaissance drones, surveillance aircraft, and other intelligence collection assets.

Within the hour Captain Peaks and his men blasted off down the road in half a dozen trucks and seized the fort without resistance. The enemy had fled, leaving the door to Kandahar wide open. Too many things were happening for me to realize it at the time, but Peaks's capture of the bridge over the Arghandab River was a clear signal to the remaining Taliban fighters scattered across the region that their war was lost. Now they had one final chance to switch their allegiance to the winning side—an accepted practice in the traditional Afghan way of war. By this time, the Taliban fighters would also have known that the Bonn Agreement had been ratified by the leading warlords of Afghanistan, and Hamid Karzai had been named the country's interim leader.

I'd heard about Taliban fighters switching loyalties, but I had no idea how it would go down. That afternoon, a group of 20 Taliban fighters appeared on the main road that bisected our defensive line. They were wearing their distinctive black headdresses, which denoted their loyalty like the uniform of any army. They carried an assortment of small arms as they casually strolled toward our position. As they got closer, we recognized them as the defenders of the old British fort who had wounded a Green Beret just days before.

As my men took aim, our Afghan partners stood up and began encouraging us to lower our weapons. My men didn't budge—they had the Taliban in their sights and were ready to fire at the slightest provocation. Our battalion leadership hadn't given us any notice that enemy fighters wanted to surrender—and these guys were all armed, and weren't waving any white flags. I had to make a decision fast, and either way looked like a catastrophe in the making.

Maybe it was a gut feeling, or the calm demeanor of the Taliban fighters walking toward us, or the sincerity of our Afghan friends' entreaties—but I eventually ordered the Green Berets to stand down. One by one, our enemies filed past us, grinning broadly and offering friendly greetings in Pashto. They had no idea how close they came to getting smoked.

We watched in amazement as the Taliban assembled in a military formation in front of the schoolhouse Karzai was using as his headquarters. Karzai strode out with chest puffed like a conquering general, inspected his new recruits, and made some remarks we couldn't hear. The Taliban then removed their headdresses and threw them on the ground, energetically stomping and kicking dirt on the jet-black turbans. One of Karzai's functionaries approached holding a stack of light-colored scarfs that each Talib took and immediately wrapped around his head. With a raucous cheer, the ceremony was over, and Karzai went back inside.

That was it. No background checks, no loyalty oaths, no probationary period. The newly ex-Taliban who had shot and wounded a Green Beret just days prior had instantly become fully fledged members of the American-Afghan alliance and partners in the War on Terror. And now they were marching back out to our ridgeline to take up defensive positions alongside us.

To a bunch of working-class Green Berets inculcated with patriotic Western values, this scenario was simply unimaginable. We were trained to deal with prisoners of war, but what do you do when your defeated foe asks to fight alongside you? How can you trust them not to shoot you in the back the first chance they get? And if these guys switch loyalties so easily, how hard are they really going to fight for our side when the chips are down?

I had only been in country for a day, and it was already becoming clear to me that Afghanistan wasn't just another country; it was another world. The rules we lived by didn't apply here. The values we assumed to be universal were totally foreign. And I had a sinking feeling that if I was ill-prepared to operate in this strange new world, the chances were that the entire U.S. Army was ill-prepared as well.

I recalled some sage advice passed down by fellow

soldiers who had served in the Vietnam War. They often-times would establish a visible defensive position during daylight, then at night would pick up and move silently to an alternate position to confuse the enemy. With one Green Beret keeping an unobtrusive eye on our newest allies as they settled in nearby, I passed on the plan to the hearty approval of the rest of the team.

That night was a fever dream. Every 30 minutes an Afghan fighter fired an old Soviet heavy machine gun into the pitch-black engulfing us, causing the entire crew to frantically prepare for an enemy attack. Each time, we'd stare intensely into the darkness, waiting for a flash of return fire or a silhouette darting across the landscape. I wasn't sure if the Afghan gunner was just trigger happy, or whether he was intentionally conducting "reconnaissance by fire"—shooting where you think the enemy might be in order to provoke a response that confirms their position. I didn't really care. At least it kept everyone awake and alert.

The next day, the order came down to deliver Karzai to Kandahar where he would be installed as the interim leader of Afghanistan. Seizing Mullah Omar's hometown and installing a new leader on his turf would demonstrate his impotence and signify an unquestionable defeat of the Taliban. Once we reached Kandahar, the war in Afghanistan would officially end in American victory. Or so we were told.

Battalion Commander Dave Fox decided to immediately move his staff to the northern outskirts of the city to clear the route and establish a secure base that Karzai could be moved to the next day. With little warning, they packed up their gear and disappeared into the midday sun.

I was now the senior military officer in charge of protecting the future leader of Afghanistan. As darkness fell, I could feel my anxiety rising as it dawned on me that Karzai's physical safety, and the outcome of American involvement in Afghanistan, was now in my hands. This would be the perfect time for one of the Taliban turncoats among our surrogate army to earn his immortality by taking a shot at Karzai.

I spent the night planning our movement to Kandahar in precise detail: routes, sequence of movement, actions we would take if attacked, defined speed limits, and plans to recover broken vehicles. I was incredibly pleased with myself, and considered it a masterpiece of military planning that would have made my Ranger School instructors proud. I looked forward to accepting the stream of accolades that my comrades would no doubt shower upon me the next day.

At sunrise, with Karzai thankfully still alive and in the protective embrace of a paramilitary force from the Intelligence community, I summoned the leaders of the U.S. and Afghan forces to brief them on the operation. Karzai sat stoically nearby in the back seat of a Toyota Land Cruiser surrounded by paramilitary officers.

I began the briefing by unfolding a map and announcing that we would be going to Kandahar. As soon as the words left my lips, someone shouted in Pashto, "On to Kandahar!" With that, a deafening cheer arose and the entire group bolted in all directions, cramming into Toyota Hilux pickup trucks. In seconds, the truck beds were packed like clown cars with screaming Afghans brandishing more weapons than a Texas gun show.

The senior American intelligence officer shouted "great plan, genius!" as everyone burst out laughing and rushed to join the scrum of trucks now blazing down the road toward the bridge over the Arghandab River.

It was a scene straight out of *Mad Max*. A line of vehicles stretched across the horizon, kicking up a swirling tempest that made it almost impossible to see or breathe. In the truck beds in front of us, the ecstatic Afghan fighters held on for dear life with one hand, and with the other they maniacally waved their rifles, machine guns, and grenade launchers above their heads.

The windows of my Toyota Tacoma had been blown out by the errant bomb just days prior, and we choked on the thick cloud of dust that filled the cabin. Behind the wheel, Master Sergeant Danny Leonard quickly donned his tanker goggles, and I could vaguely hear a steady stream of excited invective from under the scarf wrapped around his nose and mouth.

The speeding trucks in front of us bounced across the rugged desert landscape, swerving to avoid obstacles we couldn't see, periodically ejecting gear and three-foot-long rocket propelled grenades that had been resting unsecured in the truck beds. On multiple occasions, a truck hit a bump and Afghan fighters were sent flying over tailgates to the hard desert floor. If the Afghan drivers were aware, they didn't care—each was recklessly racing to be the first to reach the city.

Normally, a commander in my position would be glued to his map with a radio handpiece affixed to his ear to call in close air support in the event of enemy resistance. I couldn't hear a thing on my radio due to the screaming engine and wind blasting me in the face. All I could do was grip the dashboard with both hands and revel in the exhilarating insanity.

The melee was tamed as we reentered civilization on the north side of Kandahar, and we calmly drove single file along the well-manicured roads to Mullah Omar's compound. The bullet holes that riddled the compound walls were reminders of the first U.S. commando raid of the war in late October. But this time we weren't leaving. We were here to stay.

In a career replete with errors, blunders, lessons learned and relearned, by far my greatest failure occurred on December 9, 2001, when I failed to insist on cutting the main road that ran south from Kandahar to the Pakistan border. We had just moved from Mullah Omar's compound on the outskirts of Kandahar to the government compound in the heart of the city.

With Karzai on his way to Kabul to set up the new Afghan government, the new warlord in charge of the region was Gul Agha Sherzai. Nicknamed the Lion of Kandahar, Sherzai had a reputation as a hard-hearted, self-serving piece of shit, and he certainly lived up to his reputation.

We had a Green Beret A Team—code-named "Texas 17"—embedded with Sherzai's guerilla army that had helped them capture the Kandahar Airport during the Taliban's final, last ditch stand. Texas 17 was led by Captain Hank Smith, an accomplished team leader with good instincts that I knew and trusted. Smith asked for permission to allow his Afghan forces to put in a roadblock that night on the road that connected Kandahar with the Spin Boldak border crossing point into Pakistan. He expected any remaining senior al-Qaeda and Taliban officials to bug out now that we had captured the city, and he had a hunch it would happen that night. I agreed, and discussed the proposal with Sherzai using a Green Beret sergeant as my interpreter. Sherzai said he didn't think the roadblock was necessary.

When I told my Battalion Commander, Dave Fox, he advised that overruling Sherzai would harm our fledgling relationship and hamper our efforts to win over the local population. Fox had extensive experience working with indigenous forces, so I didn't push the issue any further.

The next day, we learned that a large convoy of senior al-Qaeda and Taliban leadership escaped Kandahar under the cover of darkness and crossed into Pakistan the previous night. I strongly suspect that Sherzai had cut a deal for their safe passage—a timeless tradition in Afghan culture that neither I nor my superiors properly understood at the time—although I was never able to confirm it. War is always a matter of luck and unpredictability, but I can't help but wonder how the course of the war might have been altered if we destroyed them that night.

Somehow, four al-Qaeda fighters didn't get the "haul ass" order and were left behind in Kandahar. They had been wounded days earlier and were stuck at the Mirwais Hospital, the major regional hospital located in downtown

Kandahar. We had plenty of other tasks to accomplish in December, so for the time being we barricaded the wounded terrorists in a six-room section of the hospital and waited to starve them out. By early 2002, we finally had the bandwidth to deal with them properly. Fox and I assigned the mission to the 12-soldier A Team known as ODA 573, and ordered them to remove the enemy from the hospital dead or alive.

At the time, we were still naive about the values, motivations, and willpower that drove al-Qaeda fighters. We assumed they would surrender once they realized they had no way out. It was an incredibly shortsighted Western-centric perspective: "you're surrounded, come out and talk and we'll arrange your flight to a lovely resort on a Caribbean island 90 miles off the coast of Florida."

Our initial parley with the wounded fighters seemed positive. They requested that the A Team swear an oath on the Koran that they would not be killed. This might seem like a trivial request to most Americans, but in the modern Army so dominated by pencil-pushing bureaucrats, it's not something our soldiers on the ground are allowed to handle. I actually had to call the lawyer at our headquarters in Uzbekistan and request a legal opinion on whether I was allowed to lie to al-Qaeda terrorists.

An hour later, I received a reply approving the ruse and attesting that lying to terrorists who wanted to murder you was, in fact, legal. The al-Qaeda stay-behinds edged out from behind their barricaded door but got skittish at the sight of the bearded Green Berets and retreated in a fury. So much for niceties. We were going to have to dig them out the old-fashioned way.

* * *

My orders were to use Afghans to do the fighting, which was a classic Green Beret tactic. We would train, advise, and assist a small group of Afghan commandos, but they would do the shooting and serve as the external face of the operation. From a public relations perspective, it made sense to have Afghans lead the way in ridding their country of al-Qaeda (AQ).

I wrote up a plan of action and briefed the participants. We would stealthily move to the hospital in the predawn hours before the surrounding mosques issued the first Muslim call to prayer. Green Beret demolition experts would affix explosive charges to a brick wall directly in front of the second-floor hospital rooms where the AQ fighters were holed up. Two Green Berets assisted by hospital staff would move patients away from glass windows in the main hospital. Upon hearing the muezzin's call to prayer, our demolitionists would wait one minute for the AQ fighters to assemble in the hall and prostrate themselves in prayer, and then blow the wall. Our well-trained and disciplined Afghan commandos would storm the breach and proceed to clear each room. The whole operation would take less than 15 minutes from start to finish, and we'd be gone before the CNN crew staying in a nearby compound would be able to fire up their cameras.

Matt Peaks' A Team, ODA 524, had spent the previous week training Afghan security forces in close-quarters battle tactics like assaulting buildings and clearing rooms. The training had been offered to 20 Afghan fighters under the guise of routine basic training.

At the end of my briefing, the assembled mass dispersed to brief their men, rehearse, and prepare equipment. I crawled off to get some sleep before commanding the first nontraining direct action raid—the premier commando mission desired by all Green Berets—of my career.

We lined up our 20 pickup trucks in the early morning darkness, dressed in our desert camo uniform tops with name tags and unit patches removed to disguise our identities as much as possible. The first surprise of the day came when we learned that our 20-soldier Afghan commando force was now down to 12. After being notified the previous evening that they would be conducting a live mission, 8 of them decided to slip away in the dark of the night with their equipment and weapons.

The second surprise occurred when the convoy leader missed the turn that would take us on a surreptitious route out of view of our targets. Our new improvised route drove us slowly past the hospital wing housing our AQ targets. I actually saw the shocked face of one of the terrorists in the window as we pulled up. With the essential element of surprise completely ruined, we moved into position.

"Execute, Execute, Execute!" I ordered into my radio. A couple of seconds later, two pounds of C-4 explosives detonated in a massive explosion that blew apart the brick wall. Our Afghan commandos darted into the dust-choked hallway and disappeared.

Every battlefield has unique sounds and smells, and a trained ear can discern a battle's progress even when you can't see what's happening. In this case, I was listening intently for the distinctive crack of fragmentation grenades that upon detonation spew out thousands of pieces of shrapnel. I heard two grenades go off, then everything went quiet. This was not a good sign. We should have heard repeated bursts of gunfire, then more grenades, then more gunfire, and so on, as the assault force methodically cleared each of the six rooms.

Soon, the report came in that half the Afghan assault force was wounded and being evacuated to the casualty collection point outside the hospital. In the excitement of the moment, the Afghan commandos had not waited for the grenades to explode before charging into the room. Instead, they had chased the grenade into the room with a predictable outcome.

I scurried over to the casualty collection point. None of the injuries was life-threatening, and the medical team went to work stabilizing them. This was going to take a lot longer than 15 minutes.

I was leaning on the hood of my pickup truck that served as my command post, thinking about what to do next, when our two battalion Warrant Officers sauntered over. They were the Green Berets who had directed the movement of hospital patients away from windows prior to the assault, and now they had a plan they wanted to pitch me.

"Hey sir, why don't we smoke them out?" they offered. They proposed taking a propane tank used to fuel stoves—the same type you use for the gas grill in your backyard—wrap it in blankets, strap on a small explosive charge, and toss it down the hall toward our AQ holdouts.

The detonation would ignite the fabric, their thinking went, and create billowing clouds of thick, black smoke that would force our enemy out into the open. Earlier in my career, I had become certified as a demolitionist and had constructed the same sort of improvised explosive device they were describing. I approved the idea to their visible delight, and they scampered off to assemble their bomb.

With the sun approaching its apogee and CNN crews filming from the roof of their compound across the street, the two Warrant Officers lit the fuse on their propane bomb and hurled it down the hallway. Thirty seconds later, we heard a low decibel thump. A few minutes after that, smoke started billowing out of the shattered windows. Lots of smoke. Much more than we expected.

In the window about 25 meters from my truck, one of the AQ holdouts kept popping above the windowsill to snatch a breath of fresh air before ducking back down. A sergeant lying behind a dirt pile shouted, "Hey sir, can I shoot this guy?" I was slightly peeved at his request having gone over the rules of engagement in excruciating detail during the briefing the day prior. "Yes, Mark, you can shoot him," I responded.

Mark settled in behind his M4 rifle and pulled the trigger. "I got him!" he shouted in amazement—it was his first kill in over 16 years as a Green Beret. A voice came across the radio from another Green Beret on the first floor: "You sure did. We heard him hit the ground like a sack of potatoes." One down, three to go. This just might work.

Then flames started dancing in the windows. My father had once regaled me with a story of his time as cop in Wilmington, Delaware, when he fired tear gas into a barricaded house and ended up burning the place to the ground. But unlike some drug den in the 1970s, this was an International Red Cross hospital and CNN was broadcasting it live. I was about to accidentally become a war criminal.

As the flames grew in volume and intensity, so did the sense of panic in my chest. Then in the distance I heard the wail of a siren. And in one of the most bizarre moments of my Army career, a shiny modern fire truck flawlessly painted in a fluorescent yellow-green hue rounded the corner, pulled into the courtyard, and parked smack-dab in the middle of my war. The crewmembers were dressed in classic red firefighter regalia, as if we had been suddenly and miraculously transported from the dystopian wasteland that was Afghanistan to beautiful downtown Manhattan.

The firefighter on the water cannon pulled the trigger and methodically blasted each second-floor window with a deluge. In a matter of minutes, the fire was extinguished, and the truck backed out of the courtyard and drove off in the direction from whence it came. I was speechless. We looked at each other as if we had just seen an apparition. And then we started laughing.

A few days later, we learned that the truck and equipment had been donated by the good people of Germany several years prior. So to the Germans—thanks for saving my ass from a court-martial.

I knew that Lieutenant Colonel Dave Fox was monitoring the radio chatter from his headquarters at the provincial government building downtown. Thus far, he had been very indulgent and allowed me to command the raid without interference. After almost burning down the hospital, I decided it was time to end the circus I had created. I called Fox and told him I was going to put in a guard post at the blown-out wall and reinstate our siege. Fox ordered me to keep everyone in place, because the cavalry was on the way.

Soon, the local police commander pulled up with 40 of his men. We had worked together on a previous operation, and I knew he was a disciplined and effective commander. His vehicles were clean and well-maintained, and all of his men wore identical uniforms—something extremely rare in Afghanistan. "Mr. Chris," he said, "I will take care of this." The two bomb-making Warrant Officers grabbed a couple of satchels full of hand grenades and led the new assault force to the second floor.

The next assault began with the thunderous crack of several grenades exploding followed immediately by a 200-round burst of machine-gun fire. I should note that firing 200 rounds nonstop is extreme overkill for a situation like this. U.S. soldiers are trained to fire short 5–10 round bursts to maintain accuracy and prevent the machine-gun barrel from overheating. But I was just happy to have a competent Afghan force for once, and at least they were getting the job done.

There were three rooms on each side of the hallway, and those of us outside the building could follow the assault as it progressed. It was the well-orchestrated ballet of death and destruction to which professional soldiers always aspire. The final concussive blasts and torrent of machine-gun fire concluded, and the report came across the radio that the second floor was secure and all enemy were dead.

Our 15-minute operation had stretched into its twelfth

hour, and it still wasn't over. Now we had to search the rooms and bodies for anything of intelligence value, and then take the bodies to the U.S. military morgue at Kandahar Airfield. I sent in the search crew along with two Explosive Ordinance Disposal (EOD) experts.

As I entered the hospital to inspect the battle scene and get a feel for how long the search was going to take, I was staggered by an explosion on the second floor. I sprinted up the stairs with my mind in overdrive. We had completed the operation with no friendlies killed, and now something bad had happened. The rubble strewn corridor was darkened with the dirty gray smoke that is the hallmark of a high explosive. I could make out two men sitting on the floor stunned. It was the two EOD soldiers.

I grabbed them and shouted at them if they were all right. The confusion slowly lifted from their eyes, and one of them, Sergeant Brian Craig, said, "They did it. They booby-trapped one of the bodies." I then noticed that they both were holding a line of green, high-tensile parachute cord. In Basic Training, you are taught to tie a rope around the foot of enemy dead and give the body a disruptive tug to trigger any booby traps. It was a lesson learned in the Vietnam War, where the Vietcong and North Vietnamese would often rig their dead with explosives to injure or kill inattentive searchers. But Craig and his partner, Specialist Justin Galewski, had followed their training to the letter. Their attention to detail saved the search party from guaranteed injury and possible death.[4]

---

[4] Tragically, Craig and Galewski were killed several weeks later while clearing a booby-trapped explosive device from a public area.

I moved on to check out the room where the AQ fighters had bunkered down. It was an absolute slaughterhouse. The guy we shot through the window had the top of his head splayed open and his innards were exposed from the grenade that his colleagues had placed under him after his death. The parachute cord was still tied to one of his feet. The other three were missing various body parts from the hand grenades and fusillade. Pools of blood and entrails were interspersed with clothing, blankets, and papers that covered the floor. Stacks of unleavened naan bread attested that they had received support from cooperative guards or hospital personnel.

I was looking forward to calling it a day when Fox called me on the radio. "I need you to go talk to the press," he ordered. I thought about using the time-honored tactic of pretending like I couldn't understand him due to radio interference. "You gotta be kidding me," I protested. "Negative. Out," he responded, and then he was gone.

It was now 4 p.m. This was not how I wanted to end the day. I grabbed the Afghan police chief and strode out to meet the press. I wore my hat with an American flag embroidered on the front and a "I Love New York" button on my uniform collar where my rank would normally be sewn. I hadn't had a haircut in eight weeks and my red beard had come in thick. I made a few anodyne comments like a baseball player talking to the press in the locker room after a big game, and hoped that would be the end of it. I had no way of knowing that it had been a slow news day, and the national media had been fixated on our hospital raid. When I called my wife via satellite phone later that night, she knew all about my day. My daughters had shouted at the dinner table, "Mommy, it's Daddy on TV!" as ABC Evening News described the action.

I crawled into my sleeping bag that evening wondering if I would be psychologically distraught or have nightmares about the day's death and destruction, the way popular media often represents the effects of combat. I slept like a log.

The next day, Colonel Mulholland, the indomitable commander of all Special Forces in Afghanistan, forwarded me a message from the Army's second most-senior general officer. He was upset with my physical appearance and failure to be in a proper uniform during the impromptu press conference following the hospital raid. He said I looked like a "swashbuckling cowboy." I laughed at the mixed metaphor and responded that I would try to do a better job representing the Army in the future. I had never been more satisfied with my decision to leave the conventional Army and their pedantry and silliness seven years earlier.

As my men and I discussed the operation, I learned that the two Warrant Officers had personally led the final, successful assault chucking grenades into rooms and assisting the Afghan machine gunner. Between that and their propane bomb-making, they clearly had performed above and beyond the call of duty and deserved special recognition.

But I had a problem—the press was extensively reporting that the operation was the first example of the new Afghan Security Forces taking control of their country. The Army's PR script was working splendidly, and commending my Warrant Officers publicly would contradict the carefully crafted narrative. A martinet could also interpret the actions of our Warrant Officers as violating orders by taking the lead from the Afghans. Screw that, I thought. They earned it. I submitted them both for Bronze Stars for Valor, and as usual, Colonel Mulholland underwrote my actions and approved them.

We had succeeded despite my mistakes. I'm still ashamed of my failures, but witnessing the unbridled power of a hive mind of creative experts was awe-inspiring. There is nothing our soldiers can't achieve, if we just let them do their jobs.

CHAPTER FIVE

"I CAN'T BELIEVE WE'RE REALLY DOING THIS"

In April 2003, we were finally in Baghdad. I had handed off the company I commanded in Afghanistan in the summer of 2002 and had been elevated to serve as the Operations Officer responsible for training, planning, and operations of the 18 A Teams of the 3rd Battalion, 5th Special Forces Group (Airborne). The Third Infantry Division and the 1st Marine Division had blasted through Iraqi defenses and captured the capital. It was World War II shit. Tom Brokaw was sitting in the back of my Humvee taping radio spots when he leaned over and said something like, "You guys must be so relieved."

I definitely was relieved. The invasion of Iraq had gone off without a hitch, and American casualties had been minimal. I was glad we made it to Baghdad in one piece, even though I still wasn't sure why we were there in the first place. I thought of my family and all of the important events I had missed in my children's young lives to accomplish this goal. I thought about all the crap my wife had to deal with because I was never home. I thought about the friends I had lost over the preceding 16 months.

I started to choke up and turned my head away so Brokaw and the other occupants of the vehicle couldn't see the tears welling up in my eyes. I was physically exhausted and emotionally spent. Why is it always some benign comment from a well-meaning stranger—a meaningless aside, Brokaw's pleasantries—that unexpectedly triggers a wave of emotion?

Baghdad had consumed my life since I returned from Afghanistan the year prior. I had been tasked by the 3rd Battalion Commander, Lieutenant Colonel Tim Williams, to support the military invasion and get us to Baghdad to assist in destroying Saddam's regime. Williams was a no-nonsense Arkansan who was incredibly bright and strongly respected by the men under his command.

Williams was assisted by an absolutely legendary Non-commissioned Officer (NCO), Command Sergeant Major Dave Strickland, a country boy from Ohio who felt personal ownership of the battalion and forged it in his image: professional, blue-collar, no frills, with enormous endurance.

Three days before entering Baghdad, we had been at Ali Al Salem Airbase in Kuwait, which we shared with 2nd Battalion, 5th Special Forces Group, as well as an Air Force Special Operations unit and a Navy SEAL team. We had arrived in February 2003 and had spent the intervening two months planning, training, and rehearsing every facet of the invasion.

Secretary of State Colin Powell had recently given a

speech at the United Nations outlining the Bush administration's belief that Iraq possessed Weapons of Mass Destruction. The fear, according to Powell, was that those weapons could easily fall into the hands of terrorists since a "sinister nexus" between Iraq and al-Qaeda existed.[5]

Truth be told, I didn't think we were actually going to invade. I assumed our efforts were part of sophisticated "coercive diplomacy"—in other words, a threat designed to get Saddam to yield to our demands without a fight. There was no way we were going to invade a sovereign country that hadn't attacked us, and in all likelihood didn't pose a significant threat to us or our allies, despite the Bush administration's alarmism.

My battalion was originally relegated to serving as the strategic reserve, but I had successfully changed our mission to leading Special Forces operations for the assault on Baghdad. Our sister battalions were responsible for hunting down mobile rocket launchers that had tormented Israel during the 1991 Gulf War, conducting Special Reconnaissance, and linking up with Shia insurgent groups in southern Iraq.

Most Americans don't realize it, but Majors are the ones who plan wars. The Colonels take the briefings from the Majors, provide a bit of guidance, and then brief the Generals as if it was their idea. I had been a planner for the invasion of Afghanistan, but that was just for a handful of

---

[5] Remarks by Secretary of State Colin Powell to the United Nations, *Washington Post*, February 5, 2003, https://www.washingtonpost.com /wp-srv/nation/transcripts/powelltext_020503.html.

Special Operations units. The invasion of Iraq was going to be a big war. Armor divisions grinding up highways. Fleets of aircraft filling the sky. A shock and awe campaign that would level Iraqi military infrastructure before the real fighting even began. It was an operation ideally suited for the U.S. military.

The lead planners were two conventional Army Majors and a recently promoted Lieutenant Colonel who we nicknamed the Jedi Knights for their masterful approach gained through successfully completing an arduous yearlong program of study only available to the best Army officers. During one planning session, I tried to elbow my way into the action by offering that Special Forces were available to assist in the division's movement with reconnaissance. One of the Jedi Knights chuckled as he patted me on the back and said, "Chris, I really appreciate it. We're going to push 180 M1A1 main battle tanks up that corridor. I think we'll be all right."

He was correct, of course. This was a tank war supported by close air support and strategic air and missile attacks. It was a tanker's dream: armor spearheads knifing into the guts of the enemy defenses; 125 mm main gun rounds destroying enemy tanks from 4,000 meters away; barrages of artillery ripping apart dismounted troop emplacements. Compared to this carnage, Special Forces would be a sideshow, at best.

The phases of military campaigns had been drilled into us. They were our holy scrolls: Phase 0 (shape), Phase I (deter), Phase II (seize initiative), Phase III (dominate), Phase IV (stabilize), and finally Phase V (enable civil authority). When we completed Phase III planning, we asked the

Colonel for guidance on Phase IV. He tersely informed us that Phase IV was not our problem: the State Department had it taken care of. But we were followers of Carl von Clausewitz's edict to "Never take the first step until you know what your last step is." We were confused. We naively asked for clarification, but our queries were ignored. We figured he must know something we didn't. We were Majors, after all, and he was a Colonel. We were the proverbial mushroom—kept in the dark and covered with shit.

But I was still a Green Beret, and I was not about to sit on my hands and admire the invasion from afar. At the very least, we could recon key locations—bridges, towns, restricted terrain—so that the armor formations knew what to expect. We were also going to link up with potential resistance leaders, primarily Shias that had been persecuted by Saddam's Sunni minority, and use them as a fifth column. It was a good contingency plan in case the invasion stalled.

The overarching plan also called for the invasion forces to isolate Baghdad, and then pause to rearm prior to the launching of the battle for the city, which was expected to be reminiscent of the bloody Battle of Stalingrad in World War II. During this pause, our idea was to use our Iraqi surrogates to infiltrate the city and scout enemy positions. There was a huge slum called Sadr City where Saddam had isolated his potential rivals behind an elaborate canal system with only a handful of bridges controlling entry and exit. My assessment was that Saddam's efforts to restrict movement out of Sadr City could be turned against him, and with a little luck, we might be able to create an enclave of resistance in the heart of his capital.

The first challenge was getting Special Forces ahead of the armored columns. In an ideal situation, Special Forces infiltrate into enemy territory several days prior to the invasion, but we weren't authorized to cross the border prior to the start of the air attacks. In my mind, this prohibition further validated my suspicion that our military buildup was part of an elaborate bluff.

I decided that my battalion would establish a Field Landing Strip (FLS)—basically, a runway with no lighting or communications equipment—deep behind enemy lines and land MC-130 Combat Talon aircraft loaded with vehicles and Green Berets. I directed the intelligence shop to find ideal locations, and they focused on the Wadi al Khirr Airfield, which was little more than an abandoned runway about 150 miles southwest of Baghdad that originally had been built by Yugoslavian contractors in the 1980s. Surprisingly, the Air Force Special Operators loved the idea. Together we strong-armed the 2nd Battalion resistors into agreement.

In early March, all Special Operations elements were summoned to present our plans to conventional Army leadership for approval and integration. I had not briefed my Group Commander, Colonel John Mulholland, on my plan. Frankly, I didn't think it was at the top of his priority list. He was rightfully focused on the 1st Battalion's SCUD-hunting efforts in the western desert, and 2nd Battalion's planned operations in the Karbala Gap as part of the kickoff to the campaign. The 3rd Battalion was almost an afterthought, since we were tasked with supporting the conventional forces capture of Baghdad, which was still eons away compared to the other missions.

The higher priority of my sister battalions afforded me the luxury of minimal oversight and attention. The more I was ignored, the more I pushed ahead on my own, avoiding the mind-numbing critiques and micromanagement that were no doubt plaguing the other battalions. I had short-circuited the entire planning system. Eventually, our scheme of maneuver was approved. We were in business.

I assembled the key leaders of all the elements that would be part of the Wadi al Khirr operation. The Intelligence Community was going to hitch a ride with us, and our teams would work closely together behind enemy lines. I was pretty pleased with myself. The plan looked solid, but it was risky. Since I regrettably wouldn't be an on the ground participant, and I was hesitant to write checks that I wouldn't have to cash myself, I asked the senior NCOs for their opinion. They had more combat experience than I had, and they were the ones who would actually have to execute the plan. They all thought it was doable.

I still thought Saddam would cave before we invaded, but we prepared with full intensity. Teams tested all of their weapons and communications systems and optimized their vehicles. They practiced contingency plans until they could be conducted automatically. Most importantly, the ground units practiced loading vehicles into the fleet of MC-130 Combat Talons—an upgraded version of the four-propellered C-130 Hercules that was the workhorse of U.S. Air Force (USAF) tactical airlift.

The loading and unloading process wasn't for the faint of heart. It required precisely backing the vehicle up the aircraft ramp while carefully following the hand and arm signals of the Load Master. There were only a few inches of space between the vehicle and side of the aircraft. There was no way to ease the truck over the threshold, so the driver was required to gun the engine and race up the ramp in reverse into the plane's belly with perfect precision. Upon landing at the FLS, the vehicles would have to deplane in less than one minute so that the pilot could quickly get airborne. It was incredibly nerve-racking and required steady hands and laser focus. And we were about to become the first Green Berets to try such a maneuver in combat.

Our SOF task force did not have ready access to the latest Intelligence, Surveillance, and Reconnaissance (ISR) assets like the Predator drone that provided high fidelity, real-time video of targets. In fact, at the time there was only a handful of Predators in theater.

But I knew a guy in the Intelligence Community who might be able to help. We had served together in Afghanistan— he was the officer who made fun of my attempted briefing before moving Hamid Karzai to Kandahar in 2001—and now he was the top guy in his organization supporting special operations in Iraq. Our respective teams had fought a number of battles together and learned to trust and respect each other. Fighting and suffering injuries and death together created an unbreakable bond that could never be replicated outside of combat.

My friend offered the use of his organization's Predator to conduct reconnaissance flights over Wadi al Khirr. The good news was that the video showed the enemy was nowhere to be found. The bad news was that the video wasn't clear enough to determine the condition of the runway. Satellite photos offered no help either, and we didn't have any spies available to conduct a close target reconnaissance.

Despite unprecedented access to cutting-edge ISR, it was still going to require Green Berets and Air Force Special Operators to check it out on the ground. At least that was the assessment before the Predator inexplicably disappeared while flying over Wadi al Khirr. Not only had our expensive technology failed us, but it may have cost us the element of surprise. Now I worried that we might have inadvertently announced our intention to capture the airfield, and we had no idea what countermeasures the enemy was preparing to take.

The Wadi al Khirr mission was shaping up to be a huge win for the Green Berets, and for me personally. If successful, it would be historic and a defining statement about the professionalism and competence of the Green Berets and our Special Forces partners. If it went poorly, I feared our Regiment would be relegated to sitting at the kid's table for eternity.

Professionally, I felt my career was on the line. It was my idea from start to finish, and I would be the one found culpable for any mistakes. My stress levels were rising. The war was about to start.

Intelligence reported that Saddam was hiding at one of his palaces, and senior military leadership decided to kick the war off early with a decapitation strike. It missed, but the war was on. So much for coercive diplomacy. All I could think was, "I can't believe we're really fucking doing this."

Great football coaches talk about how once the game begins, their job is done and it's up to the players to perform. The coach's value is in the planning and preparation. I felt the same way that day—we had our game plan, and now it was up to the players to execute it.

My best friend in the military, Major Bruce Swatek, had been designated the Ground Tactical Commander for the Wadi al Khirr mission; he was the guy in charge of executing the mission on the ground. Swatek and his crew launched the next night aboard two MH-53 Pave Low helicopters, landed several miles from the airstrip, and moved overland to confuse any enemy observers about their true intentions. Just after first light, USAF Special Tactics personnel surveyed the condition of the airstrip, and Swatek reported that it was usable. All they had to do now was stay out of trouble, and after nightfall a stream of MC-130 Super Talon transporters would deliver Special Forces A Teams and intelligence personnel to their location 70 miles behind enemy lines.

I smoked cigarettes like a nicotine junkie as I sat on the stoop outside the Operations Center thinking through contingencies. About midday, Swatek reported several vehicles moving on the road network near the airfield. They were coalescing around a government building. We quickly directed air strikes on the building and destroyed it. Swatek's men spent the rest of the day pulling security for work crews removing debris and shrapnel that had littered the runway since the first Gulf War in 1991.

As soon as it got dark, our A Teams prepared the airfield for the incoming transport planes. Everything worked as planned. We got our vehicles and Green Berets off the planes without a scratch, and they disappeared into the darkness en route to their targets. NCOs and junior officers solved problems as they arose. It went flawlessly. I was expecting an enemy response because of the missing drone and the cacophony of noise we were making, but none materialized. It was like a training exercise.

We had pulled off one of the most significant missions in the modern history of Special Forces. For me, the victory held special significance. I thought back to the Iran hostage crisis in 1980, and the botched rescue attempt that had inspired me to join the Army as a kid. That disastrous mission had been aborted after a deadly aircraft accident at a FLS in the Iranian desert, which had been code-named Desert One. It had haunted Special Forces for nearly a generation.

Twenty-three years later, our war would grind on, and individual events would get lost in the broad arc of the war. But personally, I felt that the ghosts of Desert One were exorcised that night.

Our tank columns crushed the Iraqi resistance as predicted and were now pushing the front lines further away from our Special Forces headquarters in Kuwait with each passing day. The key decisions were now being made 300 miles away near Baghdad, and if Special Forces wanted a voice in the decision-making process, I believed our battalion commander, Tim Williams, needed to be closer to the action.

We loaded up our Toyota Tacoma pickup trucks into the back of MH-53 helicopters and flew into Iraq, landing on a barren stretch of highway that had been turned into a landing strip and refueling station. Even after two decades in the military, I was blown away. There is no other military in the world that can pick up, move halfway around the world, and turn an interstate highway into a functional airport overnight.

After a few hours of sleep in an abandoned office park, we started our drive to Baghdad, following the path of the armor formations that had laid waste to any and all threats over the past few days. Several hours into our journey, we spotted a couple of Army fuel trucks crewed by the Tennessee National Guard and pulled into their empty parking lot. One of the sacrosanct principles of mechanized warfare is never turn down an opportunity to top off your fuel tank, because you never know when you'll get your next chance.

While refueling, I lit a cigarette and walked across the road to the burned-out shell of an Iraqi vehicle. In the bottom was a viscous pool of liquid of the most stunning and vibrant purple color I had ever seen. I couldn't figure out what it was. Then I noticed a half-melted helmet and realized that I was looking at the incinerated remains of an Iraqi soldier. It was one of those transformative moments that few outside the military ever experience—the realization that the essence of the physical remains of the human body is a pool of purple liquid.

I put out my cigarette and got back on the road. The number of destroyed Iraqi vehicles increased as we made our way closer to Baghdad. We also saw Iraqi civilians for the first time. Every young male was bare-chested and aggressively waving their white T-shirts over their heads.

We passed a U.S. Army tank and pulled up to talk to the tanker sitting on the turret. His sunken eyes and infinite gaze reminded me of black-and-white photos I'd seen of exhausted soldiers in previous wars. He had been fighting nonstop for 14 days, and I could tell he didn't have the energy or desire to engage in conversation, so we kept moving.

Those kids from the 3rd Infantry Division had crossed the desert with the expectation, based on their commander's assurances, that they would be able to apply violence selectively and avoid alienating the local population. Their commanders weren't evil or malicious. They had simply ascended the ranks during a time of great peace and didn't truly know the essential elements of combat: fear, exhaustion, violence, fog, and friction. As a result, the reality of the violence our soldiers were now experiencing didn't match their expectations, and it was beginning to take its toll.

We set up a rudimentary headquarters at one of Saddam's Republican Guard camps near the Baghdad International Airport. We were in a two-story building on the edge of the airfield overlooking a main road flowing with a steady stream of white Toyota Corollas that intelligence warned were being used by the Fedayeen, Saddam's irregular forces dressed in civilian clothes that were wreaking havoc. In fact, they were primarily taxis—despite our advances in technological intelligence, the fog of war remained as thick as ever. I'd like to take this time to apologize to those taxi drivers that stopped to yell at us after sniper rounds perforated their engine blocks.

But in our defense, we only had a handful of people on the ground, and we were quickly wearing thin between our normal duties and pulling security on the rooftop. If we continued at this pace, we would be combat ineffective in a few days. I called Major Scott Brower, the Battalion Executive Officer who was second-in-command of the unit who was in Kuwait and asked him to push everything forward to us. It was time to move the entire battalion to Baghdad.

That night, an MC-130 landed, and our A Teams and support personnel filed out, along with a National Geographic film crew. Our Headquarters Company Commander was Captain Paul Syverson. He was a big, blonde-haired man from Chicago with an effusive personality, a ready laugh that brought joy to all those in earshot, and an uncanny ability to connect with subordinates. Every time I observed him, I learned something new about leadership. Syverson would be killed in Iraq a year later, and I have never recovered from his loss. But that day, Syverson was ready for Brower's order to move the battalion to Baghdad. They loaded up and set off on the mother of all road trips.

Now that we had enough manpower to establish security, we were able to freely roam the Republican Guard's compound. It was eerie. Apparently, they were completely surprised by our arrival. Half-eaten meals sat on tables. Trooper equipment was laid out for inspection. A well-worn path to a ladder at the compound wall showed their route of escape. I broke into the supply room and liberated several unopened boxes of tactical load-carrying equipment and piled them in my Tacoma. The equipment would be ideal barter material. Being a conquering Army wasn't so bad.

*   *   *

The road system around Baghdad was as modern and pristine as the Beltway around Washington, DC. The regular Army had exploited the quality of Iraqi infrastructure to rapidly push armored columns into the capital a few days prior, in what later became known as the Thunder Run.

Now the 2nd Brigade of the 3rd Infantry Division was about to conduct a second Thunder Run following the same route. But in the intervening days since the first movement, Syrian mercenaries had dug in defensive positions around several key cloverleaf interstate overpasses.

The Syrians were savvy. They let the armor spearheads blast through without opposition, and when the vulnerable unarmored fuel tankers and supply and medical vehicles approached, they unleashed a well-timed ambush with rocket-propelled grenades, machine guns, and small arms fire. We had a Special Forces A Team in Toyota Tacoma pickups traveling with the supply trains. Their job was to assess the local population and identify individuals who were willing to either spy or fight for us. Now they were fighting for their lives in one of the biggest battles of the war.

Without fuel, repair parts, and supplies, mechanized formations slowly grind to a halt. The Syrians had exploited a weakness in our tactics and essentially amputated the armored fist from its supporting muscles. They could survive for a while with the fuel and ammunition they were carrying, but without resupply they would have to retreat or end up surrounded. If the Syrians destroyed the vulnerable fuel tankers sitting exposed on the road, we would be in a serious bind, and the offensive would stall due to a lack of fuel. The A Team recognized the danger and rallied support personnel who were not expecting to have to fight toe to toe. But they were American soldiers, and with a bit of leadership, they began fighting back.

Our A Team quickly began clearing the Syrian mercenaries' well-camouflaged trench lines. "Clearing trench lines" sounds antiseptic, but it is one of the most dangerous and brutal operations in the business: you jump in the trench, move toward the waiting enemy around the next bend, toss a couple of hand grenades, then storm around the corner and shoot anything still moving.

I was at our makeshift headquarters at the abandoned Republican Guard compound in Baghdad. With most of our communications equipment still in Kuwait, Lieutenant Colonel Williams and I were left virtually in the dark. Our first clue that a huge battle was occurring near us was when we received a message that all movement outside of the sprawling airport complex was prohibited due to enemy activity.

Eventually, we received reports that two members of our stranded A Team had been shot and required medical evacuation. The responsibility for getting our guys out of this mess would fall to Major Scott Brower, along with the battalion Command Sergeant Major, Dave Strickland, who were with our remaining forces at our old headquarters in Kuwait. No one was more capable than Brower. He commanded effortlessly, even under pressure, and was universally loved and respected by his men.

The two wounded Green Berets had been shot in the

legs during the trench clearing. They were stable, but one required evacuation to Kuwait for surgical care.

When the regular Army commander leading the Thunder Run realized the enormous threat to his rear, he ordered a portion of his force to turn around and clear out the enemy. The Abrams tanks and Bradley Infantry Fighting Vehicles blasted the cloverleaf with devastating effect. But two Toyota Tacoma pickup trucks that our A Team was traveling in drew the attention of a Bradley Commander. I can only imagine what he was thinking, but I suspect in the heat of battle, where muscle memory and pattern recognition are lifesaving qualities, he said, "That thing isn't like the others, and the only other civilian vehicles in the area are used by insurgents." He ordered his Bradley gunner to engage our trucks, and after several rounds from the 25 mm chain gun perforated the fuel tanks, they burst into flames. Thankfully, no one was injured.

When I heard the news, I felt sick. I was partially responsible for this friendly fire incident. We had authorized the use of civilian pickups instead of our modified Humvees, believing they would be less obtrusive in the deserts and towns of Iraq and provide a degree of stealth. They worked great in Afghanistan. What a stupid decision for Iraq. I should have been more aware of the operational environment and recommended against their use in a theater controlled by our conventional military, which wasn't used to working with our nonstandard equipment.

The news kept getting worse. Our wounded Green Beret who needed medical evacuation would have to wait, because the medevac helicopter had been grounded due to a bad weather forecast based on satellite data around

Baghdad. Our guys on the ground protested that the weather was fine, but Army protocol dictated that only a certified meteorologist could overrule the forecast.

Thankfully, during our preparations in Kuwait, I had gained a reputation for taking in strays. Basically, if you wanted to be part of the invasion and not get stuck in the "rear with the gear," I was someone who would make a spot for you. A team of Defense Intelligence Agency officers offered to support us with human intelligence capabilities we weren't trained to conduct. It seemed like good synergy to me, and I attached them to an A Team. Members of a specialized reconnaissance unit petitioned to accompany us, which I gladly supported. And a USAF Special Operations Weather Team showed up one day looking for a way to get in on the action. This one was a bit novel to me. I had no idea what they did. In fact, I didn't even know we had such a force. But I went with my gut and brought them along.

I learned the next morning that our seriously wounded Green Beret had successfully been evacuated by helicopter, and he survived. I found out later that the only reason the evacuation was approved was because our meteorologists sent up weather balloons and issued a new forecast that allowed the medevac to fly. God bless the intrepid meteorologists of the USAF.

The next day, Paul Evans, one of the best Team Sergeants in the battalion, asked me to go for a ride with his team. We wound our way past throngs of looters onto a Shangri-La compound surrounded by 15-foot walls studded with guard towers. This was Saddam's Radwaniyah Palace Complex, and when he wasn't there, his inner circle of loyalists used it as the world's biggest and most extravagant Airbnb.

The palace grounds were immaculately maintained, with human-made lakes, lush vegetation, and well-manicured paths connecting small cottages and larger buildings of varied and whimsical architectural styles. We passed a row of empty zoo cages as we made our way up a human-made hill rising several hundred feet above its surroundings. At the top of the hill was a massive stone castle with 30-foot-tall wooden doors that were slightly ajar. We got out, gunned up, and tactically entered the building in case it was still occupied by enemy forces.

The electricity was out, and it was pitch-black inside. As our eyes adjusted to the darkness, we found ourselves in a cavernous Victorian ballroom adorned with magnificent marble sculptures and exquisite handcrafted furniture. As we secured the multitude of doors and passageways on the ballroom's periphery, we heard faint laughter in the distance. We followed the laughter down a long corridor leading to a spacious room haloed in blinding sunlight.

There, we found two soldiers from the 3rd Infantry Division frolicking in a crystal-clear indoor pool, their equipment and clothes strewn by the side. It was absolutely surreal. I felt like an Allied soldier wandering through Hitler's Eagle's Nest.

"What do you think, sir?" Paul Evans asked.

"I think this is better than that shithole by the airport," I said. And with that, we had a new headquarters.

* * *

With Saddam on the run, the Iraqi people were looting government buildings like drunken Vikings. I couldn't blame them, but I also couldn't have them running around our new compound.

Sergeant Major Tom Buccino rounded up the hundreds of looters swarming through the palace grounds, and with his pidgin Arabic, worked out an agreement with the Looter Leader. Buccino gave them 24 hours to pillage whatever they wanted in the buildings situated on the compound's lowlands, but they had to leave the palace alone. Any looters found on the compound at noon the next day would be shot.

We positioned our vehicles at the compound gate at 1145 the following day. Whether true or not, Middle Easterners are sometimes stereotyped as having a more flexible relationship with things like time, deadlines, and appointments than Westerners. Our Looter Leader did not conform to this stereotype at all. Exactly, to the second, at noon, the last looter walked through the gate carrying—I kid you not—a fiberglass kitchen sink on his back. The Looter Leader stepped up to Buccino, smiled, and shook hands, then walked off toward the main road. The palace was untouched. All of the other buildings on the compound had been stripped to the cinderblock walls—plumbing, electrical fixtures, and furnishings had all been taken.

The NCOs reconned the area, positioned troops in the guard towers, and divvied up buildings for living quarters and work spaces. We set up our Operations Center in the grand Victorian ballroom, moving in ornate white dining tables along with matching pink upholstered chairs on each side.

The space was way too large for an Operations Center, and it echoed with the slightest sound. But we didn't care. We had captured the palace of our archenemy. I wanted my men to have memories of their accomplishment. It was a well-earned interlude as the initial phase of our overwhelming victory transitioned to post-combat stability operations.

By June 2003, I was exhausted. My mental facilities were grinding to a halt, and I was processing information at a glacial pace. I had worked 657 days straight without a single day off—every day since September 11, 2001.

I had recently been elevated from a Battalion Operations Officer overseeing 18 A Teams to the Group Operations Officer in charge of synchronizing and coordinating the operations and training of 54 A Teams. Our leadership was beginning to recognize that we were in for a long war—a war we were not prepared to wage in a sustained fashion—and I was ordered to return to Fort Campbell to prepare the Group for the long haul.

There were only a handful of us on the C-17 Globemaster as we left Iraqi airspace on our way to Germany. The immediacy of the war faded with each passing mile. For the first time in months, maybe years, I was alone with my thoughts. I was finally able to think about more than accomplishing the mission—but about why we undertook the mission in the first place.

And the more I thought, the more I was horrified. I couldn't escape the conclusion that I had been an active participant in an unjust war. We invaded a sovereign nation, killed and maimed a lot of Iraqis, and lost some of the greatest American patriots to ever live—all for a god-damned lie.

I was proud of what we had achieved professionally. It was truly the most masterful invasion the U.S. military had ever conducted. But at the same time, it was one of the most costly and disastrous foreign policy blunders in American history. The further we got from the war zone, the more my stress turned into burning white-hot anger.

I arrived in Kentucky to an empty house. My wife and children had gone to spend July 4th with family in Massachusetts. They didn't even know I was home. I got up Saturday morning and went to the empty gym on Fort Campbell and exercised without the threat of attack for the first time in months, then I picked up a six-pack of beer and went home. I spent the weekend thinking. I reread the Constitution. I read a short book by the famous British military historian John Keegan about the meaning of World War II. I slept, exercised, and kept mulling over my experiences in Iraq.

The rage building inside me focused on two groups. First, the neoconservatives who bullied us into an unjust and unwinnable war based on an egregiously flawed understanding of human nature. As a movement that grew out of communism in the 1970s, neoconservatives never rejected communism's original sin: the belief that human beings are a blank slate on which you can write anything you want. They went from believing they could achieve a socialist paradise by revolution, to believing they could create a democratic paradise by invasion. They were wrong on both counts, and millions of human beings are dead as a result.

Second, my anger was directed at Congress for abrogating its constitutional duties regarding the declaring, funding, and overseeing of our nation's wars. Our government was out of balance. The Executive Branch was dominating the supposedly independent and coequal Legislative Branch. The guardrails established by the founders had been crumpled like those run over by our tanks on the Thunder Run to Baghdad. And nobody cared.

Military brass was eager to accept the accolades of politicians wishing to gain political points, funds, and media appearances. To be clear, I don't think the senior military leaders at the time were craven. They just remembered Vietnam—how divisive it was for our country and how destructive it was to the military institution. But their willingness to be manipulated by politicians who were advancing their own ideological interests started a steady politicization of the Armed Forces that has only accelerated with each passing year.

As a result, today there are virtually no brakes on the American war machine. Military leaders are always predisposed to see war as a solution, because when you're a hammer, all the world's a nail. The establishments of both major political parties are overwhelmingly dominated by interventionists and internationalists who believe that America can and should police the globe. Even the press—once so skeptical of war during the Vietnam era—is today little more than a brood of bloodthirsty vampires cheering on American missile strikes and urging greater involvement in conflicts America has no business fighting. Without drastic change, the twenty-first century could be just as bloody as the last.

CHAPTER SIX

THE PRICE WE PAY

By 2005, I finally felt like a real combat soldier, like my dad and uncles and the veterans I grew up idolizing. I'd been awarded my Combat Infantryman Badge and combat patch in Afghanistan in 2001. I'd been shot at, rocketed, mortared, had a parachute malfunction in free-fall, almost crashed in a C-130, and came stupid close to stepping on an IED on a Thanksgiving Day patrol. I'd had a number of close calls and been scared plenty of times, but I'd never thought, "Well, I guess this is a suicide mission" until June 28, 2005.

I was just three days away from the end of my fourth deployment to Afghanistan, and I was scheduled to fly out of the Asadabad combat outpost that evening. The small base—a couple football fields in size—hosted a Marine company, Special Forces A Team, Provincial Reconstruction Team, and the 100-member U.S. interagency-Afghan Counterterrorism force I commanded. The base was constructed on the remnants of an abandoned Soviet outpost near the

Pakistan border, nestled between the Kunar River and the jagged peaks of the Hindu Kush mountain range. We were essentially the cork in the bottle preventing the bad guys from pushing south to the provincial capital of Jalalabad.

My kit was cleaned, packed away neatly, and ready for the journey home. All that remained in my windowless room was my rucksack, body armor, helmet with night vision goggles, and rifle.

My father had planned a much-needed family vacation to France. My mom had just overcome a bout of cancer, and with my kids finally old enough to appreciate the experience, we were looking forward to some family time. I was in a semi-euphoric "going home mode," having survived another three-month tour in Afghanistan.

With little to do before I left, I sat in a rocking chair on the covered porch that ran the length of our single-story building. Locals had concocted it out of a slurry of mud and bricks—the kind of materials laid by hands that believed their work, like civilization itself, was temporary. Across the dirt road, I noticed a sudden flurry of activity in front of an older building that housed the 3rd Special Forces Group (Airborne) A Team. It wasn't the orderly bustle that proceeded departure for a mission, but frenzied and frantic, as if someone had just poked an invisible beehive.

The A Team was commanded by Captain Christian Sessoms of Fayetteville, North Carolina. At 5'7" and 140 lbs soaking wet, with thinning strawberry blonde hair, Sessoms would never be asked to pose for a Special Forces recruitment poster. But in my opinion, he could have written a chapter or two in the "How to Be a Special Forces Badass" training manual.

When it came time to fight, his eyes hardened, his expression lost its buoyancy, and his jaw fixed like stone. His voice deepened, and his every word was meticulously focused and precise. He never lost his cool, never lost his nerve, never lost his focus on the mission in front of him. He was like a machine. Possibly a Terminator from the future. I couldn't be sure.

One night, when Sessoms and his team were on a mission up in the mountains, I heard him calmly report over the radio that a helicopter had crashed and that his team was in the process of recovering the wounded crewmembers. He sounded like he was describing a mundane morning walk to his mailbox. The next day, I found out the helicopter was hovering directly over his head when it suddenly rolled onto its back, plummeted like a rock, crashed at his feet, and burst into flames. Sessoms was the kind of guy who didn't blink when death stared him in the face.

No training exercise, no matter how realistic, can prepare a leader for a situation like that. You can't hide behind an elite university diploma or your rugged good looks. Your peacetime promotions mean shit. The rank on your collar is irrelevant. The god of war has either blessed you with the gift for combat command, or he hasn't—and these are the moments when you find out.

I had no doubt that Sessoms had the gift. But that afternoon he was visibly shaken. I met him on the dirt road between our buildings. "Chris, something bad just happened. Can't give you details yet, but get ready." That's all I needed to know. I understood he had an obligation to keep his cards close to his vest. Even though we were friends, I was outside his command. But I'd served with him long enough to know that if he said something was bad, it was *really* bad.

I walked up the street to the barracks housing the 100 Afghan commandos I commanded and ordered the senior NCO to get everybody ready to deploy. We had a practice of never detailing our plans to preclude an Afghan commando leaking it, either inadvertently or deliberately, via the cell phones that had become omnipresent by then. Within minutes, armored Toyota pickups lined the dirt street. Machine guns were mounted, rations loaded, and fuel and water cans topped off. We were ready to roll.

But I still had no idea what we were headed into, so I walked over to the A Team house and quietly slipped in unnoticed. Sessoms was on the radio and his team was huddled around maps in the operations center. I quickly surmised that a Navy SEAL element had gone missing after being compromised while performing a Special Reconnaissance (SR) mission in the Korangal Valley. Their mission was to locate the local warlord, Ahmad Shah, and either capture him or call in an airstrike to kill him. It was part of a larger U.S. Marine Corps operation called Operation RED WINGS, and the heroic deeds of those missing SEALs would later be memorialized in the best-selling book and blockbuster film *Lone Survivor*.

I was confused. We had heard about the SEAL plan several weeks prior. One of the intelligence officers I worked with had recognized the danger in going into the Korangal Valley with such a small force and predicted disaster. I went with him when he called the Joint Special Operations Task Force (JSOTF), which oversaw the SEAL unit, and he explained why the operation was a bad idea. The last I had heard, JSOTF leadership agreed with him, and the mission had been canceled. Case closed. I didn't think anything else about it.

Unfortunately, the plan had been resurrected. The problem is that SR missions always sound great in a briefing. It's such a sexy concept—sneak in and watch the enemy without them knowing it. The only hitch is that it's damn near impossible to remain undetected in populated areas—particularly if your arrival is announced by the deafening cacophony of helicopter blades, as was the case with the SEAL insertion. There are techniques to confuse your opponent about your location—you can conduct numerous false insertions, forcing the enemy to disperse to pick up your trail, or you can land several miles from your "hide site" and patrol slowly. But either way, the clock is ticking, and it's only a matter of time before you make contact with the local population or enemy forces.

SR teams know this, and that's why they prepare detailed contingency plans in case they are compromised. Among the endless scenarios to consider, the most important is what to do if civilians—noncombatants—stumble on your position. A team only has three options: (1) take civilians prisoner during the mission and release them when complete; (2) kill them; or (3) let them go. Green Beret medics love to offer a fourth option of temporarily knocking the guy unconscious with a drug cocktail, but that's because they watch too many spy movies. In real life, you don't know when the guy will wake up, assuming he doesn't die of anaphylactic shock as a result of the sedative. Option 2 is occasionally discussed but always discarded because it violates the Law of Armed Conflict and the ethos of the American fighting person; killing unarmed innocents is the last thing any soldier wants to do. Turning civilians loose is inherently and obviously risky. That leaves you with Option 1—take civilians prisoner—and that is the option that most teams end up choosing.

The evening prior, the SEALS had landed on the high ground overlooking Shah's house. We didn't know how they had been compromised. Later, we found out they had, in fact, been discovered by a local goatherd, whom they chose to let go. But for now, all we knew was that they had called for emergency exfiltration by helicopter. One of the rescue helicopters had been shot down—the really "bad" thing Sessoms had warned me about a few minutes prior. Now the SEAL team was on the run, and all efforts to contact them had failed. They had gone into Escape and Evasion, or E&E, protocol.

I wasn't terribly concerned: detailed E&E planning is a hallmark of special operations. That's why we spent so much time on it during pre-mission planning and rehearsals. Now, all we had to do was open up the sealed manilla envelope labeled "E&E," follow the game plan devised by the SEAL team, and we'd have our guys home in no time.

Or so we thought. When JSOTF reported that the sealed envelope contained an anemic one-page plan, that's when I thought, "Well, I guess this is a suicide mission." We had nothing. We didn't even know where to begin our search.

With no E&E plan, our start point—the location we needed to get to—was the crash site of the helicopter. Once we rescued any survivors at the helicopter crash site, we could then branch out looking for the SEAL team.

I went back to my headquarters across the street and

briefed the two American officers that assisted me in leading the commando force, and my boss, the intelligence officer who oversaw all counterterrorism collection activities at Asadabad.

It was clear to me that the JSOTF was in turmoil. Command of the JSOTF rotated every six months. The 7th Special Forces Group was in the process of handing over responsibility to the 3rd Special Forces Group in what is called a "Relief-in-Place/Transfer-of-Authority," or RIP/TOA. Basically, one crew was clocking out, and the next shift was clocking in. It was always a sensitive, difficult, and dangerous period. The experience and wisdom of the outgoing team is diluted by the general naivete of the incoming crew. Plus, the inherent competition between units often results in the new guys not wanting to ask questions so they don't look dumb, and the experienced guys not proactively offering advice so they don't appear arrogant.

It was the worst possible time to conduct an E&E recovery. E&E was not a routine operation. As a matter of fact, most people never experience one in their careers. In our case, intelligence collection and analysis were unavailable. Resource availability was opaque. We had no idea who was in charge because of the RIP/TOA. It was a clusterfuck, to put it charitably. But that wasn't going to stop us from doing our job.

I wasn't eager to go up into the mountains, specifically around the Korangal Valley, on the day I was supposed to start heading home for my family's French vacation. I didn't want my career or my life to end like some sappy paperback novel: "He was waiting for the helicopter to take him away to his loved ones, but they sent him on one final mission."

But I didn't have much choice in the matter. "I will never leave a fallen comrade" is part of the Ranger Creed, the sacrosanct code by which we live and die.

We all knew Ahmad Shah. I had a different view of him than the Navy SEALs. They viewed him as an insurgent. To me, he was more like a pirate or a bootlegger. But instead of running moonshine, Shah and his people illegally smuggled timber into Pakistan. Either way, he was an asshole for sure and extremely dangerous.

The Korangal was a haunted place. There was only one road in or out. You knew you were being watched, and you knew you were going to be attacked. The roadsides in the region were littered with massive tree trunks jettisoned by Shah's crew to avoid prosecution by Afghan federal authorities. His beef with us and the Kabul-based central government had little to do with politics, but everything to do with commerce. But my perspective was entirely too nuanced for the black-and-white worldview that dominated American intelligence and military thinking at that time.

Sessoms and his men developed a plan to drive as far as we could, park our vehicles, and hike into the mountains to the crash site. It looked easy on the map. A bit of elevation, but we could manage. We'd hump up there, kill whoever needed killing, put up a defensive perimeter around the downed helicopter, get the wounded and dead out, then go find the SEALs. This wasn't a high-tech, hyperplanned Special Ops mission; it was an old school, in your face, kill the bad guys and capture the flag mission. No nuance required, or possible.

Normally, we would have choppered our guys into the area with swarms of attack helicopters and planes in support, but the military restricted flights to high-altitude aircraft that could avoid enemy shoulder-launched missiles. There were no vehicles that could traverse the mountainous terrain to carry equipment, supplies, and fire support. We had a miniscule amount of artillery that we could bring to bear, but using artillery effectively in the mountains is difficult at the best of times. We had night vision goggles, spotty satellite communications, global positioning devices, and our weapons were all automatic, but in many ways we were no different than our World War II Devil's Brigade predecessors that clawed their way up the mountains of Southern Italy.

The operation would be led by a Green Beret major that would meet Sessoms's team, 50 of my commandos (the other half were left behind for reinforcements), and a handful of Navy SEALs who latched on to help their brothers in need. A group of Rangers would also meet us at the vehicle drop-off point at the base of the mountain.

A lone Army artillery First Lieutenant volunteered to accompany us to handle artillery and air support. Communications difficulty had prevented him from getting approval from his commander, but, recognizing the importance of the operation and the need for his skills, he joined us anyway. I was impressed. He wasn't going to wait for permission to do the right thing, and he wasn't going to mindlessly obey bureaucratic rules if it meant abandoning his fellow Americans. Such moral and doctrinal courage is cheap and easy during training, but profoundly meaningful when lives are actually on the line.

It was beginning to look like a Saturday morning pickup game of basketball at the park; we were going to play with whoever showed up. When I went to brief my boss, an intelligence officer with an alphabet agency, he asked that I draft a CONOP—Concept of the Operation—to send to higher headquarters in Kabul for approval by the senior intelligence officer—the same guy who had made fun of me prior to moving Karzai to Kandahar in 2001 and who authorized the Predator reconnaissance mission in Iraq in 2003 that resulted in the aircraft crashing. My boss had no combat experience, and it showed. We had four missing SEALs and 16 Americans unaccounted for who were on the downed helicopter. It was around 2:30 a.m., and we were leaving for the drop-off point in a matter of minutes. I told him I had to go and didn't have time for paperwork. I'm pretty sure he thought I was joking because he forced a little chuckle and repeated his request. I suppose I could have gotten on the radio and called back to Kabul, but the duty officer would have had to wake the leadership, and I didn't have time for all that. So I just smiled and said, "I'm sure they'll be all right with it." Then I walked out the door.

I knew I'd be in deep shit, but to me this was the kind of event that defines a career for any officer. The safe thing—the "cover my ass" decision—would have been to sit down and call higher headquarters for approval. It probably would have taken less than an hour. With a little luck, I could have caught up to Sessoms at the vehicle drop-off point in a couple hours. But Sessoms and his men were going into the heart of bad guy country. They had six vehicles and 20 or so American special operators, enough to handle a gunfight—but my 10 additional vehicles and 50 commandos might be enough to dissuade an attack in the first place. And in any case, if Sessoms did get bogged down in a gunfight without me, my Quick Reaction Force was going to blast out of the base to reinforce him, and in that case I sure as hell wasn't going to waste time filing a CONOP.

As a husband and father, I also couldn't help but think of the families back home who would expect me, or anyone in my position, to get off my ass and bring their loved ones home. Families buy into the mythology that the American military always takes care of its own. Those who have served and lived at the mercy of the military's lethargic and bumbling bureaucracy know the truth is a bit more nuanced: *Soldiers* take care of their own; the military as an organization often does not. I wasn't about to let those families down.

To be fair, though, the American military, perhaps subconsciously recognizing the aforementioned truth, does allow for the expression of individual agency. In fact, one of the most unique characteristics that distinguishes the American military from all others is that it leverages the individualism inherent to the American character. Generations of military leaders have created a culture that embraces the free will of the individual soldier. It is uniformly *the* attribute that has enabled our tactical battlefield successes over the centuries. When everything is going wrong and the day seems lost, individual soldiers, without prompting, step forward and get the job done.

I also justified my actions by reminding myself that the United States taxpayer had given me a free college education, housing, health care, a nice middle-class quality of life, and the most meaningful friendships I will ever have. Parents and spouses had entrusted me with their most precious treasures—their sons, daughters, husbands, and wives—the most humbling and awesome responsibility I could ever imagine.

What return did they expect on their investment? The appropriate forms completed correctly in a timely manner with nice penmanship?

Fuck that. I was going to get our guys and bring them home.

I called it the "fire worm." Our quarter-mile-long convoy exited the camp gate and moved through the darkness like a centipede, expanding and contracting based on the condition of the road and surrounding terrain. A group of Humvees was waiting at the rally point when we arrived just before dawn. By the time the sun peaked over the horizon, the ambient temperature was nearly 90 degrees Fahrenheit. It was going to be an absolute smoking hot day. Water would be a crucial factor, and the gallon we each carried in our rucksacks wasn't going to cut it.

The mountains towered over us like the Titans of Greek mythology: ancient, monstrous, and utterly indifferent to our survival. I asked the Green Beret major who was running the show how long it would take to reach the crash site, and he said six hours.

"But that's based on straight-line distance," I said. "I bet it's at least 12 kilometers. This is going to take us at least two days."

He scoffed at me. I was wearing the same nonregulation garb as the indigenous force I led, and with a big red beard and shaggy hair that made me look like some kind of albino Pashtun, I guess I was easy to dismiss.

Vehicles continued to pull into our makeshift parking lot. We now had five separate elements assembling—a collection of Navy SEALs, a Ranger rifle platoon, a Ranger reconnaissance detachment, two 12-soldier Special Forces A Teams with a 10-soldier B-team, and my 50-soldier Afghan commando force. The Ranger element was led by a major bristling with confidence and energy, the exact opposite of the quiet and deliberate Green Beret major who was in charge of the overall mission. Culturally, this was a disaster in the making.

The typical Special Forces operator is older and exudes a laid-back attitude necessary to work effectively with indigenous forces. Rangers tend to be younger, and because they are tasked with the most difficult assaults, they necessarily value unerring discipline and instantaneous execution of orders. The SEALs live in a world apart and don't really care about the cultural norms of the Army. And I looked like an alien Anglo-Afghan hybrid leading a band of locals whose mere presence created suspicion and distrust. It might have been nice if we had covered such a scenario in training. As it was, leaders comingled and exchanged information while everyone else butt-sniffed and slowly developed some team cohesion.

I'm not going to lie—on the inside, I was absolutely petrified. I really didn't want to go up that mountain. I was convinced I was going to be killed. The treacherous route would expose us to the blazing sun as well as our enemies the entire way. We figured Shah could put 50 fighters or more in the field to ambush us. Their advantages would be incalculable. They knew the terrain. They would be in defensive positions. They had the element of surprise. They had been fighting in these mountains for generations. The blood of their fathers and grandfathers stained the very soil on which we stood—yet here they were, unvanquished and determined.

We were better equipped and could bring in air and artillery strikes, but this was going to be bloody. We would just have to bludgeon our way through head-on.

It was the most brutal movement of my career. We set off in a mile-long column up a narrow rocky trail that quickly became an endless series of switchbacks. When you faced the mountain, you saw the feet of the person on the switchback above you. When you turned away, you could see the head of the soldier on the switchback below you. The elevation gain was probably 2,000 feet in two miles. Thirty minutes into our climb, a Green Beret sat down on the trail and announced he could go no further. I was speechless. In 2001, I had heard about a Green Beret quitting on a mountain movement, but it was almost like a legend—it sounded like bullshit, but you couldn't be sure. Seeing it with my own eyes was like stepping on a crack in the sidewalk and then coming home and finding my mother a paraplegic for life. "Holy shit—it's true!"

Then a few minutes later, it happened again—another man down. Then another, and another. Each time, the exhausted man was sent back down the hillside. We were getting slaughtered in a war of attrition against nature, and we hadn't even made contact with the enemy. This was going to be a death march.

The Green Berets were loaded down with all of their

standard equipment as if they were on a training exercise at Fort Bragg. Each was clad in 30 pounds of body armor and carried a bulging rucksack weighing over 100 pounds. It gave me flashbacks to the excruciating cross-desert training exercise I subjected my team to back in Kuwait a decade earlier. But this time, we were scaling a mountain in a real combat situation. I knew how this was going to end.

In contrast to the overburdened Green Berets and Rangers, my commandos carried the minimum amount of equipment necessary. I decided we wouldn't wear body armor because it was too heavy and suffocating in the heat. Had I been serving in a conventional military unit, I probably would have been fired for that decision. But back in 2001, I'd gone into Afghanistan without body armor and credited the extra quickness and agility it afforded with keeping me alive on more than one occasion. Each of my commandos carried 210 rounds of ammunition, a couple of grenades, water, two food rations, and a clean pair of socks. Additionally, I carried a small backpack stuffed with a satellite phone, squad radio, and various devices to signal aircraft and denote our location. Our gear probably weighed one-quarter of the Green Berets' load, and it was still exhausting.

Since I was supposed to be going home in a couple of days, I had turned in all my operational funds—I always carried several thousand dollars in U.S. and Afghan denominations for contingency purchases. Fortunately, one of Sessoms's sergeants brought a wad of cash and put out the word to the Afghans mingling around the rally point that we needed pack animals. In a matter of minutes, Afghans started streaming in to rent their mules for exorbitant fees. We were happy to pay the money to ease our burdens.

As we struggled to get our gear loaded onto the animals, I couldn't help but think of the resistance I experienced earlier in my career when I petitioned higher headquarters to pay for mule training in Tennessee. I was laughed at. The idea that the most advanced, high-tech fighting force in the history of the world would ever require pack animals for mobility was the height of lunacy. Who was laughing now?

As a small unit leader, I was obsessed with movement rates—speed was king, as far as I was concerned, especially when it came to "rucking"—the Green Beret term for walking overland while wearing a rucksack. I tested theories and equipment. I talked to anyone who seemed a fellow traveler. I kept notes. I practiced rucking incessantly.

I had spent the previous couple of months at Asadabad specifically trying to master quick movement in the mountains. I'd also worked with the Afghans for several years and had heard the stories of their mujahideen fathers. They wore tennis shoes and carried the most rudimentary items required to get nourishment and fight.

I had deduced an intractable fact: When moving over broken terrain, an organized military force can move an average of one kilometer per hour. The Green Beret major leading the task force was operating under a flawed assumption.

We finally crested the first peak of the mountain around noon and found ourselves on a flat area a little larger than a football field. The crash site was still a long way to go, but at least we'd gotten the hardest part out of the way and could start running ridgelines that were more gradual in slope. Everybody was out of water. We had no choice but to wait for resupply. Even the mules had quit in the heat. We put in a defensive perimeter and scrounged for scraps of shade to shield us from the sun. All I could find was a sad little bush that reminded me of Charlie Brown's Christmas tree. I sat down and waited. It was miserable. I felt like my brain was cooking. My fair skin was frying.

After a while, the leaders of the SEALs and Rangers realized that at our current pace it would be another day before we reached our objective. They decided to form a "flying column" of 25 of the fittest warriors who would haul ass for the crash site. I absolutely loved the idea. The Navy SEALs and Ranger Regiment reconnaissance detachment were, in my mind, the most physically fit and combat-savvy members of the Armed Forces. The only question was whether they could reach the crash site before collapsing from dehydration.

I happened to own the fastest time to the Observation Post overlooking our combat base at Asadabad. I had no doubt I could hang with, or even dominate, any of them when it came to rucking. The flying column was what I had been preparing for my entire career—a desperate mission in desperate times, built around my obsession with rucking.

All I had to do was turn over command of my Afghan unit to my junior officer. No one would have cared. He would have loved the chance to be the boss, and he was completely qualified to run the unit. We were in the middle of nowhere and out of communications with higher headquarters. I was the senior intelligence officer in the task force, and my decision wouldn't be critiqued. I loved to tell my kids when they were in the midst of a challenge that it was "time for heroes." This was one of those moments. The flying column might be something that generations of special operators would talk about. It was historic.

But I couldn't do it. If I joined the flying column, it would be about satisfying my own desires, rather than serving the interests of the mission. They didn't *need* me to go, and I had a responsibility to my men. I couldn't shirk it just because I felt like it. I started out not wanting to go on this mission at all, but I had to. Now I wanted to be the tip of the spear and couldn't.

Finally, a MH-60 helicopter landed in our midst, unloaded five-gallon containers of water, and evacuated another handful of soldiers that were too dehydrated to continue. My guys and I were last in line to the water resupply. The containers were almost empty. We got a couple of sips each.

With their canteens full, the flying column exited the perimeter and moved at a brisk pace toward the unknown.

The sun was dropping behind the mountain as we shambled up the trail. It was kind of reminiscent of the Alps in *The Sound of Music*, but without the flowers or the singing. We crested the next peak and found ourselves on a very restrictive ridgeline, with a steep drop off on either side. It was the perfect place to make camp for the night.

It didn't surprise me that the Special Forces Major that was commanding the Task Force offered my Afghan colleagues and me the distinguished honor of manning the portion of the perimeter closest to the enemy. It reinforced my suspicion that he considered us little more than cannon fodder.

The Afghans were all relaxed—a good sign that we wouldn't have to fight in the near term. I didn't know Shah intimately, but the fact that he was still alive indicated that he was a savvy operator. Insurgents that live long enough to make a name for themselves usually follow, formally or intuitively, Mao Zedong's guerilla warfare maxim of only fighting when the conditions are in their favor.

But, in fact, we had no idea what Shah was going to do. We had no meaningful intelligence on what had happened to the missing SEAL team. In the 1990s, the national security community had become obsessed with the theory that super-fast computers, ubiquitous intelligence, surveillance drones, geostationary satellites, and improved communications systems would give American commanders near-perfect battlefield information and "Lift the Fog of War"—as the title of a book by Admiral Bill Owens suggested.

Military strategists have been trying to eliminate the fog of war since Jesus was a little boy. It was, and is, a pipe dream—but Owens and his acolytes postulated that America was on the verge of accomplishing this.

I had been exposed to their theories while attending the Naval War College a few years earlier. I was skeptical, but with so many high-ranking and highly revered leaders advocating such ideas, it was difficult not to get swept away by the metastasizing mania.

But now the truth was inescapable. We hadn't heard a peep from our missing SEALS. We were the most technologically advanced military in the history of humankind, with sensors in orbit that could identify the launch of rockets, listen in on radio conversations, and identify disturbed earth from space—yet we were operating no differently than Winston Churchill in India's Northwest Frontier Province in the late 1890s. So much for lifting the fog of war.

* * *

As darkness enveloped the mountain, we got reports that the flying column had collapsed in exhaustion well short of the crash site. A new plan was made: After midnight, another Ranger platoon was going to fly in and off-load out of range of the shoulder-fired missiles templated on the high ground around the crash site. The fresh troops would then patrol the remaining distance to the helicopter wreckage.

As I drifted off to sleep that night, I decided that if this new plan was successful, I'd reassess what to do with my commando force.

The next thing I recall was a tornado descending on me, courtesy of a dual-rotored Chinook helicopter hovering directly overhead. Boxes and water cans started raining down all around me. Obviously, the soldiers on the helicopter had no idea I was on the ground below them. I scrambled for safety, angry but amused by the lunacy of the situation. Getting killed by a five-gallon water can or box of MREs would have been the perfect conclusion to this snakebit operation.

With the blessed relief of dawn, I checked in with the Task Force commander. The Rangers had made it to the crash site and established a defensive perimeter. Tragically, all 16 Americans on the downed helicopter had perished. There was no one for us to rescue.

The rest of the Task Force would now shuttle by helicopter to the crash site and start the search for the missing Navy SEALs. Unsurprisingly, my Afghan commandos were the lowest priority for movement. I knew how this was going to go—we would get left behind. I decided to save the Green Beret major the trouble.

"Hey, I'm repositioning the QRF back to A-bad so we can respond better to anything that comes up," I told the Task Force commander. He smiled and said, "Good idea." I'm sure he was glad to have me and the Afghans out of his way.

After the nightmare of the last 24 hours, I was eager to get my guys moving as soon as possible before the sun started pounding us again.

When we reached our vehicles, I dumped my sweat-soaked gear in the bed of my pickup and sat in the passenger seat in my T-shirt and fatigue pants. We always drove with our ballistic glass windows up for protection. But now I rolled mine down so I could feel the rushing wind and smoke a cigarette as I reveled in the adrenaline high. We had beaten the odds.

That evening we received a handwritten note from an Afghan written by one of the missing Navy SEALs, Petty Officer Marcus Luttrell. He was in horrible shape when rescued by Pashtun villagers, who had taken him under their protection. The intel officers studied the note carefully, searching for signs that Luttrell had written it under duress. We were concerned that it might be a trap set by Shah and his men.

While the military drew up plans for the operation, the intel team decided to send the courier back to the village to fetch a tribal elder who could arrange for Luttrell's rescue.

The next morning, we found out Shah had released a video of his men rifling through the SEALs' equipment. We couldn't be sure, but it was beginning to look like Luttrell was the only SEAL who had survived the mission—if we could get to him in time.

The intel officers huddled to discuss how to handle the tribal elder that was on his way to Asadabad to provide more details about Luttrell. We arranged for the elder to be brought discretely through a back gate in a civilian vehicle to avoid scrutiny by enemy observers at the base's main entrance. The intel team would validate his information, debrief him on enemy activity in the area, and hand off the intelligence to the Ranger rescue force.

When the elder arrived, we assigned an intel officer to be his handler. We had arranged a friendly setting so that we could quickly win his favor. Then I heard a commotion in the hallway. I stepped out and saw two Rangers marching toward our holding room with determination.

I intercepted them. "Hey, fellas, what's up?"

"Sir, please step aside. We have orders to take custody of the prisoner."

Oh shit. I knew they were just following the orders of their 25-year-old Staff Sergeant who was executing the desires of his 35-year-old Platoon Sergeant who was doing what his 25-year-old Platoon Leader told him to do based on the orders of his 35-year-old Ranger major.

"Fellas, I know you're just doing your jobs, and I respect that. But here's the deal: He's not a prisoner, and we're going to take care of this so we don't piss him off and fuck up our only chance of saving a Navy SEAL who needs our help. Why don't you have your squad leader come down here and we'll figure something out. Tell him that Lieutenant Colonel Miller is standing by." It was the first time that I revealed that I was one of them, despite my beard and long hair and lack of military uniform.

They turned and walked away deflated. Rangers only take the smartest Infantrymen. They knew they had been given stupid orders, but they still had to follow them—and now they were going to get scuffed up by their sergeant for failing to accomplish such a simple task.

While we were waiting, our handler popped in and announced that he heard the Rangers intended to tie the tribal elder onto the hood of the Humvee that led the convoy to rescue Luttrell.

So much for bridging the cultural divide. The Rangers were still operating by the maxim often attributed to Theodore Roosevelt: "If you've got them by the balls, their hearts and minds will follow." The Rangers' culture would adapt as the war progressed, but at the time, all Afghans were suspect by default, so lashing one that was voluntarily helping us to the hood of a truck made total sense to them.

The Ranger major came down, and after a few heated words, we reached a reasonable compromise: They could take our Afghan asset, but he could ride in the passenger seat instead of being strapped to the hood.

The Rangers recovered Petty Officer Marcus Luttrell without incident a few hours later. He was hanging on by a thread. He had suffered multiple bullet wounds, shrapnel had blasted through his limbs, and his back had been

broken as he tumbled hundreds of feet down the mountain. He had crawled through hell and made it out alive, the
lone survivor and a true Navy SEAL.

After the last couple of days, it felt good to finally get a
win.

I successfully got out of country the next morning without further drama. My wife picked me up at Dulles International Airport on July 4th, one day before we departed for
our family vacation in France. An hour later I was parked
in a lawn chair watching the neighborhood fireworks and
my children running around in delight. I couldn't help but
think about the stories of Vietnam veterans who at the
end of their tour were plucked out of a jungle battle and
deposited 48 hours later in their hometowns. I was older
and more experienced than many of them, but that night
I could appreciate the cognitive dissonance they must have
felt.

After my experience with Operation RED WINGS, I
never again put any credence in the techno-military evan-
gelists like Admiral Owens and numerous other "national
security professionals." I feel a bit foolish that I ever took
their utopian visions seriously. I applaud the efforts of those
who desire to limit the human waste of war by developing technologies that allow for precise targeting that limits noncombatant casualties and wanton destruction. But
they do our nation a disservice by overpromising and creating unachievable expectations for the young fighters
that are on the front lines. They are trained to believe that
they can apply extraordinary violence humanely and with

supreme discretion, only to find that such an approach is unachievable.

This gap between expectation and reality causes them to question their superiors, their training, and themselves. Adjusting to the brutality and randomness of combat requires every soldier to undergo a psychological and spiritual transformation, and it is only made more difficult when they have false expectations.

The delusions of the techno-warriors are also amplified by an inexperienced corps of journalists, media personalities, and elected officials—the vast majority of whom haven't been personally involved in the dirty, barbaric fights that are the essence of warfare. Most of the leading voices espousing network-centric warfare and all-domain operations come from the technologically enabled fields of aviation, submarines, and missiles instead of ground combat. The think tank crowd doesn't have any skin in the game, and their contributions should be met with profound skepticism. If they are wrong, no one holds them accountable, and they move on to the next "shiny object" that will elicit grants and donor contributions.

The recovery of Marcus Luttrell had absolutely nothing to do with technology and everything to do with the ancient martial virtues—physical and mental toughness, camaraderie, and the willingness to sacrifice for others.

Technology will never eliminate the essential nature of war. Combat is the most visceral and unambiguous of human activities and, as such, is driven by the vagaries of human emotion—fear, anger, hate, compassion, unpredictability. No computer or algorithm can model it or decide its outcomes. Artificial intelligence is incapable of replicating the vicissitudes and complexity of the human heart and brain. Instead of continuing to waste time, money, and brainpower focusing on the misguided and strategically unmoored theories of technology-centric war, we should retool our military to master Human-Centric War.

The most important weapon systems America can ever develop are the strength of our warriors' hearts, muscles, and the six inches of space between their ears.

CHAPTER SEVEN

THE DEADLIEST
ENEMY

I didn't know it at the time, but my 2006–2007 tour in Iraq would be my last time in combat—though I would soon square off against opponents that were far more dangerous in terms of the damage they could do to the United States. At least on the battlefield, your enemies do you the courtesy of shooting you in the face. Where I was headed, they stab you in the back.

In 2009, I was selected to attend the Army War College. The Army's incentive system rewarded War College attendance; it was a required gate for promotion to general, but with a war going on, most everyone just wanted to check the box and get on to their next assignment. The War College prided itself on being open to new ideas and welcoming unorthodox thinking, even though it wasn't. The truth is, like every other institution of higher education in America, its real purpose was to perpetuate the values, beliefs, and dogmas of the ruling regime. In the case of the military, that meant inculcating in graduates a rosy internationalist world-view and unquestioning faith in the invincibility of technology, ensuring that the next generation of leaders continued to support ever-increasing military spending.

I really didn't feel like participating in the charade and was looking for a way out when a buddy saved me by fina-gling a fellowship at the CIA. I had attended most of the Army's premiere Special Operations training courses, so why not attend the CIA's?

I spent the next three months learning the basics of recruiting and managing foreign spies. I was 45 years old, a decade-and-a-half older than the other candi-dates in the program, and had gained experience over the years implementing some of the techniques we were learning—especially after my tour in Bosnia. Most of it seemed like pretty mundane spy stuff to me: how to make dead drops, create cover identities, detect and evade hostile surveillance, use cameras and listening devices, and weap-ons training.

But what was far more interesting to me were the human aspects of the training: learning to read people's body language and demeanor, parsing their words, thinking about how their personality and beliefs shaped their behav-ior, and trying to discern their hidden thoughts, motives, and intentions. When you are in the field, you don't have time to think deeply about what makes your enemies tick— you're too busy trying to capture or kill them. Now, for the first time in my career, I had the chance to intensely study the human individual and to process, think, and learn slowly and deliberately.

I completed the course in July 2010, believing that it was a rewarding experience that wouldn't be particularly relevant to my career going forward. I was totally wrong.

About a month later, I got a call from Lieutenant General John Mulholland, the commander of all Army Special Operations Forces (SOFs). I had served under Mulholland, twice as a company commander and also battalion commander, and he was my mentor, role model, and, along with my father, the most important figure in my development as both an officer and a man. Mulholland had reached the conclusion that he needed a man at the Department of Defense to advance concepts and programs supporting the Irregular Warfare activities he oversaw. He asked me to accept a job at the Pentagon in the office of the Assistant Secretary of Defense for Special Operations and Low-Intensity Conflict. I didn't have a clue what the job entailed, but like a dutiful soldier, I accepted. He told me to report to the Pentagon in one week.

I had been in the service for 23 years and received numerous lectures on the structure and functions of the Department of Defense (DOD), but as a soldier my mind was always focused on more important and immediate priorities. As a result, I initially misunderstood Mulholland and thought he was asking me to be a traditional "assistant" to someone important at the Pentagon and that my primary responsibilities would include getting coffee and making copies. It took a second for it to dawn on me that he was actually asking me to be the deputy to the civilian head of Special Operations, two levels removed from the Secretary of Defense.

SOLDIER SECRETARY

I reported to my first tour of duty at the Pentagon in September 2010 to be the Colonel in charge of Irregular Warfare planning and policy. I'd visited the Pentagon briefly a few times in the past but had not spent considerable time there. It was one of the largest office buildings on Earth, having been speedily constructed in the run-up to World War II. Essentially a small city hosting 25,000 residents, it is completely self-sufficient with shopping, food service, medical and dental care, dry cleaning, hair salons, and fitness facilities. Some wag once said it was purposely designed so that employees never had an excuse to leave during the duty day, maximizing efficiency (and misery). My first few weeks, I would wander up and down the 17.5 miles of hallways looking at the museum-quality exhibits of famous battles, wars, and personalities. I stared at the alphabet soup of acronyms on doors, wondering what task and purpose the occupants were responsible for. It was as alien as any remote village in Afghanistan, and I didn't speak the language.

The first year was like drinking from a fire hose. I didn't understand the process, culture, alliances, or the games everyone seemed to be playing. As a result, the career bureaucrats consistently ran circles around me. But I paid attention and learned from every battle. That's the way the Green Berets trained me.

One of the things that bothered me was the layers of bureaucracy that needed to be coordinated, synchronized, browbeaten, and schmoozed just to accomplish the smallest of tasks. I was from a culture where "Yes sir, I'm on it" was the verbal affirmation of a relentless focus on producing results. Now I was overrun by legions of low-talent, low-energy obstructionists who were nevertheless quite formidable. Like the enemies I faced in Afghanistan, the DOD bureaucratic blob knew the terrain, they were deeply entrenched, and they had been defending their fiefdoms from invaders like me since time immemorial.

Every day, I'd see someone dozing off in the Cape Cod chairs in the courtyard or sleeping at a desk in the library with drool running down their cheek. They epitomized the slothfulness of our DOD. I compared the civilian organization I now represented to the uber-organized and efficient active-duty military officers of the Joint Staff that attended our interminable meetings. I shared their disdain for the civilian bureaucrats that controlled the pace of everything. Things that seemed common sense and noncontroversial to me were slowed down by the civilians who asked voluminous questions about legal precedent, rules of engagement, and funding requirements, to name a few of the endless list of questions that did nothing but obfuscate, obstruct, and confuse.

Civilian control of the military had been inculcated in me since my first high school civics class, and it always sounded logical to me. Now, seeing it up close for the first time made me nauseous.

But my views moderated over time as I worked more closely with the civilian leadership, and eventually, I gained a deeper appreciation for the role of the Office of the Secretary of Defense. Although there were absolutely some slackers and stereotypical bureaucrats deeply embedded in the Pentagon, at its best, civilian control served as a necessary firebreak to the impatient, operationally focused uniformed military. They applied a necessary brake to the frenetic pace of the active-duty military that had defined the previous quarter-century of my existence.

SOLDIER SECRETARY

*   *   *

By my second year at the Pentagon, I was finally finding my sea legs. I'd learned the arcane systems and pathologies of the bureaucracy, and now I was starting to test counter-measures to advance my office's projects and priorities.

The overarching mission Lieutenant General Mulholland had given me was to institutionalize Irregular Warfare in the DOD, which required prodding the bureaucracy to accept the realities of a post–Cold War world and enter the twenty-first century. Not an easy task, to say the least.

The problem was that the military establishment was entirely focused on waging Traditional Warfare. Traditional Warfare is exactly what you imagine: World War II–style military-to-military combat designed to obliterate enemy forces, seize terrain, and capture capitals. The U.S. military has been optimized for such activities for the past 70 years, and it still is.

By contrast, Irregular Warfare is more typical of the twenty-first century with violent struggles among state and nonstate actors not just to control geography but to gain legitimacy and influence in the eyes of the people stuck in the war zone. In Iraq and Afghanistan, destroying military forces had little if any effect on defeating the insurgents. The "key terrain" wasn't a city, river crossing, road intersection, or mountain pass, but the loyalty or compliance of the population.

When we support insurgents to overthrow a hostile government like we did in Afghanistan in 2001, success requires in-depth knowledge of the language, culture, and customs; psychological warfare to communicate supportive messages and themes; civil affairs expertise to assist in establishing governmental services like courts, health care, public safety, and development; and Special Forces to train, advise, assist, and lead security forces and tie all of the other elements together in an integrated and synchronized way. Irregular warfare lives on the Island of Misfit Toys; nothing about it really fits in with the rest of the military.

To be clear, the DOD, defense contractors, Congress, the media, think tanks, and academia uniformly *hate* Irregular Warfare (IW), primarily because there's no money in it. Language training, cultural studies, and small, easy-to-use aircraft do not significantly improve a major defense contractor's quarterly earnings statement. The proponents of Traditional Warfare justify their obsession by waving around doomsday intelligence threat assessments and hyping warfighting concepts that require expensive weapons systems and vast numbers of active-duty personnel spread throughout the world to deter aggressors and respond if molested.

They often pay lip service to IW but quickly pivot back to their talking points demanding massive military expenditures so we can continue to try to police the world in vain. Concerns closer to home, like the drug cartels that kill 100,000 Americans annually, aren't really existential threats to the United States in their view and should be handled by law enforcement rather than the military. They believe this despite the fact that the United States only engages in major conventional war every few decades and is overwhelmingly engaged in IW activities the rest of the time.

After Vietnam, the Pentagon had gutted an important component of IW known as Counterinsurgency

Operations (COIN). Many COIN units had been disbanded and defunded, with the resources reinvested in traditional warfighting capabilities that would deter the Soviet Army from marching through the Fulda Gap in West Germany.

But after 9/11 and America's early victories in Afghanistan and Iraq, COIN briefly became the "shiny object" for the national security industry in the mid-2000s. General David Petraeus led the short-lived military transformation with his production of the first COIN manual since the 1970s, and he successfully implemented his concepts as the overall commander in Iraq from 2007–2009. As a result, major defense contractors quickly bought out a bunch of start-ups that provided interpreters, reconnaissance aircraft, intelligence analysts, maintenance personnel, information technology services, and civilian advisors to government ministries, to name but a few of the new business opportunities. In the government contracting world, these services are enormously lucrative, often generating a 100 percent profit margin for the parent company.

But by the time I stepped into the fray as the head of IW policy in 2010, the shine was coming off IW, and the supporters of the "Big War" paradigm were regaining their form and strength. They had been stunned and marginalized after the 9/11 attacks and the global counterinsurgency campaign it triggered. Now they were ready to get back to business as usual, and I was the face of everything they detested.

In the Pentagon, everything comes down to money. If you have money, you have power and influence. If you

Eighteen years old and a year of college under my belt. Military Police Advanced Individual Training at Fort McClellan, Alabama, in the summer of 1984. It was the height of the Cold War and part of the bow wave of the renaissance of the Army from the dark days right after Vietnam. *(Author's personal collection)*

I enlisted in the Army Reserve right after high school and completed eight weeks of Basic Training at Fort Benning, Georgia. This photo was taken during Advanced Individual Training at Fort McClellan, Alabama, in 1984, between my freshman and sophomore years of college. *(Author's personal collection)*

Private First Class Miller of the District of Columbia Army National Guard preparing to leave my dorm at George Washington University for weekend duty, 1985. Thirty-five years later, I would mobilize my old unit on January 6, 2021, to secure the Capitol for the upcoming inauguration. *(Author's personal collection)*

United States Army Ranger School involves eight weeks of unrelenting physical stress, limited sleep, and constant hunger. It produces the finest small-unit leaders in the world. Thus, it was a defining professional experience, and enormous relief, to attend my graduation in May 1984 at Fort Benning, Georgia. *(Author's personal collection)*

This is me trying to lead my first platoon in Korea during a training exercise in the winter of 1988. We were hyper-focused on being ready to "fight tonight" and spent every waking moment training to repel an expected invasion by the North Koreans. *(Author's personal collection)*

South Korea in the winter of 1988. My partner and I were evaluating a sister unit during a large-scale training event. The orange bands on our helmets set us apart from the operational unit. This was the height of the Army's renaissance after the Vietnam War, when every major activity was critiqued by an external evaluating team. *(Author's personal collection)*

My Ranger buddy 2LT Mark "Bo" Ridley in Korea in 1988. No one graduates Ranger School alone, and I would have never made it without him. We ended up in the same battalion in Korea—1st Battalion, 506th Infantry Regiment (the unit made famous in *Band of Brothers*), 2nd Infantry Division. *(Author's personal collection)*

Commanding a joint cordon at the Pentagon's ceremonial field for the arrival ceremony of some long-forgotten foreign military head, circa 1989. Thirty-one years later, I looked out over the same field from the office of the Secretary of Defense. *(Author's personal collection)*

Deep in the Hindu Kush of Pakistan on my first training deployment as a newly minted Army Special Forces Team Leader in the summer of 1994. A Company, 3rd Battalion, 5th Special Forces Group spent the month training with the Pakistani equivalent of the Green Berets. Those bonds of fellowship served us well in 2001. *(Author's personal collection)*

It's amazing to think we roamed freely over the Swat Valley of the Pakistan Tribal Area in 1994. Al-Qaeda took the valley over in 2004, and any Westerner traveling through the region would not last long. *(Author's personal collection)*

With Captain Mark "Bo" Ridley, in Pakistan in 1995. We went through the Infantry Officer Basic Course, Ranger School, and served in Korea together, and we were now Green Beret Team Leaders at Fort Campbell, Kentucky. It was a joy having a friend across the hall in our rundown and decrepit headquarters. *(Author's personal collection)*

Learning how to operate in the desert in 1994. Fifth Special Forces Group (Airborne) maintained a constant presence in Kuwait following Saddam Hussein's expulsion in Operation Desert Storm in 1991. We adopted the tactics of the World War II–era British Special Air Service and Long Range Desert Group and updated them with modern technology. *(Author's personal collection)*

Hunting war criminals in Bosnia in 1998. The first place my physical profile didn't stick out. It was a graduate-level course in learning how to operate with a low profile. Many of the special operators that served together in the region during that time period became the small-unit leaders in Afghanistan in 2001 and the invasion of Iraq in 2003. *(Author's personal collection)*

Heading off to work at Fort Campbell, Kentucky, to board the plane to the Special Operations Forward Operating Base at Karshi Khanabad, Uzbekistan, just before Thanksgiving, 2001. Going to combat seemed like a good idea in 1983 when I was 17 years old and single. Having a wife and three kids at 36 focuses one's mind quite a bit more. *(Author's personal collection)*

The best job I ever had: Special Forces Company Commander of Operational Detachment Bravo 570. This is early morning during a raid to capture or kill four al-Qaeda fighters barricaded in a hospital. We weren't wearing body armor because we infiltrated on December 5, 2001, with minimal equipment so we could move fast. *(Author's personal collection)*

When I moved to the Pentagon, I only took one thing: this photo, inscribed with the words "When you think it can't get worse, actually it can." This is me realizing that my "superb" plan to capture or kill four al-Qaeda holdouts in a hospital in Kandahar, Afghanistan, in early 2002 had utterly failed. In true Green Beret fashion, a couple of sergeants and warrant officers came up with a new plan that worked. *(Author's personal collection)*

Kabul, Afghanistan, in 2004 at one of the only local stores that sold beer. A frequent stop for low-visibility operators and the plethora of U.S. and foreign workers. I carried a Remington 870 pump action shotgun with an 18" barrel during this tour with "another government agency"—the same style shotgun I bought as a 14-year-old in Iowa City, Iowa. *(Author's personal collection)*

The intelligence assessment in preparation for this March 2005 operation to capture a high-value target deep in the mountains of Afghanistan was that we would land in 3 feet of snow in freezing temperatures. I dressed accordingly. It turned out to be 70 degrees and sunny, and I almost became a heat casualty. This is after the successful mission, waiting for the helicopters to lift us out. *(Author's personal collection)*

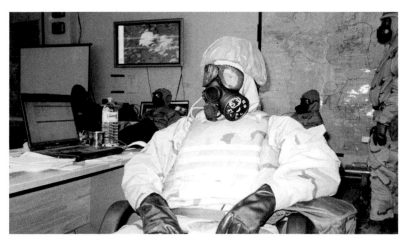

Most soldiers hate training to operate in a "Nuclear, Biological, or Chemical" environment, me included. And then Saddam started shooting missiles at Kuwait in the run-up to our 2003 invasion. I would sit in my protective gear at our headquarters in disbelief that we could potentially become the first generation since World War I to be gassed. *(Author's personal collection)*

My best friend in the Army, then-Major Bruce Swatek, as he prepared to load his Task Force into an armada of helicopters to recon an abandoned air strip in southern Iraq that we hoped to use in advance of the main invasion of Iraq in 2003. It worked. Bruce was the finest combat company commander I witnessed during the war—absolutely fearless, level-headed, and unflappable. *(Author's personal collection)*

Getting ready to back my truck onto a MH-53 USAF Special Operations Pave Low helicopter for the flight into Iraq in April 2003. The side clearance was mere inches and backing it up the ramp to the helo was not for the faint of heart. (The Load Master frowned on us hitting his helicopter.) *(Author's personal collection)*

Loading ammunition magazines in preparation for infil to Iraq from Kuwait. I was the Operations Officer of the 3rd Battalion, 5th Special Forces Group (Airborne). As the third in the chain of command, you were always solving problems and taking care of other people, and all of your personal needs are reduced to the basics. Loading magazines focuses the mind and allows you to switch over into combat mode. *(Author's personal collection)*

Retired Special Operations legend General Wayne Downing. We gave him a ride on April 10, 2003, into Baghdad the day after the city was captured by the 3rd Infantry Division. We are at the iconic Iraqi war memorial. *(Author's personal collection)*

Third Battalion, 5th Special Forces Group (Airborne) Commander Lieutenant Colonel Tim Williams in Baghdad after the 3rd Infantry Division's remarkable second "Thunder Run" that ended Saddam's regime. I was his Battalion Operations Officer (S3). *(Author's personal collection)*

As Army Special Forces, we weren't invited to join the victory drive into Baghdad the day after the 3rd Infantry Division captured the city. They reassessed when we noted that we were escorting NBC's Brian Williams. Williams's "adult escort" was the retired, legendary commander of the United States Special Operations Command, four-star general Wayne Downing, who grabbed us and said, "Give us a ride and we'll get you in the convoy." *(Author's personal collection)*

Radwaniyah Palace Complex, Baghdad, Iraq, Thanksgiving 2006. I was back as the commander of 2nd Battalion, 5th Special Forces Group (Airborne). To give the infantrymen who normally manned the gate a break on Thanksgiving Day, I pulled an eight-hour shift before going out on patrol that night. *(Author's personal collection)*

My family argued with me that the photo of the Baghdad raid was staged. The photo they had seen on TV had me cut out. I let them rant for a while before I finally yelled, "It wasn't staged. I was there! We were all watching the Predator feed on the screen on the wall!" Everyone knows when the president's photographer is in the room, and we weren't going to get caught in a "Hillary Clinton moment" like the UBL hit. *(White House photo)*

I decided to join the Army after the failed 1979 operation to rescue our hostages held by the Iranians in Tehran. This is me in December 2020 in the Oval Office advising the president on how to respond to Iranian provocations. Oftentimes in DC, pundits will say to a former member of the Armed Forces, "It could be worse—you could be in combat." I replied, "I'd rather be in combat than dealing with you dipshits." *(White House photo)*

Getting ready to walk out to the coin toss for the 2020 Army-Navy football game at the United States Military Academy at West Point. My eye glasses had fogged over because of weather and condensation from wearing a mask, rendering such a memorable and meaningful event blurry. The president was magnificent, interacting with the cadets and midshipmen in the stands after the coin toss. *(White House photo)*

Thanksgiving, Bahrain, 2020. You don't know what is going on in the military until you break bread with those actually doing the job on the front lines and listen to them. It's tradition for senior leaders to serve service members their Thanksgiving meal. I couldn't have lived with myself if I didn't go out there and serve them. *(Defense Department photo)*

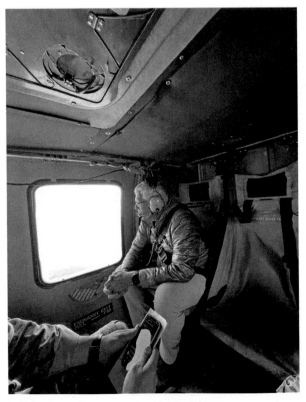

Flying over Kabul with General Austin "Scott" Miller, a mentor and the greatest general officer our country has produced in recent times, in December 2020. My hair was bright red the last time I was in Kabul in 2005. I went out to talk to General Miller to guarantee that our plan of withdrawal was solid. I never imagined that the incoming administration would botch the withdrawal so badly a few months later. *(Author's personal collection)*

Attending an Association of Southeast Asian Nations Conference via video teleconference from Hawaii. I went off script and ripped into the Chinese for their aggressiveness in the South China Sea. It was gratifying to see the Chinese general become visibly upset on the screen. *(Defense Department photo)*

I wanted to go the Capitol to help sort things out on January 6, 2021, but I knew the press would accuse me of fomenting a military coup. When I realized that local and federal law enforcement were incapable of protecting the Capitol, I ordered the largest mobilization of military forces in Washington, DC since the Civil War to reestablish control. It was personally devastating to be the person that had to militarize the Capitol because our civil discourse had broken down so fundamentally, but I was enormously gratified to witness the dedication of the members of our Armed Forces who conducted their mission with fortitude and focus. I was angered by the hypocrisy of Congressional leaders who welcomed the Armed Forces on their turf after January 6th after spending weeks lamenting that the very same troops posed a threat to the Republic. *(Eric Thayer / Getty Images)*

Jane Horton worked at the Pentagon to represent Gold Star Families—those who had a family member killed in combat—and asked me to speak with some families to learn about how our support programs were working. I was surprised that more secretaries of defense hadn't engaged with them—if our nation can't respect and support them, we have serious problems (and we have serious problems). *(Defense Department photo)*

don't, you are ignored. Budget in the Pentagon is a zero-sum game, and offices fight titanic battles over the nickels that are available for new projects each year. The first year I was clueless. The second year I was familiar with the process and personalities and was moderately successful in manipulating them to my office's advantage. By my third and final year at the Pentagon, I was dangerous. I had figured the place out. Someone once told me that military officers shouldn't stay more than three years at the Pentagon because by then the officer has mastered the system and was in danger of being permanently assimilated by the bureaucratic Borg. At the time, I didn't give it much credence.

That final year, I was responsible for conducting a quick turn study to determine how many Special Operations Forces America needed since President Obama had hastily withdrawn American troops from Iraq in 2011. Although no one outside Washington, DC, knows it, the most powerful entity in the DOD is the Cost Assessment and Program Evaluation (CAPE) office.

CAPE is the successor to the Kennedy-era Whiz Kids who brought "scientific" management to the Pentagon to bring spending under control. CAPE only dealt with data and spreadsheets. Opinions, speculation, gut feelings, experience, and common sense were applicable only if stated in writing on an official document—meaning they were never applicable.

With the Iraq War supposedly over, CAPE sought to justify future force structure based on the military's written war plans. The principal war plans were for major combat operations against countries like North Korea, Iran, and

Russia and included details on equipment and personnel requirements down to the last transport truck. The Special Forces were at a debilitating systemic disadvantage with CAPE's accounting methodology, because we only had a small role in major conventional war plans. Special Forces, after all, were designed to handle messy IW scenarios that can't be planned out years in advance. To the bean counters at CAPE, that meant Special Forces barely existed and wasn't particularly important.

I was well prepared to go into bureaucratic combat with CAPE and their platoons of PhDs. I knew that the CAPE employees were assessed by how much money they could wring out of the defense budget. I liked how their incentive system competed against the "more is better" mentality of the rest of the Pentagon, but I was adamant that they were looking in the wrong place. Instead of trying to reduce the size of U.S. Special Operations Command, they needed to consider growing it to reflect the realities of warfare in the modern world. I refused to relent to their subtle hints that the study could end if I just agreed to a reduction, and I was feeling confident that my approach was working. I knew they had to deliver a product to the Deputy Secretary of Defense rapidly, so I turned their own tactics against them. I obstructed, delayed, obfuscated, and was generally a dick.

Eventually, CAPE reluctantly recognized that they were significantly short-changing IW, and they agreed to maintain SOFs funding at current levels. I knew that I had won a battle and not the war, but it was a victory nonetheless, and I had bought crucial time to muster men and resources to withstand future assaults.

The timing turned out to be extremely fortuitous with the rise of ISIS the following year. The Obama Administration gradually accepted the awful reality that their precipitous withdrawal from Iraq in 2010 had unleashed the largest terrorist army in modern history. They decided against reintroducing American combat forces into the region, and Pentagon leadership was left with only one strategic tool: IW, waged by a small number of special operators who would train Kurdish paramilitary forces and Syrian dissidents, joined by U.S. intelligence agencies, foreign actors, and international partners. In a grinding, unforgiving war of attrition, these U.S.-enabled forces destroyed ISIS in the most effective IW campaign in American military history.

I hate to think about what might have happened if the bean counters had succeeded in gutting Special Forces funding.

The longer I stayed at the Pentagon, the more I began to think like a bureaucrat and less like a soldier. After three years, I found myself being drawn into petty squabbles about things that didn't matter. I started taking personal offense whenever someone disagreed with my opinion, and my first instinct would be to fire off a nasty email instead of actually solving the problem. The offender's name would be jotted down on the list of enemies steadily growing in the back of my mind. I was inadvertently becoming more and more preoccupied with protecting my little fiefdom—for all the right reasons, I told myself, just as all bureaucrats do.

In short, I was becoming the very thing I had always detested. I had gazed into the bureaucratic abyss, and the abyss gazed also into me. I realized that if I kept swimming in *The Swamp*, I would eventually sink into its mucky depths and be absorbed. It was time to go.

I had spent the first part of my career wondering whether I had what it took to be a combat officer. Although I had proven myself in battle, I now found myself once again pondering the same question for different reasons. I was approaching my fiftieth birthday, and when I was honest with myself, I could feel it in my joints. My kids were getting older, and I had missed huge chunks of their lives while I was overseas. My wife had endured more than her share of sleepless nights over the preceding two decades, and though I can't explain why, she enjoyed having me around. So in 2014, with my assignment to the Pentagon complete, I decided to retire after 27 years of service in the Army.

I routinely saw fellow colonels at the Pentagon who looked like they had aged more during their service in our nation's capital than during multiple tours overseas. It seemed like every retired colonel was overweight or on crutches. You didn't need a PhD in psychology to recognize that they were dealing with unresolved issues from their past, as well as the psychological and physical dislocation that comes with leaving the military. Many servicemembers' sense of self is wrapped up in their identity as a member of the Armed Forces. I suspect it is more pronounced in the officer corps.

I knew I had a lot of things to work through. For years, I had been cramming unpleasant memories into a box and storing them on a shelf deep in the recesses of my psyche, knowing that someday I'd have to unpack each one. Originally, I planned to hike all 2,200 miles of the Appalachian Trail, much like World War II veteran Earl Shaffer had done to "walk the war out of my system."[6]

Not being independently wealthy and unable to afford a four-month sabbatical, instead I set a goal to run a marathon in less than three hours. It was an aggressive goal, but achievable if I trained properly. And in any case, spending hours alone on the running trails of northern Virginia would give me time to work through the experiences of the past couple of decades and regain some spiritual, emotional, and mental fitness.

My weekly long run of 15–25 miles became my personal therapy session. I had come to believe that many of the psychological wounds of war are caused by moral guilt brought on when an individual violates their belief structure or sense of self. I'm not talking about the act of killing other fighters—that's part of the job, and military personnel are trained and toughened to deal with it. But the military doesn't prepare its people for wounding or killing a civilian or a child. If only the war my generation fought, and the motives behind it, were as clean and comprehensible as the popular media portrayed it.

I also had to deal with a simmering sense of betrayal that every veteran today must feel—the recognition that so many sacrifices were ultimately made in the service of a lie,

---

[6] Abigail Tucker, "The Army Veteran Who Became the First to Hike the Entire Appalachian Trail," *Smithsonian Magazine*, July 2017, https://www.smithsonianmag.com/smithsonian-institution/army-veteran-became-first-hike-entire-appalachian-trail-180963678/.

as in Iraq, or to further a delusion, as in the neoconservatives' utopian fantasy of a democratic Middle East. It still makes my blood boil, and it probably will until the day I die.

Leaders have the added guilt of knowing that their mistakes resulted in destroyed lives. Having your people maimed and killed is horrible, but it's part of the job of a commander. In many ways, it's the essence of the job. And yet I saw many senior officers become frozen by the shock and horror of taking casualties. I suspect it was because they came of age in an Army that had been at peace for almost 30 years.

Somewhere along the line, the slogan "Mission first, men always" gained great cachet. I've spent years trying to decipher what the hell that means, and I still have no idea. The two clauses are mutually exclusive, but people repeated it religiously. The reality is that the mission always comes first, and soldiers are the tool to accomplish it—and sometime soldiers are sacrificed to achieve the mission. Whether this is right or wrong is irrelevant; it is simply a statement of fact.

When I was a platoon leader, I recall one young (drunken) soldier tearfully saying to me in frustration, "I'm just a number to the Army. They don't care about me." "No shit," I responded. "We're cannon fodder. That's what we volunteered for." If you actually believed that being in the Army was about learning a skill or getting money for college, you got played. The best any soldier could hope for was that the mission would be worthy of the sacrifice—and for my generation, that often proved to be an unreasonable demand.

I learned early on that people confused my gregarious-ness and approachability for friendship. I felt guilty when subordinates realized that I wasn't their friend and would hold them accountable if they failed to perform. I worried that I was disingenuous and manipulative. So after a while, whenever I took command of a new team I would announce, "I'll be your buddy. I'll laugh at your jokes. I'll go to your parties. I'll drink your beer. But never confuse that for friendship. My job is to accomplish the missions we are assigned. We all are expendable." It was coldhearted and maybe a little melodramatic, but I didn't want any confusion.

During my tour as a battalion commander in Baghdad, I remember telling a Green Beret that I was friendly with to get in his truck and move out. We both knew the odds were high that his vehicle was going to trigger a roadside bomb. He thought I was kidding at first—after all, we had spent time together and had a relationship. I said, "I'm not kidding. Get in the fucking truck and move out." His face turned white as he processed the information. Then he got in the truck and moved out. Fortunately, he made it to his destination without injury. We talked about it later, and he said, "You know, you told us we were expendable."

I carry a great deal of moral guilt because I didn't have the same profound reaction to loss as the senior leaders above me. I had to consider if I was some sort of depraved degenerate or a sociopath. I was naive about a lot of stuff in the military, but the one thing I knew from all the stories I heard growing up was that some people I was responsible for were going to be shot to pieces, blown to bits, or burned to a crisp.

The cruel irony and inescapable tragedy of effective combat leadership is that you must destroy the very thing you build and love—your unit. That's not something they tell you in officer training. Maybe that's because if they told you the truth, sane people would run for the exit.

Robert E. Lee uttered the deepest words of any warrior, "It is well that war is so terrible, otherwise we should grow too fond of it."[7] There is no more dramatic place than the battlefield. Life is compressed. You only have one thing to do. There is no spouse complaining about money; no kids to be picked up from practice; no paperwork or meetings; no lawns to be mowed or dinners to be prepared. You simply become who you are. I knew I was susceptible to the battlefield's siren song—who wouldn't be?

To leave it all behind was the hardest thing I'd ever done, yet I knew I had no choice. Even the most battle-hardened war junkie eventually has to face the reality that war is a game of probability, and the probability of death becomes a certainty the longer you play. And no matter how hard I tried, I couldn't see an end to the wars America was fighting.

Less than 1 percent of the American population was fighting the war. And an even smaller percentage—a couple of tens of thousands—were statistically doing most of the fighting and bearing the brunt of the physical and

---

[7] Douglas Southall Freeman, *R.E. Lee: A Biography*, vol. 2. C. Scribner's Sons, 1935.

psychological destruction. I remember patrolling the streets of Baghdad at night and almost never running into any of the other 20,000 coalition forces.

As a result, the Army was coming undone psychologically: suicides were skyrocketing, alcohol abuse was rampant, marriages were collapsing, petty discipline problems were typical, and professional development—which was critical to maintaining a professional corps of leadership—was pushed aside due to the exigencies of combat. It was all entirely predictable—those are exactly the pathologies expected in a volunteer Army that is engaged in combat for an extended period.

I still feel completely culpable in this deceit. I rationalized that I was a mid-level leader who was getting paid to maintain a fighting force, and I wasn't a politician or policymaker. But as a field commander, I could see the results firsthand. Whenever I asked my battalion's medical doctor how the men were doing, he'd say something like, "Sir, lots of people are having problems sleeping. I think it will ease in the coming weeks, but I've never seen it this prevalent." I knew what the fuck that meant. But my response would always be, "Can we get them out the door again?" "Yes sir, I think so," he'd say. Mission first, men always.

The pathologies that develop in individuals and units constantly exposed to the stress of combat are still not well understood because our nation has never gone to war for so long with so few citizens participating. But suffice it to say that severe pathologies should be expected any time a volunteer army wages a protracted war. An army becomes a wasting asset as soon as it meets the enemy. Our Army started the war in 2001 as the most professional and disciplined in history, and with each passing day of combat, it started breaking apart. This is the inviolate nature of war.

The only thing our leaders can do to prevent the catastrophic mental health effects of prolonged war is to stop engaging in unwinnable and unending wars.

I thought it would take me a couple of months to accomplish my goal of running a sub-three-hour marathon. It proved to be a bit more laborious than I originally projected, but I finally did it. And yet I found that I still hadn't quite run the war out of my system, so I kept at it.

My running odyssey ended after snapping something in my ankle while running down the Appalachian Trail during the 2017 JFK 50 Mile race. I had reinjured the same leg I had broken my first day in Afghanistan. But I hadn't let it stop me from running into war back then, and I damn sure wasn't going to let it stop me from running the war out of my system. It must have been a blown tendon or ligament—I'm not sure, because I never went back for the MRI my doctor scheduled. But I know it wasn't broken, because I managed to finish the race in 7 hours and 48 minutes, coming in second in my age group.

I sat down at the finish line, covered in sweat and mud, and accepted that my race was run. There were no great epiphanies, no angels descending from heaven with divine revelation. All I could think was that war is a horrible waste. And that those who are thrust into its cataclysm of fear, longing, heroism, cowardice, empathy, hate, repugnance, and glory have limited control and just need to do their best. Forgiveness and understanding are difficult to call upon, but it's good to try.

But ultimately it's about acceptance—accepting that there is no logic to something that is completely illogical by its very nature. The moral and ethical compromises and their handmaidens, guilt and shame, are essential elements of the combat soldier's experience in war. I could criticize the Army for failing to properly prepare me, but that would be unjust. I probably wouldn't have listened to such warnings when I was younger.

CHAPTER EIGHT

JACKPOT

In March 2018, I was appointed to the National Security Council (NSC), serving as the Special Assistant to the President for Counterterrorism and Transnational Threats— President Donald Trump's senior advisor for counterterrorism. I had been stuck in bureaucratic hell as a mid-level official at the Pentagon responsible for inspecting military intelligence units for compliance with rules designed to protect American citizens from the wide-scale civil liberties violations of the 1960s and 1970s. A close friend from my days in the military, Chris Costa, was leaving his job at the NSC and asked me to interview to replace him. I have always counseled my children to interview when offered the opportunity because you will always learn something, and you might get the job. The fact that the interview would take place at the White House—a place I hadn't visited since my time as a lieutenant in The Old Guard—added to the significance. Apparently, I aced the interview and was offered the position.

My new boss was National Security Advisor John Bolton, the mustachioed, tough-talking war hawk who had served as President George W. Bush's Ambassador to the United Nations. Bolton has always denied being a neo-conservative, but in my opinion, he is perennially in favor of sending American troops to die in whatever godforsaken war is currently being discussed on cable news. Why Trump would hire someone so diametrically opposed to his own worldview will remain a mystery to me.

Bolton fashioned himself as a tough guy on Fox News, but in my estimation, he was a classic "chicken hawk." Like a loud-mouthed frat boy at the bar, he was quick to talk shit and cause drama, but he was nowhere to be found when the fists started flying. I really appreciate his service in the Maryland National Guard during Vietnam, but I wonder if a tour of duty in the combat zone would have moderated the tough guy persona that he worked so hard to cultivate on TV.

Unlike Bolton, I was an unabashed supporter of President Trump's efforts to end the war in Afghanistan. After being part of the initial invasion in 2001 and having served numerous tours there, I agreed with the assessment of many in the military, intelligence, and diplomatic fields that the war was a military stalemate and the only option for ending it was through negotiations. We had killed the people responsible for 9/11. How they wanted to run their country was no longer our concern—but if terrorism came back, so would we.

Three years into Trump's presidency, his efforts to end the war had been slow-rolled and selectively ignored by

Secretary of Defense Mark Esper and Chairman of the Joint Chiefs of Staff (CJCS) General Mark Milley. The Department of Defense (DOD) and the CIA were adamant that the current force structure of 8,200 military personnel was the absolute minimum required to avoid a devastating strategic failure in Afghanistan. That bullshit might work with the neophytes that hadn't actually been in the country, but I knew better.

So my NSC colleagues and I took it upon ourselves to find the answer to a simple question: How many troops did we really need to keep in Afghanistan in order to prevent a terrorist attack on American soil? Without approval or authorization, we started to war-game different scenarios.

We recruited a group of planners at the National Counterterrorism Center to host a series of tabletop exercises to develop a range of options for policymakers to consider. The CIA and military initially refused to participate; they remained adamant that 8,200 troops was the minimum required. When we advised them that the working group would continue with or without them, they changed their tune.

After numerous sessions, the group's universal consensus was the minimum military force presence needed to maintain a counterterrorism platform that could prevent al-Qaeda from reemerging in Afghanistan was roughly 800 military personnel.

I had my number. It would be a 90 percent reduction in the current force structure and would meet the criteria of President Trump's goal of withdrawing combat troops from Afghanistan. Our study couldn't override the recommendations of the DOD and CIA, but now we had an alternative that could put downward pressure on their insistence on leaving thousands of American soldiers in Afghanistan for eternity.

The narrative promulgated by the senior military officers that the collapse of the Afghan Army in 2021 was impossible to predict is totally wrong. I believe Chairman Milley and the theater commander, Marine General Frank McKenzie, are either lying or grossly incompetent. I'm not sure which is worse. Any member of the Armed Forces or Intelligence Community that served in the field alongside the Afghan Army knew that without U.S. support they would collapse.

We had trained the Afghan Army to expect massive displays of supporting fire, air support, and medical evacuation every time they went into battle. They had been led to expect logistical support to guarantee they didn't run out of ammunition, food, water, and gasoline. In reality, the Afghans were never capable of such undertakings on their own—and when our support was withdrawn, the inevitable happened.

I remember seeing old fighter jets provided by the Soviets in the 1970s and 1980s abandoned at the Kandahar airfield when we arrived in 2001. One of them had a tree growing up through the cockpit. Anyone who thought that Afghanistan was ready to join the modern community of nations was extraordinarily deluded.

Being a soldier in the Afghan Army wasn't exactly promising employment, but for those with few opportunities, the pay was appealing despite the danger. Illiteracy in Afghanistan was high, requiring a longer time to train in basic combat skills and limiting the efficacy of high-tech weapons and communications systems.

Cultural and societal norms also impact the warfighting style and mores of a people. I had observed and experienced these factors firsthand. Familial and tribal links affected everything. My experience was that the Afghan people are enormously pragmatic, and at the time I was unable to appreciate the blood links upon which their society is built.

As the U.S. Unconventional Warfare campaign in 2001 gained momentum, the Taliban quickly learned that they couldn't withstand our assaults. Every time we would arrive near their defensive positions, they would halt our advance with small arms fire. Through an interpreter, the Taliban commander would acknowledge the futility of further resistance. We would then call in an airstrike to convince the Taliban fighters that their commander was making the right decision, and they would immediately surrender and change loyalties to the insurgent forces we led. The military expected the defeat of the Taliban to take several months. Instead, 200 Special Operators and Intelligence Community paramilitary personnel overthrew the Taliban regime in a matter of weeks.

Yet we are supposed to believe that our military leaders never imagined that the exact same thing would happen in reverse once we were gone? It was obvious from the beginning. And the truth is, that's why they kept us in Afghanistan—they knew how it was fated to end, and no one wanted to be the one left holding the bag.

* * *

"What are you doing here?" National Security Advisor Robert O'Brien, Bolton's replacement, asked me in amazement.

"I'm here for the Baghdadi raid," I said.

It was about 4 p.m. on Saturday, October 27, 2019, and I had just walked into the White House Situation Room. Chairman Milley was already there. Two communications experts were connecting computer cables and checking out the live video feeds from the drones circling over Syria.

"You weren't read on to this," O'Brien said. I gave him a lighthearted pat on the shoulder and said, "You pay me to know what's going on."

I sat down across from Milley at the 15-foot-long wooden table that dominated the Situation Room. On the wall to my right were video screens displaying the drone's live stream. To my left was the head of the table where the President would sit when the operation commenced.

The CIA had tried to shut me out of the formal process leading to the raid on Abu Bakr al-Baghdadi, the leader of ISIS and the world's most wanted terrorist. I had been dealing with the CIA's jackassery for over a year now. I'd started out my tenure in March 2018 trying to be collegial and respectful, but my NSC colleagues and I had been repeatedly sidelined as the CIA hoarded intelligence in an attempt to enhance their bureaucratic power and influence.

I'd worked closely with the CIA for years, but always in the field where bureaucratic rivalries and shenanigans don't exist. When you put your lives in each other's hands in a war zone, nobody cares about politics or what organization is on your ID card. But in the nation's capital, I had to develop independent sources of information to guarantee I knew what was going on and could implement the President's strategies. In other words, my NSC colleagues and I were forced to spy on the CIA just to do our jobs.

I'd ruffled their feathers early on by loudly declaring that our new strategic objective should be to kill off the remaining seven senior leaders of al-Qaeda, then declare the Global War on Terror officially over. Obviously, we would continue to disrupt and destroy terrorist networks whenever and wherever necessary—but we needed to formally close the books on the Global War on Terror in order to focus on countering China and the emerging threats of the twenty-first century.

In true CIA fashion, their leadership smiled politely and said generally supportive things to my face while working behind my back to undermine, malign, and resist White House direction. I became so annoying that they finally summoned me to a private meeting and read me in on their intelligence and overarching operational objectives. I knew it was merely their attempt to co-opt me and shut me up. They soon realized their efforts were for naught, because I simply used the access they provided to pressure them to prioritize rescuing hostages being held by al-Qaeda in Africa, Pakistan, and Syria.

With the military defeat of ISIS in December 2018, the CIA grew even more clannish and insular. We all recognized that the Global War on Terror was winding down, and there would soon be voices in Congress calling for reductions in Counterterrorism (CT) expenditures. The CT crew at the

CIA was using the time-honored technique of hoarding intelligence so that policymakers would view them as the most important CT entity whose budget shouldn't be cut.

What was most frustrating to me was that the DOD was more than happy to play along. Defense Secretary Mark Esper, aided by Milley, and his predecessor Jim Mattis obsessively controlled the flow of intelligence outside the Pentagon, and any subordinates perceived as overly hospitable toward Trump's NSC were neutered. They had created an extremely hostile situation even for their own employees—including me, since I was still technically a DOD employee on loan to the NSC—and their dictates were draconianly enforced. On numerous occasions during NSC deliberations, frustration with DOD's intransigence would explode into open conflict. I heard it stated on more than one occasion by DOD employees that Esper and Milley would only provide their recommendations directly to the President, and never through the NSC—thereby cutting out the very people the President had hired to advise him on matters of national security and ensuring that no one could challenge the narratives they presented him.

The way I saw it, I got paid to advise the President, and if the CIA and DOD didn't want to provide the information that I needed to do my job, I needed to find another way to get it. I had run intelligence networks overseas. I figured it wouldn't be that hard to use the same tactics, techniques, and procedures within the United States Government.

As it turned out, it was a lot easier than running spies overseas because everyone spoke the same language and there were plenty of frustrated professionals loyal to the President and the Constitution who happily supported our efforts. Even with the CIA and DOD maintaining a stranglehold on information about the Baghdadi raid, we built an expansive network that was reporting to us in real time the status of the intelligence collection and planning. That afternoon, I got a call from a guy running a key portion of our spy network. "Get to Whizzer," he said, referring to WHSR, the abbreviation for the White House Situation Room. "It's going down tonight."

I gave a sly nod to Brigadier General Marcus Evans, the head of special operations at the Pentagon, who would be monitoring the details of the operation and passing updates to Milley. Evans had participated in hundreds of direct action raids since 2001 and was one of the most experienced CT leaders in the United States.

Evans would never get sideways with his boss, and I don't think he would have ever given me a heads-up about the mission, despite the fact that we talked regularly. But he flashed the slightest of grins when I walked in, acknowledging my craftiness in outmaneuvering those who had tried to keep me in the dark about tonight's raid.

The helicopter-borne assault force would launch from their staging area in northern Syria at 6 p.m. EST. The operation was one of the most high-risk raids in American military history. It was on par with the legendary Vietnam War raid to Son Tay to rescue American prisoners of war, the failed Iran Hostage mission, and the bin Laden operation. Frankly, I was surprised that the President accepted the high risk. The Syrians and their Russian sponsors had extensive surveillance capabilities that were guaranteed to spot our air armada crossing into their territory. It was entirely within the realm of possibility that they would engage our helicopters and create a catastrophe of historic proportions.

President Trump had already experienced political blow-back for approving a SEAL raid into Yemen in the first weeks of his presidency, which cost the life of Chief Petty Officer William Owens. Despite the risks involved in tonight's mission, and the misgivings of some of his advisors, President Trump ordered the mission to go forward. He could have opted for an airstrike without risking American lives, but he knew that bombing the compound would likely result in civilian casualties, and we wouldn't know for certain whether Baghdadi was killed. It would have been easy to decree, "Let's continue to monitor the situation, collect further intelligence, and wait for a more opportune time." But Trump said, "Take him out." To me, it was the definition of courageous presidential decision-making.

Vice President Mike Pence arrived in the Situation Room at about 5 p.m. and asked for an update. Evans provided a cogent, succinct overview of the operation. The Vice President then asked if it would be all right if he said a prayer. I was raised a Methodist, and I believe in the power of prayer, but I'm not particularly keen about public demonstrations. I had read many of the press reports about the Vice President's faith—most of which characterized it in negative ways. I wondered what he was going to say as we all bowed our heads. In a measured and deliberate voice, the Vice President asked the Lord to protect our warriors that were going into harm's way, to help them achieve their mission, and to bless their families. It was a simple prayer, but it had a remarkably positive effect on us and provided a sense of focus and calmness.

The President was keeping to his public schedule in order to maintain the illusion that nothing was going on that evening. He was still on his way back from a golf outing when our eight helicopters launched from their base in northern Syria. It was the moment of truth. Unlike flying through mountains or over jungles where helicopters can hide from enemy air defense radars by hugging the Earth and getting lost in the ground clutter, our helicopters were flying over a flat and featureless desert that offered no masking ability. The Syrian and Russian radars had an unobstructed view and would easily identify the airborne flotilla soon after liftoff.

Milley muttered under his breath, "Well, let's hope this isn't the start of World War III." Our airborne sensors were able to monitor the status of enemy threat radars and would automatically signal if they locked on to our helicopters for an attack. There was also a Russian fighter jet cruising over the target area that could effortlessly attack the helicopters, if ordered. The tension was palpable, and no one spoke. Some of us held our breaths. The passing seconds seemed like an eternity.

Evans, listening through his headphones to the tactical commanders running the raid, announced in a clinical, calm voice, "The Russian fighter has moved out of the area to the south." I finally took a breath. Whether it was a lucky coincidence or a sign that the Russians had decided not to oppose us, we didn't know. A few moments later, Evans said that all threat radars had stood down. We let out a whoop of joy and relief. It was game on. The Russians made the right call, undoubtedly remembering the last time they acted provocatively against us when we killed several hundred of their mercenary forces in Syria just months prior.

The Situation Room filled up as more personnel filed in. We had nothing to do for the 30 minutes it took the assault force to streak across the desert to Baghdadi's house except speculate about what Baghdadi might do. I wanted to believe that he would surrender. I viewed Baghdadi as a bully, and therefore a coward who would not have the courage to fight when his moment of truth came. But I had also seen the tenacity of al-Qaeda fighters firsthand, including during our raid at the hospital in Afghanistan, and I couldn't be sure.

I had been following Baghdadi closely since 2014, when he publicly proclaimed himself the leader of Sunni Muslims and declared the establishment of an independent Islamic caliphate. I was impressed with his mastery of propaganda and the sheer size of his balls. I initially viewed him as a worthy foe because, as a rule, I generally avoided demonizing our enemies. But I made an exception when I learned of Baghdadi's depraved treatment of Kayla Mueller, an American aid worker that had been abducted by ISIS and subjected to unspeakable depredations by Baghdadi personally.

Kayla Mueller was a sweet and innocent young woman from Arizona who was motivated by her deep Christian faith to help refugees fleeing the civil war in Syria. She was captured by ISIS in 2013, and Baghdadi had forced her to become his "bride" against her will. For 18 months, he personally subjected Kayla Mueller to nonstop torture, abuse, and sexual slavery, then beat her to death.

Early on, we thought the accusations were simply hyperbole from opportunists trying to sell us information, but following a series of daring but failed rescue attempts, we learned definitively that these stories were true. Those unequivocal findings fueled a righteous anger that drove our efforts to hunt Baghdadi down. For many combat soldiers, killing bad guys just becomes part of your work routine. There's no malice and no joy; it's simply part of the job. Tonight was different. Tonight, it was going to feel good to capture or kill this piece of shit.

In the war against ISIS, our CT forces and Intelligence Community partners had developed and implemented the most advanced Irregular Warfare campaign since Vietnam. With a limited number of American personnel in theater, they were required to work through sympathetic Arab forces and the Kurdish Peshmerga, a fierce group of fighters based in Northern Iraq.

The Kurds had been forced to adopt clandestine, underground organizations to survive Saddam Hussein's persecution, and thus became masters at intelligence operations. They had developed a robust spy network capable of moving freely behind enemy lines. They had networks of informants providing early warnings of enemy activity and monitoring the movements of high-value enemy leaders. They confused the enemy by spreading false information on social media and through local rumor mills. The United States provided Signals Intelligence, satellite imagery, and surveillance drones, creating a powerful "intelligence-strike complex." When combined with the fervor of committed, passionate professionals who were intent on bringing down Baghdadi, it was an irrepressible machine that ground steadily toward its objective.

We all rose when the President entered the Situation Room and took a seat at the head of the table. I had been at the NSC for over a year, but I had yet to see him perform his duties as Commander in Chief up close like I was about to. I wasn't sure what to expect.

Milley provided a quick overview of the operation while the President studied the drone feeds on the far wall. Drone video isn't like what's portrayed in the movies or television. It's grainy, monochromatic, and distant, and it can be difficult to understand exactly what's happening in real time, even for those with a great deal of experience.

After a few minutes, the helicopters entered our field of view and landed, and the assault force rushed out to surround Baghdadi's compound. Evans began providing a running commentary of the tactical situation on the ground. Once the assault force had cordoned off the compound and other support elements had secured key intersections to block off any enemy or civilian movement toward the objective area, a linguist announced through a bullhorn that the building was surrounded and that everyone should come out with their hands up. Making this announcement greatly increased the danger to our commandos because it cost us the element of surprise, but it was necessary to protect innocents in the compound, which we believed might include a dozen children or more. In a matter of minutes, a column of people could be seen cautiously exiting the main building. Our eyes scoured the screen for signs that Baghdadi was among them.

We waited in silence. I knew firsthand the controlled chaos the ground force commander was experiencing, and I was gratified that the President and the other senior civilian leaders were patient while the guys 4,000 miles away did their jobs. The sorting complete, Evans relayed that Baghdadi remained in the building along with two of his wives. The evacuees reported that Baghdadi had barricaded himself in a tunnel and was wearing an explosive suicide vest. Baghdadi was going to fight to the death. The commandos would have to go in and kill him and then dig him out, quite literally.

We entered a long period of waiting as the assault force readied themselves for the close quarters battle. Matt Pottinger, the Deputy National Security Advisor, was sitting to my right. I had enormous respect for Pottinger. He started his career as a journalist, but joined the Marine Corps after September 11, 2001, and had led Marines in combat in Iraq.

I leaned over to Pottinger and whispered, "Man, this is going to get sporty if he pops himself off." It was an inside joke for those who had seen the effects of a suicide vest detonation up close. Invariably, the explosion causes the bomber's head to fly off, often a great distance, and identifying the mushy remains becomes a huge pain in the ass.

Unbeknownst to me at the time, Pottinger had once spent hours in the Iraqi heat searching for the missing head of an al-Qaeda suicide bomber that had tried to kill Pottinger and his patrol. His commander had demanded that they identify the bomber for intelligence purposes, and

Pottinger and his unit were forced to spend the afternoon rummaging through dense roadside vegetation on a quest for the wayward head while enemy forces moved into position to attack them.

Pottinger was the consummate professional and rarely raised his voice or cursed, but as he told me his story, I could hear him being transported back to that roadside in Iraq. The longer he went on, the more worked up he got. The tenor and cadence of his voice began to sound like that of a Marine officer in the field, punctuated by a steady stream of epithets. I thought it was hilarious and enjoyed sharing a few minutes of comradeship with him.

The President remained fixated on the screens, periodically asking questions about what he was seeing. Soon, he wanted to know why the helicopters were suddenly firing their miniguns. Evans explained that hostile local forces were amassing and preparing to move toward the fighting, and the gunships were breaking up their formations. A few moments later, he asked about another flurry of activity near the compound. Evans explained that the assault force was sending a robot into the building to identify Baghdadi's exact location so they would know what to expect during the final assault.

People often ask me what President Trump is like in real life. I always say he's the same person you see on TV—supremely confident, relaxed, and in control. Prior to working at the White House, I assumed his public persona was mostly an act to connect with everyday Americans and that in private he was a different person. To tell the truth, I expected him to be an arrogant, entitled plutocrat. Nope. He had no airs and he said exactly what was on his mind. There was no false modesty, no diplomatic-speak, and no hesitation to ask questions. What you saw was what you got.

While we were waiting for the final assault to begin, First Lady Melania Trump entered the Situation Room. Secretary of Defense Mark Esper quickly gave up his seat and she sat down next to the President, who introduced her to us as if we didn't know who she was. Her presence was unexpected, to say the least. I wondered how it would play in the press if word got out that the First Lady had popped in to watch a major military operation. Not my problem, I figured. And after all, it was her house.

The President asked Evans to bring the First Lady up to speed. The imperturbable Ranger, who had effortlessly provided the President and Vice President concise and flawless briefings, was suddenly tongue-tied now that he was speaking directly to the former supermodel First Lady. He would start a sentence and then immediately lose his place, stammering like a schoolboy who finally mustered up the courage to talk to his secret crush. I was desperately trying not to laugh out loud. Finally, Evans just kind of gave up and stopped talking, and everyone seemed happy to allow him to escape his personal hell.

We were all becoming a bunch of armchair generals providing commentary and predictions about the coming assault. Someone asked what would happen if Baghdadi detonated his suicide vest. I heard a voice nearby say, "His head will pop off like a champagne cork." It was Pottinger. He was still back in Iraq. The First Lady looked up in horror. I couldn't take it anymore and burst out laughing.

173

But Pottinger was right, and that's exactly what was about to happen. Evans soon alerted the group that our assault force had unleashed their combat dog. The dog stormed into the building with our commandos close behind. And with that, they disappeared from sight. Despite our high-tech cameras and drones and satellites, all we could do was helplessly stare at the monochromatic video of a rooftop and wonder what the hell was happening inside. I tried to imagine the knife fight that our commandos were engaged in. It was a "no quarters" fight to the death. Everything hung on the courage and valor of a handful of Special Operators.

After a few brief but intense minutes, Evans declared that our commandos had cornered Baghdadi before he blew himself up while holding two of his own children. Two of Baghdadi's wives were also killed. But the assault force commander wouldn't declare "Jackpot"—the code word announcing that Baghdadi was dead—until the body was inspected. They would also take some tissue to check for a DNA match once they got back to friendly territory. Pottinger and I knew that some poor kid was searching through the dust- and smoke-shrouded rubble with his helmet-mounted lamp and handheld flashlight, trying to find Baghdadi's head.

After a few minutes, Milley called Marine General Frank McKenzie, who was the overall commander of the operation. McKenzie reported that the assault force commander was extremely confident that Baghdadi was dead but wasn't willing to definitively make the call without DNA confirmation. I admired the commander's discipline. He knew that the President of the United States was personally monitoring the operation, but he didn't buckle to the pressure.

Pottinger and I again imagined that unlucky kid collecting forensic material holding up Baghdadi's head and comparing it to photos, measuring the distance between the eyes and looking for other distinctive features. Milley explained that our commandos were now collecting documents, computers, and anything else that might provide useful intelligence, and that in all likelihood, Baghdadi was dead.

Out of nowhere the President asked, "What are you going to do with the bodies?" Milley explained that Baghdadi would be given a burial at sea consistent with Islamic practices, as had bin Laden.

"We killed two women," the President persisted. "What about them?" After a long pause, Milley finally sputtered something about leaving the bodies there and the civilians would take care of it.

The President wasn't happy. "Don't you think ISIS will parade their bodies around and make it look like they were innocent?" he asked.

He had a good point, and Milley should have had a simple answer, but didn't. Evans quickly called U.S. Central Command (USCENTCOM or CENTCOM) and then whispered something in Milley's ear. Milley announced that the contingency was fully planned for and that with the departure of the assault force a barrage of missiles would pulverize the building and everything in it.

Satisfied with his response, the President asked how we should announce the success. To my amazement, the First Lady took over. She offered that the President should personally make a public statement from the Diplomatic Room the next morning during the Sunday news shows. "You should talk about the dog," she said. "Everyone loves dogs." She was right, and the President agreed.

The video screens flickered as the missile barrage pounded the compound to rubble. A massive cloud expanded upward announcing the completion of the mission. The only U.S. casualty was a puncture wound to the foot of one of the assaulters who stepped on a nail. It was a complete success. I was shocked that it had gone so perfectly.

With the raiding force on their way home and the public rollout strategy decided, almost everyone in the room, including Esper, left. Milley and I remained in our seats, knowing full well that the mission wasn't a success until our commandos were back on the ground in friendly territory.

Noticeably absent from the Situation Room was Secretary of State Mike Pompeo and CIA Director Gina Haspel. Pompeo was at a long-scheduled family wedding but checked in regularly. Haspel wasn't heard from throughout the operation. I was surprised that she didn't attend in person, seeing how her organization had done the lion's share of the intelligence collection, which they had so jealously guarded. Milley ordered his communicators to dial up Haspel after the President left. He asked where she was and thanked her for the partnership. She passed on a few platitudes but ignored the query about her absence.

With the raiding force back in friendly territory, Milley started shutting down the operational links to the various headquarters around the world that were reporting. The relief was palpable and well-earned. The clinical, monotone voices of the commanders became more relaxed and conversational. Milley was closing out with Frank McKenzie, the CENTCOM Commander, when McKenzie threw out, "Hey, Chairman, you know what the assault force's name was?" Usually, task force designations are a mundane set of numbers with no particular significance. "The men agreed that they would be named in honor of Kayla Mueller." I could feel a lump in my throat, and my eyes moistened. Kayla Mueller hadn't been forgotten. Her life, and those of the other hostages who had been mercilessly killed by Baghdadi and his cronies, could never be replaced, but America had brought justice to them and their loved ones.

When I finally walked down West Executive Avenue and through the gate to the Ellipse parking area, I was able to take a breath, look around, and start sorting out the historic event that I had just witnessed. I thought about the guys who were back safely at their base in northern Syria as they wrote their reports, conducted After-Action Reviews, cleaned equipment, ate dinner, and decompressed. I wouldn't have expected at the start of the night that I would have been so complementary of President Trump. I'd subconsciously bought into the incessant media drumbeat that he was lacking in experience and temperament to lead our Armed Forces. But I saw him in action. He was exactly the kind of Commander in Chief I would want if I was going into harm's way.

I'd never been behind the scenes of a Presidential address before. I wore my Special Forces Regimental tie for the occasion. The President showed up in a cheerful mood and stood next to the teleprompter operator and read through his speech, ordering edits here and there. He paid keen attention to minute details, making sure that each word contributed to the distinctively grandiose tone that always characterized his public remarks.

"We need to get that dog here ASAP," the President said. "The American people love dogs." Overnight, a news story had revealed that a military dog named Conan involved in the raid had been electrocuted by an exposed live wire and knocked silly. I knew I would be the one responsible for getting that dog back to the United States but decided I would enjoy the day's festivities anyway.

As the President spoke, I realized that his primary audience wasn't the American people or the international community; it was ISIS and those who were susceptible to their appeals. The President warned those considering joining ISIS that their decision would result in death. It was atypical, but I understood what he was doing. He talked about hearing Baghdadi whimpering and described the raid as if it were an action movie. I didn't hear Baghdadi whimpering and the video feed was closer to a 1950s black-and-white TV show than a big budget Hollywood production.

But the President wasn't making a typical public announcement; he was waging psychological warfare against our terrorist enemies. He wanted to publicly humiliate Baghdadi so that potential recruits would understand there was no glory in following in his footsteps. And instead of delivering lukewarm platitudes decrying the futility of embracing ISIS's extremism, he put it in raw, unvarnished terms that everyone could understand: If you join ISIS, you will die whimpering like a dog. I chuckled at his New York City tough guy routine but knew that those with more refined sensibilities would cry about his exaggerations.

I was waiting for the President in the East Wing hallway when he finished his remarks. The first thing he said to me was, "Hey, don't let 'them' walk back my comments. You got it?"

"Don't worry sir, I got it," I said.

I went to my office and drafted a message for distribution to the CT leaders at the CIA, DOD, and FBI congratulating them on the successful operation and how it was a transition point in our global campaign to defeat al-Qaeda. I highlighted that the President's announcement was worded very deliberately and was calculated to reinforce our campaign against Islamist terrorists. I followed up on Monday with personal phone calls. Miraculously, no disgruntled or clueless government employee said anything significant to undermine the President's statements.

CHAPTER NINE

THE SOLDIER
SECRETARY

By the summer of 2020, President Trump was growing frustrated with Secretary of Defense Mark Esper. The White House had come to believe that Esper was being manipulated and controlled by the defense bureaucracy, and the larger swamp often referred to as the Military-Industrial Complex. For one thing, Esper was refusing to draw down troops in Iraq, Afghanistan, and Syria as the President wanted, leading to tensions with the Commander in Chief. The President had already had a number of Secretaries who disagreed with his America First worldview and his determination to bring the troops home. As he neared the end of his first term, he was becoming increasingly impatient with yet another Secretary he believed was obstructing his agenda.

As a result of this growing rift, the White House suspected that Esper knew he would be immediately canned even if President Trump won a second term. It was obvious to everyone that Esper had no future in the Trump administration—but Esper would also receive a cold reception in the private sector, given his controversial presence at an infamous photo op in Lafayette Square in June. After left-wing rioters set fire to St. John's Episcopal Church near the White House, police had used tear gas to clear crowds out of Lafayette Square. Shortly thereafter, Trump made an appearance holding a Bible in front of the church, flanked by Esper, Attorney General Bill Barr, and others. The press went absolutely ballistic, declaring that high-ranking government officials were participating in what some critics said was a political photo op.

Some of the President's advisors were concerned that Esper might resign and publicly turn on the President before the election, hoping his betrayal might rehabilitate his public image and increase his chances of landing a plum job on his way out the door. Esper had already held a press conference in which he blamed the President for the Lafayette Square incident. Some top administration officials viewed him as a weak leader groveling for the approval of the press—in other words, with suspicion and disdain.

The more pronounced the tension between Esper and the President became, the more White House aides were anxious that he might indeed choose to go out in a preelection "blaze of glory." A number of administration officials had tried the same tactic in the preceding years with varying success, including the previous Secretary of Defense, James Mattis, whose public resignation letter was perceived by many as highly critical of Trump's America First worldview.

The President's advisors thought it might be better to bite the bullet and fire Esper before he could turn on them.

The question was, if President Trump fired Esper, who should replace him? The President's choices were limited. In order to appoint an Acting Secretary, the law required him to select someone who already held a Senate-confirmed position. The President also wanted someone he already knew and trusted—an even smaller universe. That was how John McEntee, the head of the Office of Presidential Personnel and one of the President's most trusted aides, ended up talking to me.

I had been on standby throughout the late summer and early fall, knowing that the President often mused about firing people for months before eventually doing so, if it ever came to pass at all.

I had been told to expect that I could be appointed Acting Secretary in early September. But then a coordinated hit piece dropped that week in *The Atlantic*, rocking Washington and the presidential race. Anonymous sources with an axe to grind—some speculated it was Mattis—alleged that the President had called U.S. service members "suckers," among other inflammatory accusations.[8] The President came to the conclusion that firing Esper in the midst of that media firestorm would be a bad idea. For one thing, it might be interpreted as an act of retribution and lend credence to the story. At the very least, it would add to the perception of a chaotic administration entering the final

---

[8] Jeffrey Goldberg, "Trump: Americans Who Died in War Are 'Losers' and 'Suckers'," *The Atlantic*, September 3, 2020, https://www.theatlantic.com/politics/archive/2020/09/trump-americans-who-died-at-war-are-losers-and-suckers/615997/.

stretch before the election, right when they wanted to be projecting competence and order.

The election came and went, and I heard nothing. Esper remained in his post. I assumed I would continue my service as Director of the National Counterterrorism Center until President-elect Joe Biden named a successor.

But it turned out the issue had in fact come to a head just days before the election, when Esper slow-rolled yet another order issued by President Trump. In late October, the President had greenlit a hostage rescue mission in Africa. A few days later on October 31, with a Navy SEAL team moments away from jumping out of an airplane, Esper unexpectedly slammed on the brakes because the DOD and State Department had failed to notify Nigerian officials about the operation.

White House aides monitoring the operation in the Situation Room in real time were livid. Ultimately, our commandos got the go-ahead, just minutes before the plane would have had to turn around or risk running out of fuel. They executed their mission brilliantly. But for Trump, this was the straw that broke the camel's back. In his view, Esper had an attitude problem. Like several secretaries who had held the position before him, Esper appeared to be confused about which one of the two men was Commander in Chief.

Finally, on November 9, six days after the election, came the Presidential Tweet: "I am pleased to announce that Christopher C. Miller, the highly respected Director of the National Counterterrorism Center (unanimously confirmed by the Senate), will be Acting Secretary of Defense, effective immediately. Chris will do a GREAT job! Mark

Esper has been terminated. I would like to thank him for his service."

And just like that, it was go time.

Esper's staff was visibly in a state of shock when I walked into the Pentagon. I stepped off the private elevator that transports the secretary of defense from a secure parking area in the bowels of the Pentagon to the outer office and noticed a large pile of framed photos, boxes, and other office junk. Apparently, everyone in town knew Esper was on his last leg except him. He clearly had not abided by the political appointee's maxim to have no more than one box full of personal material in your office so that you can easily depart if your services are no longer required by the President.

Events in Washington can often be surreal for regular people who suddenly find themselves surrounded by the trappings of power and influence. You frequently have to pinch yourself to take stock of what you are seeing and where you are. But even by Washington standards, this was pretty wild. A year earlier I was a retired soldier and a mid-level government bureaucrat. Now I had fallen ass-backward into becoming the leader of the largest, most powerful organization in the history of the world.

When I walked into my spacious new office at the Pentagon, it felt like walking into Saddam's palace in Iraq all over again. A military aide informed me that one of my two large desks, a massive nine-foot slab of solid mahogany, had belonged to the great General John Pershing, the commander of American forces in World War I and the highest-ranking general of all time. The other had belonged to the legendary Civil War General William Tecumseh Sherman. For a former Army private, just sitting at those desks was a deeply moving and profound experience.

You might think I would have suffered from Imposter Syndrome. But I didn't. I wasn't intimidated a bit. I had been more nervous taking over my first Army Infantry platoon in the Demilitarized Zone in Korea as a 22-year-old second lieutenant in 1988. Frankly, leading soldiers as a small unit commander is enormously more difficult than the job I had just assumed. After leading men and women in combat in Afghanistan and Iraq, I don't scare easily, particularly when it comes to dealing with the bureaucratic and political knife fighters, court jesters, and inside the Beltway pretenders that dominate the miasma of Washington, DC.

Within minutes, I was escorted into a top secret room to be briefed on my role in responding to a nuclear or terrorist attack. The briefers seemed bothered by my lack of nervousness; I was completely nonplussed by the responsibilities they described. Obviously, those duties were an inherent part of the position I had accepted a few hours earlier. I had devoted a great deal of thought to those responsibilities in the preceding weeks and months, and I was prepared to carry out any action that may be necessary to protect the nation.

Entering the role of Acting Secretary at this late date in the Trump administration, it would have been easy to just play "prevent defense" and enjoy the enormous perks that come along with the position—planes, helicopters, chauffeurs, security detail, and a 23,000-person staff. As Secretary of Defense, I had more assets at my disposal than any other person on the face of the Earth, save for the President himself. I could have kept the seat warm and set myself up for a lucrative position in the defense industry after leaving office. That's certainly what almost everyone in the Department, and virtually everyone in Washington, probably expected me to do—because that's what everyone in Washington does.

But that would have been cowardly and antithetical to my history of public service. It would have been offensive to my own sense of honor and the expectations of my family, friends, and colleagues. I had dedicated virtually my entire life to the defense of our country. What's the point of rising to a position of extraordinary power and influence if you aren't going to put it to good use?

So starting on November 9, I set out on a race against the clock to accomplish several major goals.

First, I wanted to bring my generation's war against al-Qaeda to an end once and for all—and bring home our troops from Afghanistan, Iraq, and Somalia. This was personal for me. I had spent the last two decades fighting the menace of terrorism, and we had achieved all we could achieve in those theaters. Trump was right: It was time to end the forever wars.

Second, I wanted to solidify and institutionalize the military's new focus in the Trump Administration on countering transnational threats such as drug cartels. Every year, their poisonous narcotics kill 10 times the number of Americans killed on 9/11 and during the entire War on Terror. I wanted to shatter the idea inside the Pentagon that crushing the cartels and securing the nation's borders were somehow not the military's job.

Third, as a former Special Forces soldier, I believed it was critical to elevate the influence of U.S. Special Operations Forces such as the Navy SEALs, the Army Green Berets, the Marine Raiders, and Air Force Special Tactics personnel. These elements are absolutely vital to winning in the new age of warfare we have entered—the age of unrestricted warfare, which I will describe in Chapter 11.

And finally, I wanted to serve out my tenure with minimal drama: no new wars, no military coups, and no troops in the streets deployed against American citizens. All of these objectives were undergirded by a fervent commitment to give a voice to members of the Armed Forces, their families, and veterans who were not being heard. Even in the circus atmosphere of the Trump era, I assumed these final goals would be the easiest to achieve. I had less than three months until the inauguration of Joe Biden on January 20. What could possibly go wrong?

When President Trump asked me to replace Esper, his only guidance to me was to "bring the troops home." We didn't have a long, philosophical conversation about foreign policy doctrines or discuss the finer points of military matters. That wasn't his style. He was guided by a core set of beliefs and provided broad guidance with the expectation that I would carry out his orders and execute his vision.

I had carefully studied the President's behavior and communications regarding foreign policy as part of my duties as a member of the National Security Council. If I couldn't support him or disagreed with his views on how to protect the American people, I wouldn't have taken the job.

That's how I was trained as a soldier and as a Green Beret. I thrived in a climate where the boss provided general vision and clear goals while trusting you to execute them.

The narrative in foreign policy intelligentsia circles was that Trump was vacuous and his national security strategy rudderless. The truth is, he was remarkably consistent: He was a neo-isolationist who wanted to reduce our military involvement overseas, defend our territorial integrity, remove us from entangling alliances, and compete economically against China. End of story. It wasn't complicated and didn't require membership on the Council on Foreign Relations to describe him or his doctrine. All one had to do was listen to what he said: "America First," "Build the Wall," "End the Forever Wars."

And to be clear, "neo-isolationism" is not a dirty word. It is a perfectly valid school of foreign policy thought, and a perfectly reasonable response to decades of globalist intervention and overreach. It is simply the acknowledgment of reality: America is not, and cannot be, the world's police force.

Trump's neo-isolationism came as a shock to the foreign policy establishment because it was the first of its kind since the 1920s, and it was anathema to the national security apparatus created after World War II. In the 70 years since the Allied victory, the foreign policy establishment had grown to include a large standing military that had never existed in peacetime; think tanks populated by PhDs; university researchers driving technological development; a network of laboratories for atomic and advanced weapons; defense contractors to design, manufacture, and profit from the weapons of war; and the accretion of a political class permanently indebted to this Military-Industrial Complex—just as President Dwight Eisenhower had warned.

This huge establishment, with tentacles that stretched to every corner of the globe, was necessary to defeat the global threat of communism and win the Cold War. But long after the collapse of the Soviet Union in 1991, the structures and systems of the massive security state persisted despite 30 years of relative American hegemony. The establishment has no incentive to change its behavior or doctrine, and the status quo is spectacularly lucrative. Trump's presidency represented a mortal threat to the DC foreign policy blob, and above all, that's why they hated him.

I started out my career as a committed internationalist, but like Irving Kristol's "liberal who has been mugged by reality," I was mugged by the neoconservatives who led us into an unjust war in Iraq.[9] I don't think a prudent national security practitioner should ever become a rigid ideologue. Foreign policy should be based on a nation's self-interest and the international conditions at the time, not an ideological crusade like "making the world safe for democracy," as presidents from Woodrow Wilson to George W. Bush have sought.[10,11] If the geopolitical situation changed and required a different approach, I'd pivot in a heartbeat. And,

---

[9] Douglas Murray, "'A Liberal Mugged by Reality'," *The Spectator*, September 26, 2009, https://www.spectator.co.uk/article/-a-liberal-mugged-by-reality-.

[10] Woodrow Wilson, "Address to a Joint Session of Congress Requesting a Declaration of War against Germany," April 2, 1917, https://www.presidency.ucsb.edu/documents/address-joint-session-congress-requesting-declaration-war-against-germany.

[11] George W. Bush, "President Bush Discusses Freedom Agenda," July 24, 2008, https://georgewbush-whitehouse.archives.gov/news/releases/2008/07/20080724-6.html.

right now, the world is in an epoch of transition after a 30-year interlude. What we are witnessing is the final collapse of the war of twentieth-century political ideologies and the rise of a new world order defined by economic, information, and technological competition supported by military force. This is the obverse of the last 90 years where strength and power were defined by military tools.

This state of affairs is disorienting for many. Mattis and Esper, for example, were unreformed and unrepentant internationalists. Their ideological blinders ensured that their actions weren't in consonance with President Trump's objectives of ending the military's enervating and feckless involvement in operations overseas, demanding greater burden-sharing by allies, countering transnational threats like illicit narcotics that directly affect the American people, and retooling our institutions for the next era of competition and conflict with China. Their inconsistency with the President's goals inevitably led to their termination.

My team and I landed in Djibouti on Thanksgiving Day. It's traditional for senior military leaders to visit the troops at Thanksgiving. You chat them up, dish out some turkey and dressing, and take their place on the serving line so they can enjoy the day. Most VIPs serve a couple of plates, snap a few photos, and leave. That's not how our crew was going to work; we were going to serve every last soldier.

We were also there to assess the situation on the ground. In the pantheon of national security priorities, those involving Africa barely make the to-do list. With few exceptions, policymakers usually view Africa as a strategically unimportant region where the intractable problems of poverty, corruption, and violence can only be managed as opposed to fixed. It thus receives minimal attention and resources.

Africa had exploded into the public's attention when a 12-soldier Special Forces team in Niger was ambushed by a local terrorist group in 2018, killing four Americans. President Trump had been angered at the fact that American soldiers were placed in harm's way in such a low priority region and ordered the removal of military personnel from Africa. But two years later, we were still there. His orders had once again been slow-rolled by the Pentagon. I was there to finally get the job done.

I felt obligated to go to the field and listen to our commanders, ambassador, and intelligence professionals to guarantee that the drawdown was doable. When al-Shabaab, the local terrorist group, had begun strengthening ties with Osama bin Laden in 2008, we dramatically expanded our operations against them and established a counterterrorism task force headquartered in Djibouti. By 2020, the task force in Somalia had ballooned to about 1,000 U.S. personnel.

The problem was that no one in the Pentagon could explain what our mission in Somalia was. Al-Shabaab was focused on domestic politics and posed no existential threat to the United States. Why were we there? From an initial offshore capability to monitor al-Shabaab and strike them from the air, we now had an onshore force of airplanes and accompanying crews, as well as security and support personnel. There was even a crew of firefighters.

I knew how this aggregation of personnel had occurred. Every military commander wants more assets and capabilities. The rapid turnover of civilian leadership in the Pentagon allows military planners to add forces slowly. Because Special Operations typically have a small footprint, they often fly under the radar of senior leadership. As time goes on, the money and manpower devoted to the mission grows, while the actual need for such resources declines as key objectives are achieved.

When I reviewed the force laydown in Somalia, I counted fewer than 100 combat personnel actually fighting al-Shabaab; the remainder provided intelligence and logistic support. Although I don't think President Trump knew all of these details, he certainly understood the indefensibility of maintaining such a large force inside a nation soon to be deluged by another civil war.

I had developed a method to bypass the tightly scripted briefings that most VIPs are subjected to whenever they visit troops. Any time I was in the field, I always requested to eat with the troops so I could get the truth straight from the people doing the work. The generals and senior officials never attended these functions, and I could ask any questions I wanted. When provided a genuine opportunity to speak candidly, the common sense of the American fighting person will never disappoint.

I was counting on the Navy SEALs in Mogadishu to give me their unfiltered opinions. Navy SEALs don't bullshit around. It hurts my ego as a Green Beret to say this, but the SEALs are pound for pound the toughest Special Operators in the United States military, with an almost pathological need to speak the truth.

I sat down with two dozen of them for my fourth Thanksgiving meal in 36 hours. I was shocked to learn that they were not living with the Somali counterterrorism forces they were advising. The State Department had hired a defense contractor to provide the day-to-day training and support to our Somali partners. The SEALs merely dropped by from time to time to observe their progress.

When the Somali forces conducted an operation, the SEALs provided advice, intelligence, and fire support if they decisively engaged al-Shabaab. The SEALs had been on just two such operations in the three months they had been in Somalia, neither of which netted any enemy fighters. They told me they were being micromanaged by their superiors, who had become risk-averse as a result of the ambush in Niger. The senior SEAL, with numerous combat deployments, assessed their contributions as minimal. I felt badly for them. Most of the SEALs were on their first deployment, and they wanted to fight. Instead, they were stuck in a Kafkaesque nightmare.

As I listened to their feedback, I noticed a Noncommissioned Officer staring daggers at me. After a while, I finally turned to her and said, "You don't like me. Why not?"

"It's not that I don't like you," she replied. "I just want to know why you're really here."

I looked her square in the eye and said, "To get you the fuck out of here. This is a waste of talent. We don't need to be here anymore. It's time to go home."

Her face softened. I asked her, "Did you just expect me to give you some politically correct bullshit?"

"Yes sir, that's what you all do," she said.

"Not anymore," I said.

Per the President's directive, I gave the order to withdraw all American troops from Somalia by January 15, 2020, five days before the end of the Trump administration. Combined with our work to reduce American forces in Afghanistan to 2,500—the smallest military presence since the war began in 2001—I had done all I could to fulfill the President's promise and to end my generation's wars with honor.

That trip to Africa was an epiphany for me. I had started the job thinking that my constituents—the people I was supposed to support—were the generals and admirals. I knew they thought I was unqualified for the position I held, having never been a member of their high-ranking club or an uber-connected political insider. But I tried to make nice anyway.

I had served in the military or the Pentagon for over 36 years and had friends, colleagues, and like-minded supporters planted at every key node of the sprawling Department of Defense. They often reported to me on the inner workings of their commands and what their general or admiral said in private about me, the President, or the President's goals. It didn't take long to realize I was wasting my time and energy trying to convince them to support the Commander in Chief's agenda.

My visit to Africa drove the point home. Our troops were being badly mismanaged by distant and disconnected leaders, and they had resigned themselves to this fate. When I showed up, they finally felt like they had someone on their side who would listen to them and look out for them.

After Africa, I realized that the only constituency that mattered were the soldiers, Sailors, Airmen, Marines, and Guardians who do the actual work and make the physical and psychological sacrifices to protect the American people. When I voiced my revelation to the team I trusted, one of them said, "You're the Soldier Secretary. You're the only one who's been in their shoes."

The nickname stuck. It made me uncomfortable because I didn't want the job to be about me, and to me it sounded sappy, like something a PR rep would come up with. But I couldn't disagree with it. I wasn't a traditional Secretary of Defense. I didn't want to be. That's why our military is in such a jam right now. There are too many senior officials in uniform and at the Pentagon who are more concerned with not rocking the boat than with supporting the troops they lead.

It was late December, and I was standing in my kitchen after another long day at the Pentagon, thinking about our preparations for the upcoming protests on January 6 related to the 2020 election. I was completely zoned out and hadn't noticed my wife stomp into the kitchen behind me.

"Don't you do it!" she said forcefully.

"Don't do what?" I asked.

"Start a war with Iran," she said, relaying a story the media was spinning about Trump wanting to attack Iran.

I laughed with relief, knowing that for once I wasn't going to be in trouble. "That meeting was ages ago," I said. "They're just now getting around to that?"

Days prior, I had been summoned to the White House on a Sunday evening for a no-notice meeting with President Trump about Iran increasing its uranium enrichment purity. Typically, there are a flurry of pre-meetings, phone calls, and prep sessions before an Oval Office meeting with the President, but since it was the weekend and the President deemed it urgent, those formalities were pushed aside. Frankly, I preferred the President's ad hoc meetings because they forced people out of their comfort zones. Advisors were required to use their own intellect and voice their own beliefs, rather than relying on spoon-fed talking points crafted by their staffs to advance a personal or organizational agenda.

Secretary of State Mike Pompeo, National Security Advisor Robert O'Brien, Chairman Milley, and I were seated in a semicircle around the Resolute Desk. Milley was agitated, worried that the President was going to order an attack on Iran's nuclear program.

The President arrived through his private entrance and sat down behind the Resolute. Instead of the usual introductory small talk and banter that preceded most meetings, he went straight to the point: "What are the Iranians doing?" he asked. Milley launched into a detailed description of the uranium enrichment process and how Iran's announced plan didn't markedly change the timeline for their procurement of enough fissile material to produce a nuclear weapon. In reality, he assured the President, there was very little to worry about.

President Trump listened attentively as Milley spoke. When he was finished, he mulled the information over for a moment then asked, "Why don't we just bomb the hell out of them?"

Milley didn't volunteer an answer, and neither did Pompeo. After a pregnant pause, I realized it was my turn at bat. I thought the President's question was appropriate, even though it was bombastically phrased. He didn't declare, "Let's bomb Iran." He was asking a sincere question.

"Mr. President, we certainly could bomb Iran," I said. I told him I loathed the Iranian regime for the suffering they had inflicted on the region and on American troops since 1979. I noted that we definitely had the capability to destroy their enrichment program, but that it would likely start a protracted regional war. I described how many sorties of bombers would be required, how many we expected to lose, and how many American servicemembers would be killed.

I then highlighted that he was the first President in nearly a century to avoid getting us into a new war, or further embroiled in an ongoing one. As a former soldier, I admired that he had done everything in his power to get us out of these stupid wars, and I feared attacking Iran would damage his image and legacy, as well as our country. It wasn't bullshit. It was what I really believed.

The President leaned back and nodded without saying anything, then turned to the others in the group one by one. As always, the President asked questions, listened, pressed for more information, and guaranteed that every attendee had the opportunity to speak. He then concluded the meeting as he always did, by asking for each person's recommendation.

We unanimously recommended that a large-scale attack was unwarranted and ill-advised. The President told us he agreed wholeheartedly that attacking Iran was a bad idea. He just wanted to hear us explain why.

In late December, all systems were flashing red. One year earlier, the President had ordered a daring strike that killed

Iranian General Qasem Soleimani, the leader of Iran's Islamic Revolutionary Guard Corps and the world's most wanted terrorist. As we approached the one-year anniversary of Soleimani's death, intelligence reports were warning of an impending Iranian attack on American forces stationed in the Middle East.

I couldn't tell if the Iranians were just screwing with us to ruin our holidays or if they were serious. Their threats made no sense. The Trump Administration was on its way out. All they had to do was lay low and wait for the incoming Biden Administration, which would be desperate to reestablish negotiations to prove how enlightened and sophisticated they were.

Nevertheless, we had no choice but to take the threats seriously and to do everything possible to deter Iran from killing any Americans. Pompeo worked the diplomatic circuit to send them a warning. Milley worked his back channels. The most notable tools I had available to signal our intentions were strategic bomber flights near Iranian airspace and the presence of our aircraft carrier the USS *Nimitz* near their shore.

On Wednesday, December 23, the National Security Council principals met to discuss a recent rocket attack on our Baghdad embassy. Matt Pottinger, the Deputy National Security Advisor, chaired the meeting to discuss the attack, Iranian threat streams, Iraqi militant group activity, and the tools available to us to prevent the Iranians from doing something foolhardy in the coming weeks.

The next day, Pottinger led us into the Oval Office to brief President Trump on the situation. We confirmed that his red line—the event that would result in a U.S. military strike against Iran—was the killing of an American by Iranian forces or their Iraqi surrogates. The President cut straight to the heart of the matter, saying, "They haven't been listening to your threats. Why would it change? I'm the only one they haven't heard from." He instructed us to draft a tweet for him to send. The meeting was over.

Pottinger and I went back to his office, and in about 15 minutes, we had a tweet drafted and returned to the Oval. The President pulled out his black Sharpie and started editing. He read the statement out loud. He changed words and asked how they sounded. He wanted something that flowed. That afternoon he tweeted, "Some friendly health advice to Iran: If one American is killed, I will hold Iran responsible. Think it over."

Critics always complained that Trump's Twitter diplomacy was "unbecoming" of a U.S. president. Maybe so, but it was extremely effective. His message was short, simple, and clear. There could be no confusion within the Iranian regime about our red line. Now it was up to them.

Every morning I received a world map overlaid with the locations of all American forces. I had noticed a scheduled strategic bomber task force flight over Iraq and toward Iran. Such events had occurred regularly since the increase in tension after the Soleimani strike and were meant to signal our capability and resolve. The U.S. military develops a list of flexible deterrence options for a laundry list of scenarios and foreign actors to make sure sufficient resources— planes, ships, missiles, troops—are postured and prepared.

Something nagged at me though. The bomber flight made perfect sense in previous weeks, but now tensions between the United States and Iran were running extraordinarily high. In my mind, the greatest danger was now a miscalculation by the Iranians that resulted in them shooting at our planes, and thus stumbling into a larger conflict. We had shown plenty of strength in recent weeks. Now we needed to deescalate the situation to prevent a tragedy.

During our morning meeting, I asked Chairman Milley about the upcoming bomber task force mission. I gently queried him about the flight route and parameters, noting that I suspected the bombers would turn away from the Iranian border well out of their antiaircraft missile range since we didn't want an accident to happen. Milley picked up immediately on my concern and said, "Let's get Frank McKenzie on the line."

General McKenzie, commander of all forces in the Middle East, said that the route took them right up to the limit of Iranian airspace before turning south over the Arabian Gulf. I prompted, "Does that make sense right now with everything going on? What are the chances of the Iranians misinterpreting the flight and shooting at us?" McKenzie immediately noted that was a possibility, recalling how an Iranian air defense artillery battery commander had gone rogue previously and shot down a U.S. drone without authorization, and Iran had also downed a Ukrainian commercial flight in January 2020. He pivoted effortlessly and said, "Mr. Secretary, I'll have that flight swing south about 100 miles from the border."

I had successfully ensured that our planes were out of harm's way, but the USS *Nimitz* was altogether another matter. The giant aircraft carrier, with a crew of 5,000, had been at sea for the longest deployment in the history of the modern Navy. McKenzie and Milley were insistent that we needed a carrier in the region to deter Iran; I, along with the leadership of the U.S. Navy, disagreed and wanted the *Nimitz* to return to its home port in Washington State.

For a variety of reasons, by the time I became Acting Secretary of Defense, the Navy was only capable of putting two of our 11 carriers at sea at any given time. The whole situation seemed ludicrous to me and evidence of professional negligence for a military that spends $740 billion annually.

I had already extended the *Nimitz*'s deployment twice based on the entreaties of McKenzie and Milley, and I made it clear that I had no intention of extending it a third time. I told them they needed to figure out a way to replace the air and missile capability provided by the *Nimitz* and its support vessels. I felt we were breaking faith with the Sailors and Marines on the *Nimitz*. They were already missing the December holidays with their families. We were punishing a crew because Joint Staff and USCENTCOM plans were flawed, hiding our lack of planning behind a guise of "wartime necessity." I knew it would result in discipline issues, family stress, and reenlistment problems—and ultimately, we didn't need them to be in the theater anyway.

I don't think Milley or McKenzie expected me to hold fast. They submitted voluminous new analyses and assessments. They won over no converts. I ordered the *Nimitz* to return home before New Year's.

The next morning the *New York Times* and *Washington Post* ran stories about my decision. I was surprised that Milley's and McKenzie's people would go to the press over such an inconsequential thing—this wasn't a life-or-death, war-or-peace issue—in fact, it made war less likely by removing a prime target for an Iranian attack. This was a petty, bureaucratic turf war—the only kind of war they were actually good at winning.

Milley and McKenzie had pushed the story for an audience of one: President Trump, who they correctly assumed would be unsatisfied with public reports of his military looking "weak."

A few days later, the President brought up the *Nimitz* during a meeting about Iran's increasingly hostile rhetoric. He didn't say it directly, but I could tell he was concerned about appearing weak to the Iranians. I told him I would return the *Nimitz* to the region and order it back on station near Iran.

Milley and McKenzie had won. Clearly, their professed acclamations of the sanctity of civilian control of the armed forces had limits. Like so many others in the Pentagon, they were more than happy to defer to civilian leadership when civilian leadership agreed with their perspective. But if they disagreed, the knives immediately came out.

This behavior has characterized our nation's military leadership for the past few decades, but never more so than during the Trump Administration. The Pentagon fought tooth and nail against much of President Trump's foreign policy agenda—from ending the war in Afghanistan, to withdrawing American troops from Syria and the Middle East, to pressuring NATO allies to increase military expenditures. But they welcomed with open arms billions of additional dollars provided by the budgets President Trump signed into law.

Of all the swamps in Washington, DC, the Pentagon is the deepest, darkest, and most dangerous of them all—and the one most in need of draining.

CHAPTER TEN

"THE CAPITOL HAS FALLEN"

A suite of secure communications equipment is installed in the home of the Secretary of Defense. What my children referred to as the "BatPhone" rang late in the afternoon on December 30, 2020. When that phone rings, it's not a coworker calling to shoot the shit; it's the White House or the National Military Command Center calling about a matter of national security. John McEntee was on the line, asking what the military plan of support was for the upcoming demonstrations on January 6. President Trump was still contesting Joe Biden's victory nearly two months after the election and was planning on holding a huge rally encouraging Congress to reject the election results.

McEntee was technically in charge of personnel, but in reality, he was more like a Deputy Chief of Staff. When he moved his mouth, the President's words came out. I enjoyed working with McEntee and found him to be level-headed, focused, and loyal to the President's goals. He has subsequently been characterized by the press as a political hatchet man, but I suspect this is because few in Washington seem to understand how the executive branch is actually supposed to work. The president is the democratically elected Chief Executive, and all executive branch employees carry out his policy objectives; if they are unwilling or unable to do so, they should find another job. That's how functional organizations operate, and that's how the executive branch is designed under our Constitution. I never got a whiff of anything nefarious from McEntee. Instead, I found him to be an open-minded acolyte who asked questions and listened more than he spoke.

When he called asking about January 6 preparations, I offered in reply that I was looking at it closely and would be working with local officials to determine what was required. McEntee, in typical fashion, said that he would relay that to the President and looked forward to hearing the details soon.

McEntee had always been a straight shooter with me. Several weeks prior he had called and told me the President was upset with Secretary of the Army Ryan McCarthy. McCarthy had issued a public statement announcing that the Army would stay out of politics, which some interpreted to mean that the military might not implement the Insurrection Act if ordered. McCarthy's statement had come in response to bizarre comments from retired Army Lieutenant General Michael Flynn suggesting the President should impose martial law and "rerun" the election in certain swing states. I had always respected Flynn for his military achievements, but by this point he was sounding like he was losing his grip on reality, and his comments were only adding fuel to the fire.

I honestly expected that I was about to be told to fire McCarthy, which would have presented a serious and unwanted leadership dilemma. Instead, McEntee told me to call McCarthy and tell him to lay low. "The President isn't going to impose the Insurrection Act," he said. "But to be clear, if he wanted to, he could."

I hung up and exhaled a massive sigh of relief. McEntee and the President were right about executive authority, and they were right to be upset. By making a well-intentioned statement vowing to stay out of politics, McCarthy had inadvertently stepped directly into the political fray and provided ammunition that one side could use to attack the other.

With the end of 2020 approaching, I was relieved and thankful for McEntee's mature advice for handling the McCarthy miscue and perspectives on the President's philosophy on the use of the military in domestic affairs, but I still slept very poorly that night. Before accepting the position of Acting Secretary of Defense, I had established a few "red lines"—things I would never do and would resign over being asked to do. The most important was the improper use of the military. I was concerned that I was going to be ordered to mobilize military forces for duty in Washington, DC, as had occurred in June—but that this time, after months of escalating tension and mounting bitterness clouding people's judgment, all hell would break loose.

I didn't object to the domestic deployment of military forces in principle. It was totally within the President's Constitutional authority to order such a deployment. There are times when it certainly is appropriate, and even required. In fact, the military has a long history of domestic operations, from exploring and advancing the frontier, to major construction projects like flood control, to training civilians prior to World War II in the Civilian Conservation Corps, to quelling civil unrest as recently as the Rodney King riots in Los Angeles in 1992. The popular idea—mostly pushed by the media since the 1960s—that the military should only be used for warfighting on foreign soil contradicts both common sense and the history of our nation.

I decided that the Department of Defense (DOD) would support any request for military support issued by a governor or the President as long as one of the following three conditions was met:

1. There was the likelihood of large-scale violence beyond the expected capacity of local, county, state, and federal law enforcement;
2. All other civilian law enforcement capabilities were exhausted;
3. Civilian control of the government had broken down.

However, as the Acting Secretary, I had to face an uncomfortable reality. I was dealing with a shell-shocked group, and even in the most justified of circumstances, I knew there would be extreme hesitancy within DOD for any sort of military involvement. The uniformed military and their civilian counterparts that responded to the Black Lives Matter (BLM) riots in June 2020—culminating in the infamous clearing of Lafayette Square—were suffering from a form of bureaucratic PTSD. Rioters were being hailed as civil rights heroes, and law enforcement—including the National Guard—was being crucified in the media, and it had taken a heavy mental toll.

I also knew that my options were limited because any discussions concerning military contingency planning would immediately be leaked to the press, causing yet another firestorm. For months, the media had been selling the idea that the U.S. military was a threat to the republic and a pawn in a secret conspiracy by President Trump to stay in power. "Could Trump declare martial law to try to steal the election?" blared a headline in the *Washington Post*.[12] "The administration could deploy federalized National Guard troops to stop vote counts," *The Nation* wrote.[13] MSNBC contributor John Heilemann suggested that using federal troops to stop mob violence amounted to a "trial run" by the President to "steal this election."[14]

Even worse, 10 former Secretaries of Defense had recently launched a broadside at me and the Department, feigning concern that we would ignore our oaths of allegiance to the Constitution and become Trump's shock troops. Those former secretaries actually went on the record and accused members of the Armed Forces of preparing to

---

[12] Amber Phillips, "Could Trump Declare Martial Law to Try to Steal the Election?," *Washington Post*, December 24, 2020, https://www .washingtonpost.com/politics/2020/12/24/could-trump-declare-martial -law-try-steal-election/.

[13] Sasha Abramsky, "Is Trump Planning a Coup d'État?," *The Nation*, September 7, 2020, https://www.thenation.com/article/society/trump-coup -elections-gop/.

[14] "MSNBC Contributor Suggests Federal Response in Portland May Be Trial Run for Trump to 'Steal This Election'," Fox News, July 21, 2020, https://video.foxnews.com/v/6173805496007#sp=show-clips.

march into the streets and subvert the very Constitution that every single member of the U.S. military has pledged their lives to defend.[15] To this day, I don't know if they simply had been swept up in the media narrative, like so many Americans, or whether they were knowingly helping the media sell that false narrative to an unsuspecting public. Either way, their actions were inexcusable.

As a result of all of this, I had no doubt in my mind that if I had pre-deployed military forces against the expressed wishes of the District of Columbia Mayor, I would have created a civil-military crisis not seen since the attack on Fort Sumter in 1860.

And every day, the media drumbeat was growing louder.

On December 31, Washington, DC, Mayor Muriel Bowser's homeland security advisor requested support from the District of Columbia National Guard. "Byzantine" would be an understatement of phenomenal proportions to describe the role of the DOD in the District of Columbia and its National Guard. Since the District is essentially a province of the federal government without typical state-like authorities and status, the Secretary of Defense, through the Secretary of the Army, ultimately oversees the DC National Guard.

---

[15] Ashton Carter, Dick Cheney, William Cohen, Mark Esper, Robert Gates, Chuck Hagel, James Mattis, Leon Panetta, William Perry, and Donald Rumsfeld, "All 10 Living Former Defense Secretaries: Involving the Military in Election Disputes Would Cross into Dangerous Territory," *Washington Post*, January 3, 2021, https://www.washingtonpost.com/opinions/10-former-defense-secretaries-military-peaceful-transfer-of-power/2021/01/03/2a23d52e-4c4d-11eb-a9f4-0e668b9772ba_story.html.

I had heard through private conversations that Army Secretary McCarthy was loathe to approve the request, even though it had come through Mayor Bowser, a Democrat, and not President Trump. I understood their concerns about public perceptions, but I considered their opinions irrelevant because Mayor Bowser's request met my decision criteria, and I was the ultimate decision-maker.

Secretary McCarthy and his uniformed counterpart, Army Chief of Staff Jim McConville, briefed Chairman Milley and me on the morning of Monday, January 4, about Mayor Bowser's request for National Guard support. A friend of mine in the DC National Guard had provided me with a bootleg copy of the request several days earlier and, unbeknownst to McCarthy, McConville, and Milley, I had already decided to approve it.

Bowser requested 340 unarmed DC National Guard troops to be posted at 30 traffic control points (TCPs) around the White House. These TCPs were designed to block vehicular traffic into the city's core and the designated demonstration sites. After several vehicular terrorist attacks over the past two decades, law enforcement typically blocked the roads with dump trucks or other heavy vehicles. Three National Guard Soldiers and one DC Metropolitan Police Officer would be at each location. Their purpose was to show that law enforcement was present, to direct traffic, to monitor the crowd, and to intervene, if required, in disturbances.

Four National Guard soldiers along with one DC police officer and one transportation cop would also be at six Metro subway stops with the same type of responsibility as those at the TCPs. Additionally, 40 National Guard soldiers would be located at Joint Base Andrews in Maryland as a Quick Reaction Force (QRF) to respond to unexpected events or reinforce elements in need. Some have criticized the location of the QRF because of its 10-mile distance from the city center, but experience has shown that these forces are more capable near an airfield where they can be airlifted by helicopter in case the road network or bridges are blocked. I also approved the activation of a 20-person specialized element that could detect and monitor chemical, biological, radiological, and explosive hazards in support of local authorities. All the elements would be supported by 52 command and control, logistics and liaison specialists.

The intelligence picture was typical, which means analysts saw what they wanted to see based on their preexisting biases, and thus, nothing was actionable. If you think your Intelligence Community has refined, all-knowing prescience, I regret to inform you that's not the case. The coin of the realm is "credible and imminent" threats. The threshold for such a threat is that an individual or group has specifically said that they intend to attack a certain thing at a certain time. Everything else is "information," "speculation," or "unsubstantiated chatter" and does not meet the threshold of "intelligence." That's how it works. The bar for "intelligence" versus "information" is deliberately high to avoid poor decision-making like that which resulted in the U.S. invasion of Iraq in 2003.

As a Green Beret, I had learned to ask myself, "If I was the enemy commander, what would I do?" I would then list the most dangerous enemy course of action and the most likely. My assessment was that the most dangerous course of action by any troublemakers was that organized cells of demonstrators would provoke a soldier to respond in a way that would appear in the media as a violent attack against "peaceful demonstrators exercising their rights." The incident would then be amplified on social media. I thought the most likely course of action was demonstrations with small-scale violence during the day, and that when it became dark, small cells of hard-core protesters and counterprotesters would attack each other and damage property.

Genius wasn't required to deduce that violence was likely that day. BLM protesters and Antifa radicals had been burning American cities throughout the summer. Tensions were boiling over after nearly a year of pandemic lockdowns. The expectation we had at the DOD, reinforced by discussions with counterparts at the Department of Justice and Department of Homeland Security (DHS), was that right-wing elements would converge on DC, demonstrate during the day, and then when it was dark disperse and street fight with their counterparts on the left. Disconcerting, sure, but hardly historic in nature compared to the mob violence that plagued America's streets in the preceding several years.

We could scarcely have imagined what was to come.

On January 3, I met with President Trump in the Oval Office to discuss international threats unrelated to anything happening on the home front. At the end of our meeting, he asked about preparations for January 6. Specifically, he wanted to know if there had been any requests for National

Guard support, and I informed him of Mayor Bowser's request.

"You're going to need 10,000 people," President Trump said bluntly. I wasn't sure what to make of his prediction. Where did he get that number? I chalked it up to his fondness for hyperbole.

"Well, the Mayor only asked for 340," I responded. "But we're giving her everything she requests."

"Good. Give her whatever she wants," the President said. "But you're going to need 10,000."

Later that day, I convened the first of two Cabinet-level meetings aimed at achieving three goals. First, I wanted to make sure that federal and local agencies had a uniform understanding of the threat. The U.S. military is rightfully prohibited from conducting intelligence collection activities domestically, so we were relying on the FBI and local law enforcement to develop an accurate assessment of the threat. Second, I wanted everyone to understand roles and responsibilities. Third, I wanted to guarantee that everyone understood that the DOD was standing by to provide any support requested, consistent with the Constitution.

I didn't like being the one to convene these meetings. The DOD should not play a lead role in domestic law enforcement. However, as a lifelong soldier I knew that it was often difficult to get different (and often competing) organizations—like traditional Army commanders, Special Forces units, and intelligence operatives—all operating from the same playbook. It was easy for me to see that preparations for January 6 were not wired tight. Despite the potential perception of a militarization of domestic affairs, I felt it my professional responsibility to take these unprecedented actions.

Secretary of the Interior David Bernhardt and Acting Attorney General Jeffrey Rosen were on the call. Acting Homeland Security Secretary Chad Wolfe wasn't available, but one of his deputies provided a solid overview of the expected threat. Bernhardt oversaw a big chunk of property in Washington, DC—the National Mall, the area around the White House, and a number of the major roads and bridges—and had a large police force. Rosen oversaw the FBI and would be the lead federal agency. Milley, McCarthy, McConville, and I represented the DOD. DC Metropolitan Police and the DC National Guard were also monitoring.

Milley asked why Interior was allowing a protest on Capitol Hill and recommended revoking the permit. DC officials explained that permitted demonstrations couldn't simply be canceled, and American citizens, of course, have the right to free speech and to peaceably assemble.

I pressed DC officials about the number of cops that would be on duty on January 6 and their disposition. Our entreaties were met with a borderline condescending lecture by the DC Metropolitan Police official on the call that the planned force of 8,000 to 10,000 law enforcement officers were capable of handling up to a million demonstrators. The underlying message from the law enforcement community was, "We got this. Let the pros handle it, and please stay out of our way." I concluded the meeting by reminding the participants that DOD stood ready to provide any additional support requested.

The final estimate per DC Police and DHS was a maximum of 35,000 demonstrators, giving us a ratio of one cop for every 3.5 protesters—a pretty serious power imbalance in our favor. The use of the National Guard in static positions would free credentialed law enforcement officers to be mobile and able to respond to outbreaks of violence or unexpected contingencies as the National Guard did not have the authority to arrest people.

On January 5, Mayor Bowser sent a letter to Army Secretary McCarthy stating, "the Metropolitan Police Department [MPD] is prepared for this week's First Amendment activities...the District of Columbia is not requesting other federal law enforcement personnel and discourages any additional deployment without immediate notification to and consultation with MPD if such plans are underway."

It was encouraging to hear that local law enforcement had the situation under control. It was looking like we just might be able to achieve my goal of no troops deployed on American streets.

For some unknown reason attributable only to the prehistoric portions of my brain, I packed an overnight bag on the morning of Wednesday, January 6. On my way out the door, my wife noted the addition to my daily load usually consisting of a satchel and a classified zipper lock bag. "Could be a long couple of days," I said. That was the first time I had taken a change of clothes to the Pentagon.

My wife wasn't a Trump supporter. She didn't like my job. There were numerous times in the preceding 60 days that I was pretty sure she didn't much like me. The previous seven weeks had tested our 30-year marriage like never before. She thought I was an idiot for accepting the job. By the time an unruly mob started amassing in front of barricades around the perimeter of the Capitol, I was starting to wonder if she was right.

Shortly after 1 p.m., I learned that the outer perimeter of the Capitol had been breached. I'd been in a few riots, and this initially didn't appear to be a major problem. It's always tough to defend a large perimeter, but there were only a couple of ways into the Capitol where the cops could concentrate their force. There were still plenty of law enforcement personnel to move around and reinforce where the attackers were strongest.

It was impossible to tell what was going on with any degree of precision by watching the four news channels streaming into my office. And, frankly, the die had been cast by the plans and decisions that had been made the days prior. It was up to the cops on the Capitol grounds and the thousands of reinforcements positioned around the city.

My office quickly became the Operations Center for the DOD response. Kash Patel, my chief of staff, had assigned a notetaker to keep track of the flurry of activity and phone calls. The Army, as the organization directly responsible for communicating with the DC National Guard, was using their Pentagon command center and feeding information to my staff. Milley, McCarthy, and McConville swung by regularly to provide updates. It was clear to me that the civilian authorities and politicians weren't communicating effectively. It was a pretty standard "fog-and-friction" situation, and to the uninitiated it created cognitive dissonance—scenes of rioters entering the Capitol juxtaposed with the ongoing certification process on the other screen.

I had been in enough chaotic situations to know that the worst thing senior leaders can do is interpose themselves into the maelstrom with requests for information and the provision of "good ideas" and guidance. I had experienced the tyranny of commanders in headquarters watching video feeds direct forces on the ground. Good leaders recognize the distortion created by social and mass media and stay out of the way of the commanders in the fight who are dealing with information overload.

It was clear to me at 1:07 p.m. with the reports of pipe bombs at the Democratic National Committee and Republican National Committee headquarters that we were likely dealing with a larger conspiracy. But I was still confident in the predictions by the MPD in the days prior that they had adequate forces to handle the situation. Milley, McCarthy, and McConville converged on my office at 2:30 p.m. McCarthy told me that they were working through several requests for National Guard support and that his staff was trying to get everyone on the same page. I knew the challenges he and his people were facing trying to make some order out of the chaos.

My confidence that the system was working evaporated at 2:44 p.m. when the press announced that a rioter had been shot and killed inside the Capitol. That's when I knew civilian law enforcement had overpromised and underdelivered and that it was now my problem. Milley and McCarthy were freaking out. Milley was prone to histrionics, and I had learned to ignore him, and McCarthy was acting like the United States Army Ranger captain he had been when our paths first crossed in Kandahar, Afghanistan, in September 2001. I wanted to yell at them to calm the fuck down, but then I would be no better than them. I knew I had to be calm and controlled to compensate for their loss of composure. My people were watching how I would respond. It's easy to be a good leader when nothing is at stake, but this was the quintessential moment, and how I responded would set the tone for the coming weeks. I sat quietly for a moment and collected my thoughts as the chaos swirled around me.

"The Capitol has fallen. We own this now" I announced. "Let's get forces moving towards the Capitol. We need to lock down the city." McCarthy departed like a whirling dervish. Milley took a breath and changed his demeanor to match mine. It was all business now.

McCarthy returned at 3:00 p.m. and confirmed that the Army had received a request from DC Mayor Bowser for additional support. It was the justification I needed. I didn't pay much attention to the details of her request because I determined it was now a DOD mission and instead ordered the complete mobilization of the DC National Guard and movement to the Capitol of all available forces immediately. The order was issued at 3:04 p.m. We were taking over. It was necessary but disappointing—what a complete and utter failure by civilian law enforcement. Thirty minutes later McCarthy requested to go downtown and help sort things out at the Capitol. I knew that the Acting Deputy Attorney General and Deputy FBI Director were converging on the Capitol and that McCarthy would be well-suited to be part of the triumvirate that would mass federal forces in support of the outmanned and outmaneuvered local police.

I knew it would take some time for our forces to arrive at the Capitol. Deploying forces in an urban environment is deceptively complex. Even when you're moving at lightning speed, it can take hours to assemble soldiers, equip them correctly, conduct an abbreviated planning session, and brief everyone on their task, mission, purpose, limits, and rules of engagement. It becomes even more time-consuming when you have to coordinate and synchronize with the police and other domestic agencies on the ground and ensure that soldiers are deputized by a civilian law enforcement official prior to employing them. This is not a mere symbolic exercise.

The National Guard's arrival needed to impress upon the mob that the situation had fundamentally changed with the presence of disciplined, organized, and overwhelming strength. They needed to understand that the balance of power had shifted decisively back in favor of the forces of order, and it was in their best interest to give up quickly. I believed that's exactly what would happen; the only question was how soon we could get them to the Capitol.

As our troops prepared to mobilize, I had to consider other threats that might be brewing both at home and abroad as a result of the chaos. First, could this be part of a larger operation—a feint for the main attack someplace else? We had reports of a potential plot to bomb the Washington Monument and threats from small aircraft. I was also concerned that the Capitol assault could trigger copycat attacks throughout the United States, and I didn't want to overcommit resources until the situation became clearer.

Second, how might the Iranians, Russians, Chinese, North Koreans, or nonstate terrorists take advantage of the situation? The longer the siege drew out, the weaker our national government looked, and the more emboldened our foreign enemies would be to test our resolve.

And finally, we would immediately need to start arranging resources to prepare for the inauguration, which was a mere two weeks away. Clearly, the DOD would be required to play a much larger role in reestablishing and maintaining security in Washington, DC, for the immediate future.

At 4:08 p.m., Vice President Mike Pence called and asked for a situation report. The Vice President was serving as presiding officer over the joint session of Congress that had convened to certify the results of the presidential election, and he had been moved by Secret Service to a secure location in the Capitol. I had no idea that he had stayed. Surprisingly, he was absolutely unfazed; it was as if he was calling from his office at the White House asking about a routine item. Pence asked how long I thought it would be until the Capitol would be safe enough for Congress to reconvene and continue the Electoral College certification process. I advised him that I had fully mobilized the National Guard and that troops would be arriving in about an hour.

At 5:20 p.m., National Guard personnel arrived at the Capitol and began operations in support of domestic law enforcement entities there. Order was restored by 8 p.m. that evening, and the Electoral College results were certified.

In the active-duty military, our fastest responding units have a three-hour window to deploy. On January 6, the National Guard successfully deployed in 2 hours and 20 minutes. To my knowledge, it was the fastest National Guard response in American history.

SOLDIER SECRETARY

* * *

I have to confess—of my 73 days in the Pentagon as Acting Secretary of Defense, January 6 was the most familiar to me. It felt like combat again. It was stressful, because combat always is, but I also felt completely comfortable and in control.

I accept total responsibility for everything that happened in the United States military and DOD while I was the Acting Secretary of Defense. That's the essence of leadership. As a leader in the military, you are responsible for everything that does or doesn't happen in the organization you lead. You don't shirk responsibility and accountability; you own it. That's what the American people pay you for. I absolutely wish that, like the western movies of yore, the citizen-soldiers of the National Guard rescued the Capitol Hill and Metropolitan Police from being overrun by violent protesters and put an inviolate barrier around the Capitol precluding their storming of the building. But this isn't Hollywood, and conflict and fighting don't lend themselves to clarity and happy endings.

I remember a reporter asking me, "What was your worst day as Secretary of Defense?" It was obvious he expected me to say January 6. Yes, the events of January 6 were terrible, but it wasn't even close to the saddest of the 73 days I served as the Secretary of Defense. My worst experience by orders of magnitude was meeting with the families and loved ones of six soldiers who died in a helicopter crash on the Sinai Peninsula. Those soldiers were there to maintain the peace between Israel and Egypt. They were literally on a mission of peace. But while they were on a routine flight, their helicopter malfunctioned and crashed, tragically killing them all.

It was my first time back at the military morgue at Dover Air Force Base in Delaware since I had picked up Captain Paul Syverson's body for transport for burial at Arlington National Cemetery. I had sent Syverson to his death 18 years prior. This time, I was spared the pain of inspecting the body to guarantee that I was delivering the correct remains to the family.

The families of the six fallen servicemembers sat somberly on sofas in a waiting area. Vice President Pence, Second Lady Karen Pence, Secretary of the Army Ryan McCarthy, General James McConville, and Chairman Milley joined me to pay our respects.

A Casualty Affairs Officer briefed us on each of the fallen and the family members present, then we split into three groups and rotated through the room talking with each grieving family. Words were worthless. Their hearts were broken, and there was nothing any of us could say to put them back together.

These patriots had volunteered to serve simply because they loved their country. They didn't care about DC's games. Unlike so many in this godforsaken capital city, they weren't interested in amassing or maintaining personal power. They didn't trample others just to get a rung higher up the ladder. They didn't treat their compatriots like pawns to be sacrificed in the service of some grand strategy. They served selflessly, courageously, and with honor. And now they were gone.

In America, year after year, we lose our best people but always seem to keep our worst.

Yes, the riot at the Capitol on January 6 was stupid and criminal and an absolute disgrace. But it was far from anything resembling an "insurrection" or, as the Democrat slogan repeated ad nauseam suggests, an "attack on our democracy."

The actual attack on democracy is what has been happening in the halls of the very same building for years or even decades, perpetrated by elected leaders of both parties.

They led us into one pointless war after another, costing us thousands of American lives and trillions of dollars in wealth. They funded the rise of China through trade give-aways, destroying our middle class and creating the monster that now looms over the free world. They opened our borders to an endless wave of crime and drugs that kills more than 100,000 Americans annually. They squandered the strong and proud America they inherited and left our nation weaker and more divided than we have ever been before.

On the one-year anniversary of January 6, Democrat politicians delivered maudlin speeches, held candlelight vigils, and in what could be a first, announced plans to erect, rather than tear down, a national monument. Vice President Kamala Harris preposterously equated January 6 with both Pearl Harbor and 9/11.[16]

After left-wing mobs gutted entire cities, killed dozens of American citizens, and inflicted billions of dollars in property damage throughout 2020, politicians' tearful

---

[16] Rebecca Morin and Matthew Brown, "Kamala Harris Speech: January 6 Will 'Echo' in U.S. History Like Pearl Harbor, 9/11," *USA Today*, January 6, 2022, https://www.usatoday.com/story/news/politics/2022/01/06/harris-jan-6-like-pearl-harbor-9-11/9116617002/.

remembrances reeked of disingenuousness. But the absurd spectacle served a very specific purpose: to justify the ever-increasing concentration of power in the hands of our corrupt and incompetent political elite.

They may hold positions of leadership, but they are not really leaders. They may be entrusted with great responsibility, but they never take responsibility when it really counts. Our ruling class is incapable of ruling. And they should not be trusted with America's future.

In the final chapter, I'll discuss what we can do to right the ship.

CHAPTER ELEVEN

A NEW WAY FORWARD
FOR AMERICA

merica is engaged in a war for its soul and its future. Like ancient Rome at its apex, the United States military is massively overextended while our own borders are unprotected, and the American "empire of ideas" is ripe for collapse. Our national security apparatus, designed to fight a twentieth-century war against an enemy that no longer exists, coasts along on autopilot, enriching the few while endangering the many.

The purpose of government is to secure the rights, liberty, lives, and property of American citizens, which of course requires a strong military that is prepared to meet the challenges of the twenty-first century. I hope the following proposals provide some insights to advance our public discourse on these critical matters of war and peace.

ACTION ITEM 1

Restoring National Unity with Universal Service

American society is more balkanized and divided than it has been in generations. The culture war rages with an intensity that only seems to grow with each passing year, splitting Americans into warring factions based on politics, gender, religion, race, sexual orientation, and geography. For the first time in our nation's history, Americans can wall themselves off in a virtual world that only reinforces their thoughts, biases, and political views.

These barriers will not disappear on their own; in fact, they are likely to grow even stronger over time. To restore the bonds of love and loyalty that once united the American people, we must reinvigorate and expand the AmeriCorps program, requiring every 18-year-old to perform service to the nation for 18 months. Military service would be one option, but each cohort would also have the choice of serving in health care, education, infrastructure rejuvenation, environmental programs, or the National Park Service. In addition to a small living stipend, participants could pick from a menu of post-service benefits like college tuition assistance, small business or home loans, or specialized job training. The stories of the great melding effect of draftees during times of war is the model for how service creates unbreakable bonds of affection and understanding that last a lifetime. Implementing such a program would cost less than one $14 billion aircraft carrier and would likely be further offset by reduced government personnel costs and increased post-service economic and educational opportunities.

ACTION ITEM 2

Reinvigorate America's Brand to Outcompete Xi's and Putin's

The Communist Party of China is offering a different model of governance to the world, and many countries have found it attractive. China's high tech surveillance state, combined with a semi-free market that generates big profits for industrialists and government apparatchiks alike, provides a road map for wannabe despots.

The best way we can counter the growing appeal of autocracy globally is by strengthening our democracy at home. Our competitive advantage is America's economic strength and vitality and the broad appeal of liberty, equality, and freedom. On this foundation is a superstructure of world-class higher education and a legal regime that is transparent and encouraging of innovation and risk-taking. But we aren't organized as a government and society to compete effectively. By integrating and synchronizing all elements of the United States Government (not just the military) along with industry, finance, and civil society, we will correct the fundamental deficiency in our current approach to China.

The last time we transformed our national security structure was 35 years ago, after the Cold War. Senator Barry

Goldwater and Representative Bill Nichols reformed the Department of Defense to institutionalize cooperation and synergy between the separate military services and created empowered generals and admirals to serve as autonomous proconsuls around the world. The model served our nation well during the interwar period.

We are now in a new strategic era defined by competition with China and opposition to Russian expansion in which success requires not just the military, but all elements of the government and society to be engaged in a coordinated and deliberate manner. "Goldwater-Nichols II" is about forcing intergovernmental coordination and synchronization by mandating personnel move between Executive Branch departments and agencies if they want to be promoted forcing a more "multi-tool" national security professional that is more broad than the typical system where senior leaders "burrow" into one area. Additionally, the military needs to consolidate its five geographic combatant commands into two—one for the Atlantic region and one for the Pacific. That will streamline functions and coordination and reduce the bloated headquarters staffs that create needless work and friction.

ACTION ITEM 3

Cut Military Spending in Half

President Trump severely undermined his own goal of ending American military adventurism abroad by supporting massive increases in military spending *before* reforming military culture and structure. I think his heart was in the right place, but it was like giving homeless alcoholics a $100 bill along with a pamphlet for a rehab program and expecting them to do the right thing. Don't be surprised when you find them the next day shit-faced and lying in the gutter.

Our military is too big and bloated and wasteful. It continues to optimize for traditional twentieth-century warfare between large standing armies, while our enemies deploy asymmetric strategies that neutralize our advantages in size and strength. Our colossal military establishment was essential for our Cold War victory, but the Cold War has been over for 30 years. If we are truly going to end American adventurism and retool our military to face the challenges of the next century, we should cut military spending by 40–50 percent.

It wouldn't be quite as dramatic as it sounds. A 40–50 percent reduction would return military spending to pre-9/11 levels. We're no longer waging wars in Afghanistan and Iraq—yet our defense budget today is larger than it was in 2007 when I served my last tour in Iraq.[17] Why? So Raytheon, Lockheed, and Boeing can get even richer? We could cut our defense budget in half and it would still be nearly twice as big as China's.

It is time for defense, intelligence, and political leaders to accept that the Global War on Terror is over. Al-Qaeda and ISIS have been defeated. Yes, terrorists still exist and

---

[17] Stockholm International Peace Research Institute, Constant (2020) USD, https://milex.sipri.org/sipri.

always will, but we would be more than capable of destroying them even with half our current budget.

And don't fall for the politicians' favorite line of bullshit that "we have to fight them over there, or we'll have to fight them over here." It's complete nonsense. Terrorist groups don't have intercontinental ballistic missiles. The only way they can strike the American homeland is if our politicians let them enter our country through willful neglect, which is exactly how 9/11 happened. No amount of military spending would ever have prevented 9/11 or any other terrorist attack in the West. The way you defeat terrorism is not by spending ungodly sums on ships and jets, but by strictly enforcing our border—which, by and large, our political elite refuse to do.

I'm awestruck by the technological sophistication of our premiere fighter airplane, the F-35—it is a testament to the genius of America—but investing in such small numbers of traditional aircraft that will face off against swarms of inexpensive and expendable unmanned aerial vehicles is the product of legacy thinking.

Our enemies aren't going to fight us head-to-head like they did in World War II. It's eminently logical—if you are an opponent of the United States, why would you try to compete with us head on and risk defeat when you could use the tools of disinformation, economics, subversion, resistance, and cyberwar to slowly attrit our will, spirit, and expensive conventional military systems?

Consider China's creative approach. China isn't building a huge and expensive navy to square off against the United States—they are simply buying up port facilities around the world that the U.S. Navy relies on. Instead of dumping $14 billion on a single aircraft carrier, China is spending a few million dollars to develop cyber tools, missiles, and automated vehicles that can render our fleet inoperative from a great distance.

America's new Ford-class aircraft carrier is a sight to behold but provides only marginally improved capability beyond the World War II era grandparent. But at $14 billion a copy (the previous version went for a quarter of that) and designed so that only two or three can be at sea at one time, not to mention its vulnerability to attack by low-cost missiles, it makes no sense to me. The Army is investing enormous sums to replace its helicopter fleet. While at the Pentagon, I asked in all sincerity if there had been a breakthrough in rotary-wing aeronautics that transformed helicopters. No, I was assured, the physics hadn't changed; the powers that be just wanted a new family of helicopters to replace a battle-tested fleet that works just fine.

To offset the exorbitant cost, these big defense programs are designed to have extremely long life cycles—50 years, in the case of the Ford-class aircraft carrier. No one knows what warfare will look like half a century from now, yet we are placing huge bets on the ships and planes we are building today. Instead of remaining nimble, we are locking ourselves into a course of action that we cannot easily reverse.

The only way to force true innovation, wiser investments and the retirement of outdated warfighting concepts is by starving this out-of-control, insatiable beast. Money is the only thing that influences the Pentagon processes. Cutting our defense budget in half will force the military to evolve into the lean, tough killing machine America needs it to be in the twenty-first century.

ACTION ITEM 4

Secure the Border with Military Force

China is waging chemical warfare against the United States, killing scores of Americans without firing a single shot. The vast majority of the world's supply of fentanyl, a deadly synthetic opioid, is manufactured in China and smuggled into the United States via Mexico. Fentanyl kills nearly 70,000 Americans every year,[18] ten times the number of U.S. troops that died fighting in Afghanistan and Iraq throughout the entire Global War on Terror. Fentanyl is now the leading cause of death for Americans between the ages of 18 and 45.[19]

Protecting the territorial integrity of a nation is, by definition, a military problem that requires a military solution, and has been since the dawn of time. Clearly, our current strategy of relying on half-built barriers and sparse patrols is not working, and American citizens are dying as a result.

Drug cartels regularly fire upon U.S. law enforcement personnel from across the Rio Grande River. This is

---

[18] National Institutes of Health, "Overdose Death Rates," January 20, 2022, https://nida.nih.gov/drug-topics/trends-statistics/overdose-death-rates.

[19] Mark Bullion, "Fentanyl Number One Cause of Death for Adults 18–45, Recent Government Data Says," ABC 12, December 17, 2021, https://www.abc12.com/news/fentanyl-number-one-cause-of-death-for-adults-18-45-recent-government-data-says/article_ed0bfe28-5f79-11ec-8aa0-af3f6cbff03c.html.

a military provocation that should be met with a military response.

To protect the American homeland, we should increase our border defenses by increasing military capabilities along our southern border. But, more importantly, increased and sustained use of military intelligence assets and special operations forces to collect intelligence and destroy drug cartels and their facilitators wherever they lurk.

ACTION ITEM 5

Fighting on Our Terms

When preparing to fight, you always attempt to identify your opponent's critical strengths and critical weakness. Our critical weakness is an overreliance on large, expensive forces and weapons dependent on satellites to guide them or tell them their location. Our autocratic opponents do not fear our military forces—as a matter of fact, our aggressive acquisition and deployment of large, high-tech forces reinforces their propaganda that America poses an existential threat.

What they fear is internal instability that can create popular opposition to their rule. The fundamental, unitary goal of all autocrats is to maintain power. The freeing of information from state control via the internet and its concomitant hypervelocity is their Achilles' Heel and presents opportunities to foment dissent and rebellion. These capabilities that fall under the military rubric of "Irregular" or "Political" Warfare (the Chinese call it "Unrestricted Warfare") strikes terror into the hearts of tyrants who understand that instability and internal dissent are more threatening to their survival than large flotillas of ships and planes.

The winner of these conflicts will be decided by which actor wins sufficient loyalty of the populace, and not through force-on-force fighting—this is the definition of Irregular War. We failed in all our undertakings in the past 20 years. However, we know how to compete and win in these environments in which the key "weapons system" is the gray matter between the ears of the participants.

Our nation was founded by fighting irregularly. We turned the British Army's strengths—disciplined, large military forces with the latest technology and dominance of the sea—against them. Innovation, deception, wiliness, and flexibility of thought and action, undergirded by a physical and mental toughness, were our competitive advantages and created America.

It's time to reclaim that heritage—to fight smart and to use our strengths against our opponent's weaknesses. We need to re-create the World War II Office of Strategic Services and embrace civilian academics, businesspeople, special operators, and intelligence officers, as well as others with creativity, grit, and resourcefulness for nontraditional warfighting (such as cyber, information/psychological warfare, special operations and covert action, economic warfare, nontraditional intelligence analysis and analytics, diplomatic engagements, and so forth). Doing so will enhance our security by embracing our history, culture, and strategic core competencies.

ACTION ITEM 6

Create a Smaller, More Nimble Force

The world is in a state of geopolitical transition. I believe we are entering an era of what the Chinese call "unrestricted warfare" that spans every possible domain, including conventional military engagements, trade wars, and information and psychological warfare. Adjusting to this new reality will be difficult and time-consuming. When things are unstable and unpredictable, the best strategy is to hedge—to place a lot of small bets and not overcommit to anything.

The United States Armed Forces are almost unitarily focused on large-scale warfare epitomized by huge land, air, and sea forces augmented by space and cyber capabilities to clash with opposing forces in titanic battles á la World War II.

The United States defeated the Soviet Union in the Cold War through a strategy that forced them to spend so much money on countering our weapons systems that they went bankrupt. The Reagan-era Strategic Defense Initiative (more commonly known as "Star Wars") was the cornerstone of that strategy. It's worth contemplating that the Chinese may be using the same strategic approach against us that we used to defeat the Soviet Union. Could we be doing exactly what they want us to do while they spend a fraction of what we spend? We spend about a trillion dollars a year on our military—the equivalent of the next 10 nations combined. We have embarked on a plan to upgrade our conventional warfighting capability through the acquisition of exquisite, bespoke weapons systems that are ungodly expensive. The cost of operating and maintaining them is enormously costly. And we field two million people in uniform in an era in which future personnel costs—pay, health care, retirement benefits, veterans care—will consume an ever larger portion of the defense budget.

Civil War General William T. Sherman was arguably the most effective commander of that horrible conflict. He made the unpredictable, and for many, heretical decision to abandon his railroad supply lines and strike overland to destroy the Confederacy's warfighting capability. His strategic approach was to constantly put his opponents on the "horns of a dilemma" by forcing his opponents to defend numerous locations because they couldn't figure out his main objective until it was too late. Our strength is that we have the people and the capability to transform our Armed Forces into a light, mobile, stealthy, and nimble force that can put our enemies on a modern-day "horns of a dilemma" instead of fighting in a way they expect.

We have overcommitted with large, expensive bets. We have a military of high-cost, massive units equipped with exquisite capabilities deployed worldwide. While waiting for the outcome of the current global reordering, we can hedge with a new national security strategy that embraces low-cost, technology-enabled, forward-deployed, diplomatic intelligence and special operators to "sense" the environment for threats against our national interests. When these scouts identify the need for a U.S. military response, they can call forward intervention forces ranging from small, hard-to-observe, hypertechnology-enabled teams of commandos, and intelligence officers to mobile and highly lethal strike forces, to rapidly deployable high-tech conventional forces able to be reinforced, if required, by large reserves if a major adversary is stupid enough to mass their forces to fight us conventionally.

In essence, we should exchange size for stealth and speed—relying less on big weapons platform and hordes of soldiers, and more on small groups of Special Forces operators and agile, hyper-lethal strike forces.

ACTION ITEM 7

Upgrade Our Nuclear Arsenal

The only thing keeping Russia a great power is its arsenal of nuclear weapons. After witnessing our 2003 invasion of Iraq, North Korea and Iran realized that their best insurance policy to prevent the same thing from happening to them was to develop their own nuclear weapons and missile delivery programs. The United States attempted to deter their acquisition activities through diplomacy while taking a "procurement holiday" in refurbishing our nuclear forces.

Just like in football, there is always a fundamental tension in warfare between the offense and defense, and quality versus quantity. For the past 200 years, success in traditional large-scale combat typically required mass—lots of soldiers and weapons with huge mountains of supplies to support them—augmented with sophisticated weapons and offensive action. But modern technology has shifted the balance in favor of defensive action. Cheap sensors and readily accessible satellite-provided information make it much easier to locate and destroy large military formations. Today, whatever side can best protect their computer and satellite networks, infrastructure, population, and key weapons systems will prevail.

We currently rely on a nuclear triad of bombs and missiles delivered from ground-based silos, airplanes, and submarines. This triad served us well for 75 years but needs a rethink for the modern era. We must continue to upgrade the undersea and airborne legs of the nuclear triad, which started during President Trump's tenure, recognizing that mobility is the *only* way to survive in the future strategic environment dominated by cheap sensors and missiles networked to easy-to-obtain satellite technology. The ground portion of the triad is obsolete and must be eliminated because it can't survive an attack by hypersonic missiles—the most modern and potentially devastating weapon system of the twenty-first century that all great powers are developing and procuring en masse.

The savings achieved by eliminating the ground-based leg of the nuclear triad can be reinvested in developing new and improved nuclear weapons.

New warfighting concepts and systems leveraging the Technological Revolution will support the ultimate game changer that will deter aggression against us—effective defenses to protect us from missile attack by the plethora of nation's that will have the capability in the next 20 years. Many mocked the Reagan Administration for taking on such a seemingly outrageous and unachievable technological challenge. Due to the enormous dedication and ingenuity of generations of committed patriots undergirded by an unparalleled industrial base, we are on the cusp of creating a shield around the continental United States eliminating the threat of existential attack.

ACTION ITEM 8

Demolish and Rebuild the Intelligence Community

The underpinning of every national security decision is intelligence. The United States has the most elaborate, large, and sophisticated intelligence system in the world. It consists of 18 organizations collectively known as the U.S. Intelligence Community (IC) that collect information through human spying; listening in on electronic conversations; studying the electronic "dust" that is associated with every transmission; identifying changes in the physical environment; surveying and mapping the globe; and monitoring publicly available information like the popular press, academic journals, and social media. I experienced how the IC works (and doesn't) as a young neophyte in 1983 to ultimately having access to the most sensitive and exquisite intelligence in the world from 2018 to 2020.

The vast majority of what the IC produces is worthless and a colossal waste of time and resources. The preeminent World War II historian Max Hastings noted,

"Intelligence-gathering is inherently wasteful....Perhaps one-thousandth of 1 percent of material garnered from secret sources by all the belligerents in World War II contributed to changing battlefield outcomes. Yet that fraction was of such value that warlords grudged not a life nor a pound, ruble, dollar, Reichsmark expended securing it."[20] Unlike in the 1940s, when intelligence-gathering and analysis required legions of humans, we now can automate the process of sifting through torrents of publicly available data and quickly identify patterns. As in so many other professions, a large swath of the IC can be replaced by automation.

We also entrust enormous power and responsibility to the IC leadership with extraordinarily little oversight. From spying on American citizens, to framing innocent people for crimes, to spreading lies and disinformation in the media, to conducting mind control experiments on Americans without their consent, history has proven time and again that the IC should not be trusted with such incredible power.

Congress tapped the brakes on these extra-constitutional excesses in the mid-1970s, but the brakes were permanently removed after 9/11. When Congress retroactively approved the wide-scale, warrantless surveillance of Americans in the name of fighting terrorism, it compromised its independence forever. Both congressional oversight committees are now subservient tools of the IC, leaving little standing in its way as it continually seeks to expand its power at the expense of our citizens' rights and liberties.

The most urgent task is to separate the National Security Agency—the most capable spy agency in the world—from

---

[20] Hastings, The Secret War, Harper, 2016, p. XIX

the military and make it a stand-alone, civilian-run organization reporting directly to the Director of National Intelligence. The current practice of having a military leader of such a dangerous and powerful spy agency is inappropriate for our republic. To lessen the potential for overreach, the Director of the National Security Agency should be a civilian appointed by the President and confirmed by the Senate.

The way to regain civilian control of the IC is to break the back of the existing coterie of self-identified "professionals" through the assignment of additional personnel appointed directly by the President. Such "political appointees," as they are called, are common throughout the federal government and ensure that the bureaucracy is working to achieve the President's objectives. However, political appointees are rare in the IC, except for a handful of executive leadership positions—meaning the IC is virtually exempt from civilian control provided by the executive branch.

Furthermore, the 18-member IC should be consolidated into four elements: military, diplomatic, economic, and information (focused on collecting online intelligence and waging cyberwarfare). Only then will we regain control of this hydra-headed monster.

ACTION ITEM 9

Return the Military to the American People

The military is the only organization that can take over the country. In 1993, when I was a junior Army officer, I read a paper by a mid-career Air Force officer called "The Origins of the Military Coup of 2012."[21] He created a scenario using news accounts of actual events that individually seemed totally innocuous, but, when strung together in his fictionalized style, presented a scenario that ultimately resulted in a disgruntled coterie of generals taking over the government. His essay was brilliant, thought-provoking, and totally unrealistic at the time.

Three decades later, having personally experienced the state of civil-military relations at the highest level of government, as well as having served as a soldier in the ranks, I'm much more afraid. Our military is idolized by the vast majority of the people in the country, and it's undeniable to me that many in the uniformed military either subconsciously or deliberately subscribe to a belief in their superiority. They perceive society and our institutions of government and their inherent friction and seeming chaos as anathema to their sense of order. Their ethos of honor, courage, and commitment are essential and laudable, but that does not separate them from the values and diverse beliefs of the citizenry they serve.

Military service is no more noble or meaningful than any other government job. It's a business. There's no draft; people volunteer and sign a contract. Part of their contractual obligations is to fight and perhaps be grievously injured or killed. But we have placed our military on a pedestal, and criticism is perceived—and spun by the military's supporters—as unpatriotic. Contributing to this imbalance

---

[21] Charles J. Dunlap Jr., "The Origins of the American Military Coup of 2012," *Parameters* 22, no. 1 (1992), https://doi.org/10.55540/0031-1723.1623.

is the guilt by many Baby Boomers over their treatment of Vietnam War veterans. Additionally, the establishment of the All-Volunteer Force and the associated dissociation of most upper-class Americans from their military has led to a fetishization of military service.

With few exceptions, the press treats servicemembers and military leadership with deference and respect. Politicians fawn over them at congressional hearings, and heed their recommendations as gospel truth.

The current generation of military leaders are exploiting this situation to increase the size and influence of the military without effective guardrails and meaningful debate. This quid pro quo—political support in exchange for essentially uncontested funding—is beneficial for both parties in the short term, but is guaranteed, if allowed to continue, to result in a Constitutional crisis for the next generation.

Fixing this problem starts by helping society better understand its military. Proximity matters. Currently, the full-time active-duty military is sequestered in a few humongous military bases, primarily in the South, with housing, schools, health care, social services, restaurants, recreation, and shopping centers that preclude inhabitants from having to interact with the community outside the base's protected gates.

Since we are already cutting the defense budget by 50 percent, as previously recommended, it makes sense to transfer many of our active-duty forces to the part-time National Guard and Reserve that are embedded in every city and large town in America. This would better link our citizens and soldiers socially, economically, and culturally. Doing away with government housing and schools on the remaining active-duty installations will enhance connectivity and understanding. Universal service combined with two years of mandatory Reserve Officer Training Corps (ROTC) participation by all students at colleges and universities receiving federal funds will further remedy this disassociation of our society from its military. This larger cohort of citizens conversant with military affairs will reduce the power imbalance between the political influence of the military leadership and their galaxy of self-anointed experts that support them and their civilian overseers.

An additional measure to strengthen our Republic is a return to a two-year term of service for the senior military officer, the Chairman of the Joint Chiefs of Staff, with the option for a two-year extension. (Recently, Congress legislated the Chairman's term to a single four-year term.) This provides the President and Secretary of Defense the ability to regularly review the performance of the Chairman.

The Army and Navy Academies were necessary in the nineteenth century. The nation needed engineering schools to build canals and reservoirs and roads to tame the frontier and to master the seas. The Army and Navy were also small, requiring a modest cohort of officers. In the twenty-first century, we have a plethora of world-class engineering schools and an extensive cadre of professionals to maintain and improve infrastructure.

Today, ROTC provides 75 percent of the officers to the military services. The military academies, hermetically sealed from the society they are designed to protect, are no longer necessary. The one billion dollars we currently spend on the military academies can be invested in ROTC programs at public universities.

Participation of military leaders in politics is nothing new. But the days of Ulysses S. Grant and Dwight Eisenhower, when the winning commander of an existential war was expected to become President, are behind us. Contemporary examples of senior military commanders posturing for the presidency have not been so successful. FDR called Douglas MacArthur one of the most dangerous men in America, and Harry Truman successfully resisted his political aspirations. During the 1960s, legendary World War II and Cold War airman Curtis LeMay was widely regarded as a menace to the republic, and his political aspirations as George Wallace's Vice President went unfulfilled. Effective officers engender tremendous loyalty from their followers. And during wartime, success often requires megalomaniacal personalities. These two elements can be used, as we have seen in the past, to gain political power. Fortunately, no retired military officer entering the political arena has called forth his uniformed supporters to physically assist in his installation. But hope is not an acceptable course of action, as the military aphorism says, and additional guardrails must be installed in our political system.

Most senior military officers stay out of politics and continue to imbue the foundational military principle of selfless service. Those wanting to enter politics or profit from the Entertainment-Media-Political Complex as talking heads exploiting the knowledge they gained from their time in uniform should sacrifice their military rank, as well as their retirement pension, which is typically north of $200,000 annually.

There is no more visible example of Congress's failure to provide effective oversight of the military than their decision to confirm Generals Jim Mattis and Lloyd Austin as the civilian leaders of the military. In the 70 years prior to General Mattis's selection, only one general, George Marshall, was granted the necessary Congressional waiver to become Secretary of Defense soon after his military retirement. Four-star generals and admirals are enormously talented and have proven themselves capable of leading huge organizations in the most difficult, complex, and challenging environments. As with any group of success-ful people, they are typically loyal and supportive of each other. These bonds of fellowship and affection are laudable in a military context but are not appropriate in civilian gov-ernment. This development should be extremely troubling to all Americans.

In isolation, these issues may seem small, but together, they greatly increase the odds of military coup in the future.

ACTION ITEM 10

Fire the Generals

America has lost every major conventional war since the 1953 stalemate in Korea. A huge portion of the current leadership in every branch of the Armed Forces needs to be gracefully escorted into retirement.

Our successes in the post–World War II era have resulted from operating irregularly—Greece, El Salvador, Colombia, al-Qaeda, to name a few. Conservatism and prudence are quite appropriately hallmarks of the military; rapid change untethered to facts often results in preventable loss. But we have all the information we need to recognize that we are at a pivotal transition point in the history of our Nation and the World, and without transforming our national security architecture and practices, we risk cataclysmic defeat. Personnel is truly policy, and we aren't selecting the right type of people to lead our military.

General George Marshall, the World War II Army leader, ruthlessly culled nonperformers from the general officer ranks. But today, the military is the only realm where lifelong failures are rewarded with high-salaried board of director positions and lucrative punditry positions.

The military has proven incapable of policing its own and transforming its culture and standards. Internal accountability is typically absent and only occurs following public outrage. We can't wait to lose another war before bringing about this overdue renaissance.

It starts with an update to the officer personnel bible known as the Defense Officer Personnel Management Act (DOPMA) and each service's internal policy that establishes the detailed requirements for being promoted as an officer. DOPMA was established by law in 1980. It was created during the Cold War to guarantee a large population of officers to lead the masses required to fight a global World War III. It was very much a product of the Industrial Age and the organizational concepts in vogue at the time.

A DOPMA update is needed that includes stringent professional testing requirements and interviews—none exist now—for promotion and selection for command. Additionally, the military should mandate 360-degree, "whole person" reviews to weed out toxic or incompetent officers, and employ proven psychological and cognitive performance testing to guarantee that the desired traits of character, flexibility, innovation, and toughness are rewarded. These reforms will do much to create the military officer corps our fighting people and citizens expect.

Although a DOPMA refresh will result in a more professional and capable officer corps, human frailty can never be expunged because leadership is an essential human business. When instances of misconduct, malfeasance, or incompetence are identified, an independent entity that is not affiliated with the chain of command must investigate. The current process of using individuals beholden to the accused or their superiors results all too often in tepid recommendations to avoid bringing attention or discrediting the chain of command. Very rarely are investigations or inquiries conducted without the presence of undue influence by the accused or their superiors, since a negative result is detrimental for promotion. Using an outside official to investigate serious acts of officer misconduct or incompetence will reestablish trust within the officer ranks and between commissioned officers and the sergeants and warrant officers they command.

Accountability for the most senior general officers—the ones that develop strategy and provide guidance and advice to their civilian bosses—is woefully lacking in the current culture. The way we fight our wars by rotating units and leaders through the combat zone for yearlong tours isn't helpful for developing and instituting a consistent approach. If commander's decisions were subject to retroactive review—and if they were found strategically flawed and contributed to losing a war—they should be demoted to the last rank they successfully served, much like what happens for officers convicted by court-martial of felonious behavior. In our current military, a junior officer that messes up supply or equipment paperwork is routinely fired and forced out of the service. It seems obtuse that an administrative error is more harshly punished than losing a war, which brings national shame and embarrassment, not to mention the profound waste of our human and financial treasure.

Adopting these recommendations is necessary to start the process of restoring the might of the American military, ensuring we are prepared for the challenges we are certain to face in the decades to come, and rebuilding our sense of national unity.

But even if none of them are adopted—few people understand better than I how the defense and political establishment is resistant to change—I am still incredibly optimistic about the future of our military and our nation.

I'm optimistic because I have been blessed to witness the character and courage of our people in the most desperate and inhospitable conditions having been put in intolerably difficult positions by the incompetence and, sometimes, malevolence of their leaders. Rank-and-file Americans are unlike any other people on the face of the Earth blessed with enormous common sense and refined bullshit detectors. Those who volunteer to serve are among the most courageous, compassionate, and strongest men and women our nation has to offer.

No matter what the future holds, I know that when chaos reigns, standard operating procedures and the well-laid plans of higher headquarters and the Pentagon aren't worth the paper they are written on, résumés count for nothing and all seems lost, our servicemembers will always rise to the occasion and figure things out. And, without fail as they have done since before the birth of our republic, they will grab the initiative and, in the timeless words used by so many sergeants and junior officers over the years at the point of decision where our nation's future hangs in the balance, make "chicken salad out of chicken-shit" and save the day. We owe it to them to clean out the accretion of chickenshit that has built up over the years to ease their burden as much as we can.

ACKNOWLEDGMENTS

It's been a privilege and honor to partner with Vince Haley and Ross Worthington, who brought Ted Royer into the mix. David Vigliano and Tom Flannery from Vigliano Associates got us a shot. Alex Pappas risked his career and hired us and with Kathryn Riggs led the Hachette team that patiently guided us through the insanity of publishing and marketing a book. Ezra and Tony were sources of inspiration and insight.

I wish Ted and I had the time to send original manuscripts out far and wide for review like all of the rich, famous, and important people do. Regrettably, we were under intense time constraints to get the book done and delivered to the government censors for their interminable review and were unable to exploit the incredible generosity of so many that offered their assistance. Any and all errors are strictly due to my weak cognition. Ted deserves all credit for distilling my voluminous and tortured thoughts into a coherent narrative that perfectly captures my emotions and beliefs.

I was blessed to have served under bosses that put up with my nonsense. I learned from each of them—Mulholland, Cleveland, Paxton, Pagan, McDonnell, Bucci, Williams, Bowers, Fears, and O'Brien.

Acknowledgments

I was privileged to serve with a remarkable group of peers—Ridley, McGarrity, Covert, Brower, Sonntag, Mitchell, Raskin, Sanders, Raddatz, Nutt, Cadigan, Duggan, Sullivan, Notel, Leahy, Swatek, J. White, Ridley, Becton, Costa—men of courage and conviction that forced me to work harder and be a better officer and person. Joe Russell and Doug Gardner, although Marines, toughened me mentally and physically. And to my civilian friends John Casko, Rich Noyes, Steve Phillips, and Ben Klubes, who challenged and sharpened my thinking and character.

But it was the sergeants (no offense bosses and buddies) that made all the difference; why they were willing to mentor and teach me is one of the greatest mysteries of my life. Alvin, Peacock, Mulcahy, Bynum, Larry H., Vatovec, Jeffries, Bob S., Steve H., Corbett, Lovelace, Jim M., J. Ross, Strickland (may he rest in peace), to name but a few—I'm sorry for those that I failed to mention, but you know who you are. (Send me a nasty email and I'll get you in the paperback edition!)

Alpha Company, 3rd Battalion, 5th Special Forces Group (Airborne) you honored me with your patience and love and turned me into a semicompetent leader. The warriors of 2nd Battalion, 5th Special Forces Group (Airborne) and the men and women that were attached to us in Iraq in 2006–2007 that tolerated me—I was humbled and honored to serve with you in battle.

I tell my children that there is intrinsic value in public service that transcends financial reward. That sounds great until you have to tell them they can't attend an event or purchase a desired item because you don't have the money. The crews at the National Security Council (Michael C. and

Drew Teitelbaum in particular), Pentagon, National Counterterrorism Center, and SecDef's office that selflessly serve
for meager pay and little acknowledgment exemplify this
ethos. Thank you for serving and avoiding the siren song of
the fabulous wealth you could easily earn in the commercial sector. (Joe and Kash and Andrew—ODA!)

To Charlie G., Richard T., Al B., Joe T., and Griffin D.,
who risked their careers to bash the bureaucracy into doing
the right thing (sorry I can't list your full names providing
you the recognition you deserve);

To our veterans that were poisoned at Karshi Khanabad;

To those that had been denied rightful acknowledgment
for their service (I'm hopeful the United States will finally
recognize the heroism of Colonel Paris Davis);

To the Department of Defense employees and their families that were attacked by Directed-Energy Weapons (aka,
Havana Syndrome) and had been ignored by their leaders;

To those patriots that, without accolades or acknowledgment struggle relentlessly for our Nation by offering
alternatives to the lazy, corrupt thinking that is disguised as
"expertise" to guarantee that our children and grandchil-
dren will enjoy the blessings of liberty.

Mom, Dad, and Sis—you put in the foundation.

The Maags and Bouchets, who live the definition of
"unconditional love."

And, most importantly, my family—I love you more
than you will ever know. Kate, who did it all and raised
our kids into miraculous adults—no words are available to
describe my appreciation, respect, and love.

INDEX

A Teams, of 3rd Battalion, 5th
SFG
clearing trench lines by, 102
Miller, C., as Operations
Officer of, 87
A Teams, of 3rd SFG in Iraq
War, 112, 114
A Teams, of SFGs
commander qualities in, 28
deployment two common
shots per day, 33–34
E&E plan memorization, 30
in Kuwait, 26
Miller, C., as commander
on, 27
radio men two common
shots per day, 33–35
Texas 17 embedded with
Sherzai, 74–75
accountability, generals lack of,
250–251
Acting Secretary of Defense,
184–186
on AQ war end, 187
on Armed Forces voice, 188
responsibility of, 222

on SOFs influence elevation,
188
transnational threats focus,
187
ADA. *See* Air Defense Artillery
School
Afghan Army
familial and tribal links in,
161
Milley and McKenzie on, 160
Taliban and, 161
2021 collapse of, 160
U.S. support necessary for,
160
Afghan security forces
Kandahar Hospital raid
shooting by, 77, 79, 81–82
ODA 524 training of, 77
in SR SEALs recovery
team, 119, 120, 123, 125,
130–131
Afghanistan
antiquated gear in, 59–60
Bonn Agreement in, 68–69
CT platform of 800 military,
159

Afghanistan (*Continued*)
  hostile elements 2021
    overthrow in, 29
  invasion plan, 89–90
  Karzai as interim leader of,
    69–72
  Miller, C., ankle injury of
    2001 in, 53–54
  Objective Rhino in, 55
  Sayyd Alma Kalay village in,
    57–58
  SOFs daylight flight, 56–57
Afghanistan War
  assessment of, 158
  DOD and CIA on, 159–160
  Esper and Milley, 159
  Trump, D., efforts to end, 158
Africa
  Djibouti assessment,
    191–192
  Esper hostage rescue mission
    halt, 184
  SOF team ambush in 2018,
    192
  Trump, D., military
    personnel removal order,
    192–193
  Trump, D., on hostage
    rescue mission in, 184
Ahmad Shah
  ambush possibility of,
    123–124, 129
  background on, 118
  Operation RED WINGS for
    location and capture of,
    114
Air Defense Artillery (ADA)
  School, at Fort Bliss

Miller, C., Basic Training
    trainer assignment at,
    16–17
  Miller, C., ROTC intern at, 17
air support, Iraq War with
    missile strikes and, 90
aircraft carrier costs, 233
allegiance, Taliban switching
    of, 68–70, 161
All-Volunteer Force, of
    military, 245
Alpha Company, in The Old
    Guard, 18–19
Ambrose, Stephen, 12
ambush, Shah possibility of,
    123–124, 129
America First worldview, of
    Trump, D., 181
  Mattis criticism of, 182
America new way forward
    proposals, 252
  American people military
    return, 243–248
  border security with military
    force, 227, 232, 234–235
  brand reinvigoration,
    229–230
  fighting on own terms,
    235–236
  fire the generals, 248–251
  IC demolish and rebuild,
    241–243
  military spending cut,
    230–233
  nuclear arsenal upgrade,
    239–241
  smaller, more nimble force
    creation, 237–239

universal service for national
  unity, 228–229, 246
American forces
  Iran potential attack on,
    199–203
  world map for locations of,
    200
AmeriCorps service
  requirement, 228
antenna theory, radio men
  and, 34
antiquated gear, in
  Afghanistan, 59–60
AQ. *See* al-Qaeda
Arghandab River British fort,
  Peaks attack plan to seize,
    67–68
Arlington National Cemetery,
  Tomb of Unknown Solder
  at, 17
Armed Forces. *See also*
  American forces
  Acting Secretary of Defense
    on voice of, 188
  domestic deployment of,
    207–208
  large-scale warfare of,
    237
  national security strategy,
    238–239
  politicization of, 109
  as smaller, more nimble,
    237–239
Armed Services Vocational
  Aptitude Battery
  (ASVAB), 3
Army. *See also* veteran
  unresolved issues

incentive system of, 7
juvenile system judge and
  delinquent choice of, 6
martial task training, 7–8
Mission first, men always
  slogan, 150, 153
people barriers torn down
  through, 5–6
retirement from, 148, 152
train how you fight slogan
  of, 61–62
Army Special Forces, 23
Army War College
  general promotion
    requirement of, 137
  internationalist worldview
    of, 138
  on technology invincibility,
    138
Asadabad combat outpost
  A Team SFG at, 111
  Marine company at, 111
  Provincial Reconstruction
    Team at, 111
  U.S. Interagency-Afghan
    Counterterrorism force at,
    111
assessment, of Afghanistan
  War, 158
Assistant Secretary of Defense
  for Special Operations and
  Low-Intensity Conflict, at
  DOD, 139, 140
ASVAB. *See* Armed Services
  Vocational Aptitude
  Battery
autocrats, internal instability
  fear of, 235–236

automated vehicles, of China,
233
automation, of IC, 242

Baghdad, Iraq
Battalion move to, 100
First Marine Division
capture of, 87
NSC on embassy attack in,
199–200
plan to isolate, 91
Republican Guard
compound in, 99, 102
road system around, 101
Syrian mercenaries at,
101–102
Third Infantry Division
capture of, 87, 99
Thunder Run into, 101,
103
al-Baghdadi, Abu Bakr
death and DNA
confirmation, 174–175
explosive suicide vest worn
in raid for, 171, 173–174
as ISIS leader, 162
Mueller torture and death
by, 168–169
as Sunni Muslim leader,
168
al-Baghdadi raid, of 2019
assault force surrounding of
compound, 170
Esper and, 164, 173, 176
Evans, M., and, 165, 166,
167–168, 170–171,
173
Haspel and, 176

helicopter-borne assault
force for, 165
Milley and, 162, 165, 167,
170, 174–176
O'Brien and, 162
Pence prayer before,
166–167
Pompeo and, 176
Pottinger and, 171–174
Syrian and Russian radars,
166, 167–168
Trump, D., drone viewing of,
170–174
Trump, D., Presidential
address on, 177–178
Trump, M., in White House
Situation Room, 173,
175–176
Band of Brothers (Ambrose),
12
Barr, Bill, 182
Basic Training, at Fort Benning
emotional experience of,
4–5
gas mask training, 8–9
Basic Training trainer, Miller,
C., at Ft. Bliss ADA
School, 16–17
Battle of Hamburger Hill
in Vietnam War, Zais,
Melvin, at, 12–13
Be Ready to Fight Tonight
motto, of Second Infantry
Division, Korea, 12
Bernhardt, David, 215
betrayal, as Army service
unresolved issue,
149–150

Biden, Joe, 205
bin Laden, Osama
  capture operation for, 165
  al-Shabaab ties with, 192
Black Lives Matter (BLM)
  riots, military response to,
    208–209
Bolton, John
  as Bush, G. W., UN
    Ambassador, 158
  as National Security Advisor,
    158
bomber task force mission,
  Iran and, 199–200
  McKenzie on, 201
  Milley on, 201
Bonn Agreement, Afghanistan,
  68–69
border defense, with military
  force
  China fentanyl supply and,
    234
  drug cartels and, 234–235
  terrorism and, 232
  U.S. unprotected borders,
    227
Bosnia
  assignment in, 47–50
  Dayton Accords threats in,
    48
  targets search for trial, 48
Bowser, Muriel, 210–211, 216,
  219
brand reinvigoration, in
  America
  China competition and,
    229–230
  Goldwater-Nichols II, 230

military consolidation
  to Atlantic and Pacific
    regions, 230
national security structure
  transformation, 229–230
Russia expansion opposition,
  230
U.S. Government
  integration and
  synchronization, 229
British Long Range Desert
  Group, in WWII, 30
British Special Air Service, as
  SFG model, 58
Brokaw, Tom, 87–88
Brower, Scott, 102
  on Battalion move to
    Baghdad, 100
Buccino, Tom, 106
bureaucracy, Pentagon layers
  of, 140–141, 147
Bush, George H. W.
  Gulf War and, 21
  new world order vision of,
    21
Bush, George W., 158, 190

Camp Dodge, 3, 4
CAPE. *See* Cost Assessment
  and Program Evaluation
Capitol elected leaders, attack
  on democracy examples,
    224
Carter, Jimmy, 2
ceremonial unit, of The Old
  Guard, 17
Chairman of the Joint Chiefs of
  Staff (CJCS), Milley as, 159

China
  competition with, 229–230
  cyber tools, missiles and
    automated vehicles of,
    233
  fentanyl supply by, 234
  as high tech surveillance
    state, 229
  port facility purchases,
    232–233
  semi-free market of, 229
  unrestricted warfare of, 236,
    237
China Communist Party,
  governance model of,
  229
Churchill, Winston, 129
CIA
  on Afghanistan War,
    159–160
  AQ hostage rescue efforts,
    163
  human aspects training at
    fellowship of, 138
  NSC sidelining by, 162–164
CIB. *See* Combat Infantry
  Badge
civilians
  contact options, 115
  Law of Armed Conflict
    violation on contact with,
    115–116
  military control from, 141
  Secretary of Defense Office
    importance of control
    from, 141
  SR SEALs Korangal Valley
    compromise, 116

CJCS. *See* Chairman of the
  Joint Chiefs of Staff
clearing trench lines, in Iraq
  War, 102
Clinton, William "Bill," Dayton
  Accords and, 48
coercive diplomacy, in Iraq
  War, 89, 95
COIN. *See* Counterinsurgency
  Operations
Cold War, 11
  end of, 15, 52
  Strategic Defense Initiative
    and, 237
combat command, Sessoms
  gift of, 112–113
Combat Infantry Badge (CIB),
  9, 111
  for armed opponent close
    combat engagement, 10
  of 5th SFG team members,
    27
  WWII creation of, 10
commanders. *See also specific
  commander*
  A Team SFG qualities of, 28
common shots, radio men two
  per day, 33
  failure of, 34–35
Concept of the Operation
  (CONOP), SR SEALS
  recovery team request for,
  120, 121
conflict involvement, media
  support of, 109
Congress
  constitutional duties
    abrogation, 109

military oversight failure, 247–248

CONOP. *See* Concept of the Operation

Cordon Platoon, of The Old Guard, 19–20

Cost Assessment and Program Evaluation (CAPE) office, in DOD
  SOF funding agreement, 146, 147
  SOF importance study for, 145–146
  SOFs disadvantage, 146

Costa, Chris, 157

Counterinsurgency Operations (COIN), of IW, 143
  after 9/11, 144
  Petraeus manual of, 144

counterterrorism (CT)
  Afghanistan platform of 800 military, 159
  Djibouti, Africa task force of, 192
  expenditure reductions, 163–164
  Global War on Terror and, 163
  Somalia task force of, 192–193

Craig, Brian, 83

CT. *See* counterterrorism

Currahees, of Korea Second Infantry Division, 12

cyber tools, of China, 233

Dayton Accords, Bosnia threats to, 48

DC Metropolitan Police Department (MPD), January 6 riot and, 215, 218

DC National Guard. *See* District of Columbia National Guard

D-Day, in WWII, 10

debriefing, after E&E exercise, 40

decapitation strike, in Iraq War, 95

defeat, of Taliban, 161

Defense Officer Personnel Management Act (DOPMA) update, 249–250

Demilitarized Zone (DMZ), South Korea, 10–11

Department of Defense (DOD)
  on Afghanistan War, 159–160
  Assistant Secretary of Defense for Special Operations and Low-Intensity Conflict at, 139, 140
  CAPE office in, 145–147
  IW institutionalization, 142
  January 6 riot response, 217–218
  military support conditions, 208

Department of Homeland Security (DHS), January 6 riot and, 213

Index

deployment
  A Teams, of SFGs two
    common shots per day,
    33–34
  Armed Forces domestic,
    207–208
Devil's Brigade, in WWII, 119
DHS. *See* Department of
  Homeland Security
digital war, 62–63
diplomatic elements, IC
  consolidation of, 243
District of Columbia National
  Guard (DC National
  Guard)
  Bowser support request for
    January 6 riot, 210–211,
    216, 219
  January 6 riot response,
    219–221
  support approval, 211
  TCPs posted around White
    House by, 211–212
  Trump, D., on January 6 riot
    numbers of, 213–214
Djibouti, Africa
  CT task force in, 192
  Miller, C., assessment of,
    191–192
DMZ. *See* Demilitarized Zone
DOD. *See* Department of
  Defense
domestic deployment, of
  Armed Forces, 207–208
DOPMA. *See* Defense Officer
  Personnel Management
  Act
drug cartels

Acting Secretary of Defense
  on threat of, 187
border defense with military
  force against, 234–235

economic element, IC
  consolidation of, 243
E&E. *See* escape and evasion
Eichelberger, Robert
  MacArthur service with, 22
  Shortal book on, 22
Eisenhower, Dwight, 190, 247
election, of 2020. *See also*
  January 6, 2021 riot
  Flynn on rerun of, 206–207
  Trump, D., Biden victory
    question, 205
EOD. *See* Explosive Ordinance
  Disposal
escape and evasion (E&E), for
  SR SEALS mission
  lack of, 116
  RIP/TOA and recovery
    difficulties, 117
escape and evasion (E&E) plan
  exercise, of 5th SFG, 29
  A Team memorization of, 30
  Air Force jets flight toward
    Iraq, 33
  debriefing after, 40
  GO TWA contingency plan,
    38
  hide site for, 35–36
  140-pound backpacks load
    dictated in, 32–33, 36–37
  results with praise after,
    41–43
  SiLLS stop in, 32

two radio men in, 33
Esper, Mark
  Africa hostage rescue
    mission halt by, 184
  al-Baghdadi raid and, 164,
    173, 176
  as internationalist, 191
  on Lafayette Square incident
    and Trump, D., blame, 182
  as Secretary of Defense, 159
  Trump, D., frustration with,
    181–182
  Trump, D., Secretary of
    Defense removal, 184–185
Evans, Marcus, 165, 166,
  167–168, 170–171, 173
Evans, Paul, 105
Executive Branch
  Armed Forces domestic
    deployment by, 207–208
  description of, 206
  Legislative Branch
    domination by, 109
Explosive Ordinance Disposal
  (EOD), experts at
  Kandahar Hospital raid,
  83

familial and tribal links, in
  Afghan Army, 161
fentanyl
  China supply of, 234
  deaths from, 234
Field Landing Strip (FLS), at
  Wadi al Khirr Airfield in
  Iraq, 92
5th SFG. *See* Special Forces
  Group, 5th

fighting on own terms
    proposal
  autocratic enemy internal
    instability fear, 235–236
  IW and, 236
  Office of Strategic Services
    recreation, 236
fire worm convoy, for SR
    SEALs recovery team, 122
First Marine Division, Baghdad
  capture by, 87
1st Battalion SCUD-hunting,
  in Iraq War, 92–93
FLS. *See* Field Landing Strip
Flynn, Michael, 206–207
Fort Benning, Georgia, Miller,
  C., Basic Training at, 4
Fort Bliss, ADA School at,
  16–17
Fort Campbell, Miller C.,
  Green Beret training at,
  25
Fox, Dave, 67, 71–72, 75,
  81–82
fragging, 13
friendly fire incident
  in Iraq War, 103
  at Sayyd Alma Kalay, 58

Galewski, Justin, 83
gas mask training, in Basic
  Training, 8–9
generals
  Army War College
    requirement for
    promotion to, 137
  DOPMA update and,
    249–250

generals (*Continued*)
  firing of, 248–251
  lack of accountability of,
    250–251
Global War on Terror
  closing of, 163, 231–232
  CT and, 163
GO TWA contingency plan, in
  E&E exercise, 38
Goldwater, Barry, 229–230
Goldwater-Nichols II, for
  intergovernmental
  coordination, 230
Grant, Ulysses S., 247
Green Beret
  A Team, Texas 17 with
    Sherzai, 74–75
  demolition explosives, at
    Kandahar Hospital raid,
    77
  Miller, C., at Fort Campbell
    training, 25
  SR SEALs recovery team
    exhaustion, 123–124
guard duty, 61–62
Gulf War (1990-1991), 52
  Bush, George H. W., and, 21
  Kuwait invasion by Hussein,
    21
  Powell and, 21
  Scowcroft and, 21

Harris, Kamala, 224
Haspel, Gina, 176
Hastings, Max, 241–242
helicopter
  -borne assault force, for
    al-Baghdadi raid, 165

replacement costs, 233
Sinai Peninsula crash of,
  222–223
SR SEALs mission rescue,
  116, 118, 130
hide site, for E&E, 35–36
high tech surveillance state, of
  China, 229
Highway of Death, during
  Operation Desert Storm,
  36
Howe, Russ, 12
human aspects training, in CIA
  fellowship, 138
Human-Centric War, military
  focus on, 135–136
Hussein, Saddam
  decapitation strike at palace
    of, 95
  Kurds persecution by, 169
  Kuwait invasion by, 21
  Radwaniyah Palace
    Complex of, 105–107
  Sadr City and, 91

IC. *See* Intelligence Community
incentive system, of Army, 7
individualism, military
  leverage of, 121
Infantry, 3. *See also* Second
  Infantry Division, Korea
  Germany mechanized, 11
  Third Infantry Division
    capture of Baghdad, 87, 99
information element, IC
  consolidation of, 243
Insurrection Act, McCarthy
  and, 206–207

Intelligence, Surveillance, and
Reconnaissance (ISR)
assets, of Predator drone,
94–95
Intelligence Community (IC)
demolishment and rebuild
automation of, 242
citizen surveillance and,
242
Hastings on wastefulness of,
241–242
military, diplomatic,
economic, information
elements consolidated in,
243
intelligence-gathering
operations, 46, 49
internationalists, 109
Army War College and
world view of, 138
Esper and Mattis as, 191
interventionalists, 109
invasions
Afghanistan plan, 89–90
Iraq War military masterful,
108
of Kuwait by Hussein, 21
Iran
bomber task force mission
in, 199–201
nuclear arsenal of, 239
Tehran American Embassy
revolutionaries and, 1–2
Trump, D., meeting on
uranium enrichment
purity, 196–197
Iran, American forces potential
attack by

bomber task force mission,
199–201
Milley on, 199, 202–203
NSC on Baghdad embassy
attack, 199–200
Pompeo on, 199
strategic bomber flights and,
199
Trump, D., meeting on,
199–200
USS *Nimitz* and, 199,
202–203
Iran hostage crisis (1980), 46,
97, 165
Iraq
Obama 2010 troops
withdrawal, 145, 147
Petraeus as 2007-2009
commander in, 144
Iraq War
clearing trench lines in,
102
coercive diplomacy in, 89,
95
costly and disastrous foreign
policy blunder of, 108
decapitation strike at
Hussein palace, 95
First Division Baghdad
capture, 87
1st Battalion SCUD-hunting,
92–93
friendly fire in, 103
military masterful invasion
of, 108
neoconservatives
responsibility for, 108
Sadr City and Hussein, 91

Iraq War (*Continued*)
  2nd Battalion in Karbala
    Gap, 92–93
  Shia insurgent groups in,
    89, 91
  shock and awe campaign, 90
  SOFs elements, 92
  Special Operations elements
    in, 92
  start of, 95–96
  as tank war with air support
    and missile strikes, 90
  Thunder Run into Baghdad,
    101, 103
  as unjust war, 107–108, 190
  Wadi al Khirr Airfield
    mission in, 92–97
Irregular Warfare (IW)
  COIN units disbanded in,
    143–144
  description of, 142–143
  DOD and institutionalization
    of, 142
  enemy internal instability
    through, 236
  ISIS destruction by, 147, 169
  military expenditures and,
    143
  planning and policy task for,
    140
  post-WWII era successes
    from, 248–249
ISIS
  al-Baghdadi as leader of, 162
  IW campaign destruction of,
    147, 169
  Kurds participation in war
    against, 169–170

  military defeat in 2018 of,
    163
  Mueller abduction by,
    168–169, 177
  Trump, D., on penalties of
    joining, 178–179
Islamic Revolutionary Guard
  Corps, Soleimani as leader
  of, 198–199
ISR. *See* Intelligence,
  Surveillance, and
  Reconnaissance
IW. *See* Irregular Warfare

January 6, 2021 riot, xi, 225
  Bernhardt and Rosen on,
    215
  Bowser DC National Guard
    support request, 210–211,
    216, 219
  DC MPD and, 215, 218
  DC National Guard response
    to, x, 219–221
  DC National Guard TCPs
    posting, 211–212
  DHS and, 213
  DOD response, 217–218
  Harris on, 224
  McCarthy and, 211, 216,
    218–219
  McConnell and, ix, x
  McEntee on military
    preparations for, 205–206
  Milley and, 215–219
  Pelosi and, ix–x
  Pence on, 221
  QRF for, 212
  Schumer and, ix

violence likelihood at, 213
Wolfe and, 215
Joint Direct Attack Munition,
    at Sayyd Alma Kalay, 58
Joint Special Operations Task
    Force (JSOTF)
    RIP/TOA rotation and SR
        SEALs recovery, 117
    on SEALs Korangal Valley
        mission, 114–115
juvenile court system, judge
    on delinquent Army
    choice, 6

Kandahar, Afghanistan
    AQ and Taliban leadership
        escape from, 75
    AQ at, 67
    Karzai delivery to, 71–72
    Omar army and AQ at, 67
    Sherzai warlord south of,
        74–75
Kandahar Hospital raid, for AQ
    fighters
    Afghan security forces
        shooting order in, 77, 79,
        81–82
    EOD experts at, 83
    fire at, 80–81
    Green Beret demolition
        explosives at, 77
    by ODA 573, 75–86
    press release on, 84–85
    surprise element ruined in,
        78
Karbala Gap, 2nd Battalion in
    Iraq War, 92–93
Karzai, Hamid, 56

as Afghanistan interim
    leader, 69–72
delivery to Kandahar, 71–72
SFG early warning at health
    clinic, 61, 66
Keegan, John, 108
Killed-in-Action burials, by
    The Old Guard, 22
Knox, Al, 29, 40–41
Korangal Valley SR
    mission. *See* Special
    Reconnaissance SEALs
    mission
Kristol, Irving, 190
Kurdish Peshmerga (Kurds), in
    Northern Iraq
    underground organization
        of, 169–170
    war against ISIS by, 169–170
Kuwait
    A Teams presence in, 26
    invasion during Gulf War, 21
Kuwaiti Army, 5th SFG
    training and advising of,
        26

Lafayette Square incident
    Barr and, 182
    Esper blame of Trump, D.,
        for, 182
Law of Armed Conflict
    violation, 36
    mission civilian contact and
        kill option, 115–116
leadership
    democracy attack examples
        of Capitol, 224
    guilt for war casualties, 150

leadership (*Continued*)
  Kandahar Taliban escape of, 75
  Paxton Socratic style of, 42
  politics participation of military, 247
Lee, Robert E., 152
Legislative Branch, Executive Branch domination by, 109
LeMay, Curtis, 247
Leonard, Danny, 73
"Lift the Fog of War" (Owens, B.), 129
Lone Survivor (film), 114
Luttrell, Marcus, 131–134, 135

MacArthur, Douglas, 247
  Eichelberger service with, 22
Majors, war planning by, 89
Man-Portable Air Defense Systems (MANPADS), 56–57
marathon running by Miller, C., for veteran unresolved issues, 149, 154
Marshall, George, 248, 249
martial task training, 7–8
Mattis, Jim, 164, 248
  as internationalist, 191
  Trump, D., America First criticism by, 182
MC-130 Combat Talons, in USAF tactical airlift, 93–94
McCarthy, Ryan
  Insurrection Act and, 206–207
  January 6 riot and, 211, 216, 218–219

McConnell, Mitch, ix, x
McConville, Jim, 211, 216, 218–219
McEntee, John, 183
  on January 6 riot military preparations, 205–206
McKenzie, Frank
  on Afghan Army collapse, 160
  on al-Baghdadi death and DNA confirmation, 174–175, 177
  on Iran bomber task force mission, 201
  on USS *Nimitz*, 202–203
mechanized Infantry, in Germany, 11
media
  conflict involvement support, 109
  on idolized military, 245
  on Trump, D., martial law election conspiracy, 209–210
mental health. *See also* veteran unresolved issues
  of volunteer army in protracted war, 153–154
meteorology knowledge, of radio men, 34
Middle East. *See also specific country*
  5th SFG desert environment, 25
military
  active-duty transfer to National Guard and Reserve, 245–246

All-Volunteer Force of, 245
BLM riots response from, 208–209
border defense with force of, 227, 232, 234–235
civilian control of, 141
Congress failure to provide oversight of, 247–248
consolidation to Atlantic and Pacific regions, 230
DOD conditions for support of, 208
Human-Centric War focus, 135–136
IC consolidation of element of, 243
individualism leveraged by, 121
internal accountability absence in, 249
IW and expenditures of, 143
media on idolized, 245
National Security Agency separation from, 242–243
optimism about, 251–252
politics participation and leaders of, 247
return to American people, 243–248
technology-centric war, 135–136
Traditional Warfare of, 142
Trump, D., suckers calling accusation, 183–184
two-year terms of service and, 246
U.S. overextension of, 227
on war as solution, 109

military academy, ROTC programs investment and closing of, 246
military campaign phases
Phase O shape, 90
Phase I deter, 90
Phase II seize initiative, 90
Phase III dominate, 90
Phase IV stabilize, 90
Phase V enable civil authority, 90
military spending cut proposal
aircraft carrier costs, 233
enemy warfare tools changes, 232–233
Global War on Terror closing and, 231–232
helicopter replacement costs, 233
military wastefulness, 231
outdated warfighting concepts and, 233
to pre-9/11 levels, 231
Trump, D., and, 230–231
Military-Industrial Complex, 21, 181
Eisenhower on, 190
Miller, Christopher
as A Teams 3rd Battalion, 5th SFG Operations Officer, 87
as Acting Secretary of Defense, 184–188, 222
at ADA School, at Fort Bliss, 16–17
Afghanistan ankle injury of 2001, 53–54

Miller, Christopher (*Continued*)
America new way forward
proposals, 228–252
American forces potential
attack by Iran and, 199–203
AQ at Kandahar Hospital
raid by ODA 573 and,
75–86
Arghandab River British fort
attack plan and, 67–68
Army retirement, 148, 152
at Asadabad combat outpost,
111
as Assistant Secretary
of Defense for Special
Operations and Low-
Intensity Conflict, at DOD,
139, 140
on Baghdad, Iraq, 99–103
al-Baghdadi raid, of 2019,
162–178
at Camp Dodge, 3, 4
as commander of A Teams,
of SFGs, 27
as Company Commander of
5th SFG, 51
as Detachment Commander
of ODA 573, 26–28
Djibouti, Africa assessment,
191–192
E&E plan exercise, of 5th
SFG, 29–43
at Fort Benning Basic
Training, 4–5, 8–9
at Fort Campbell Green
Beret training, 25
January 6, 2021 riot and,
205–225

Korangal Valley SR mission
and, 114–134
marathon training for
military unresolved issues,
149, 154
Naval War College master's
degree program, 51
in Second Infantry Division,
Korea, 11–15
as Special Assistant
to the President for
Counterterrorism and
Transnational Threats, of
NSC, 157
Wadi al Khirr Airfield
mission and, 92–97
Miller, Kate, 53, 84, 88, 108,
148, 196, 216–217
children with, 51
evening ritual with, 51–52
meeting and marriage to,
15–16
Milley, Mark, 164
on Afghan Army collapse,
160
al-Baghdadi raid and, 162,
165, 167, 170, 174–176
as CJCS, 159
on Iran bomber task force
mission, 201
on Iran potential American
forces attack, 199,
202–203
January 6 riot and, 215–219
at Trump, D., meeting on
Iran, 197
on USS *Nimitz*, 202–203
missiles

of China, 233
Iraq War with strikes of,
90
Mission first, men always
slogan, 150, 153
modern warfare, SOFs and
realities of, 146
Mogadishu
SEAL conversation in,
193–194
SOF operators death in,
49
moral guilt, as Army service
unresolved issue, 149,
151–152, 155
MPD. *See* DC Metropolitan
Police Department
Mueller, Kayla, 168–169, 177
Mulholland, John, 92
on DOD IW, 142
as SOFs commander, 139

National Counterterrorism
Center, 184
on Afghanistan 800 military
personnel, 159
National Guard troops. *See
also* District of Columbia
National Guard
active-duty military transfer
to, 245–246
National Security Agency,
military separation of,
242–243
National Security Council
(NSC)
Bolton as Advisor for, 158
CIA sidelining of, 162–164

Miller, C., as Special
Assistant to the President
for Counterterrorism and
Transnational Threats, 157
national security structure
Goldwater and Nichols DOD
reforms, 229–230
of smaller, more nimble
Armed Forces, 238–239
Naval War College, Miller, C.,
master's degree program
at, 51
Navy SEAL team (SEAL),
88. *See also* Special
Reconnaissance SEALs
mission
characteristics of, 123
conversation in Mogadishu,
193–194
Korangal Valley SR mission
and missing, 114–134
Trump, D., approval of
Yemen raid by, 166
Yemen raid and Owens, W.,
death, 166
neoconservative
Bolton as, 158
Iraq War responsibility of,
108
neo-isolationism foreign
policy, of Trump, D.,
189
new world order vision, of
Bush, George H. W., 21
Nichols, Bill, 229–230
Nimitz, USS, Iran and
American forces potential
attack, 199, 202–203

9/11. *See* September 11, 2001
nontraditional warfare, Office
 of Strategic Services and,
 236
Noriega, Manuel, 52
North Korea, nuclear arsenal
 of, 239
NSC. *See* National Security
 Council
nuclear arsenal
 of North Korea and Iran,
 239
 Russia power and, 239
nuclear arsenal upgrade, 239,
 241
 ground element obsolete, 240
 satellite technology for, 240
 Technological Revolution
 support of, 240

Obama, Barack, 145, 147
Objective Rhino, in
 Afghanistan, 55
O'Brien, Robert
 al-Baghdadi raid and, 162
 at Trump, D., meeting on
 Iran, 197
ODA. *See* Operational
 Detachment Alpha
Office of Strategic Services,
 nontraditional warfare of,
 236
The Old Guard. *See* 3rd United
 States Infantry Regiment
Omar, Mullah, 55, 74
 army at Kandahar, 67
101st Airborne Division, in
 Vietnam, 12–13

140-pound backpacks load,
 E&E exercise, 32–33,
 36–37
Operation Desert Storm
 Highway of Death during,
 36
 Strategic Reconnaissance
 teams in, 30
Operation Just Cause (1989),
 to depose Noriega, 52
Operation RED WINGS. *See also*
 Special Reconnaissance
 SEALs mission
 for Ahmad Shah location
 and capture, 114
 Lone Survivor film, 114
 SEALs missing in, 114
 technologies and, 134–135
Operational Detachment
 Alpha (ODA) 573
 AQ at Kandahar Hospital
 raid by, 75–86
 Miller, C., as Detachment
 Commander of, 26–28
Operational Detachment
 Alpha (ODA) 574, 62–63
 Afghan security forces
 training by, 77
 Arghandab River British fort
 assault by, 67
Owens, Bill, 129, 134
Owens, William, 166

PACE. *See* Primary, Alternate,
 Contingency, and
 Emergency
pack mules, for SR SEALs
 recovery team, 125–126

Patel, Kash, 217
Paxton, Chip, 41
  Socratic leadership style of,
    42
peacetime, live ammunition
    carry prohibition in,
    31–32
Peaks, Matt, 66
  Arghandab River British fort
    attack plan, 67–68
Pelosi, Nancy, ix–x
Pence, Mike
  on January 6 riot, 221
  prayer before al-Baghdadi
    raid, 166–167
Pentagon
  budget and money influence
    at, 144–145
  description of, 140
  layers of bureaucracy in,
    140–141, 147
  Trump, D., foreign policy
    fight from, 203–204
Pershing, John, 185
Petraeus, David
  COIN manual of, 144
  Iraq commander 2007-2009,
    144
Phase O shape, in military
    campaign, 90
Phase I deter, in military
    campaign, 90
Phase II seize initiative, in
    military campaign, 90
Phase III dominate, in military
    campaign, 90–91
Phase IV stabilize, in military
    campaign, 90–91

Phase V enable civil authority,
    in military campaign, 90
politicization, of Armed Forces,
    109
politics, military leaders
    participation in, 247
Pompeo, Mike
  al-Baghdadi raid and,
    176
  on Iran potential American
    forces attack, 199
  at Trump, D., meeting on
    Iran, 197
Pottinger, Matt, 171–174,
    199–200
Powell, Colin
  Gulf War and, 21
  Highway of Death aerial
    firepower attack called off
    by, 36
  on Weapons of Mass
    Destruction, 88–89
Predator drone
  ISR assets of, 94–95
  Trump, D., viewing of
    al-Baghdadi raid by,
    170–174
  Wadi al Khirr
    reconnaissance flights
    over, 94–95
press release, on Kandahar
    Hospital raid, 84–85
Primary, Alternate,
    Contingency, and
    Emergency (PACE)
    methods, 60
Provincial Reconstruction
    Team, at Asadabad, 111

al-Qaeda (AQ)
Acting Secretary of
Defense on end to war
with, 187
CIA and hostage rescue
from, 163
at Kandahar, 67
kill objective for seven
senior leaders of, 163
leaders escape from
Kandahar, 75
naivete about values,
motivations, willpower
of, 76
raid for fighters at Kandahar
hospital, 75–86
Quick Reaction Force (QRF)
for January 6 riot, 212
on SR SEALs recovery team,
121

radio men, in A Teams
antenna theory and, 34
knowledge of, 34
meteororology knowledge
of, 34
two common shots per day,
33–35
wave propagation theory
and, 34
Radwaniyah Palace Complex,
of Hussein, 105
as compound, 106
looting of, 106
Operations Center in,
106–107
Rangers, 9
characteristics of, 123

reconnaissance detachment,
on SR SEALs recovery
team, 123, 127
rifle platoon, on SR SEALs
recovery team, 123
Reagan, Ronald, 240–241
Relief-in-Place/Transfer-of-
Authority (RIP/TOA),
JSOTF command rotation
and, 117
Republican Guard compound,
in Baghdad, 99, 102
Reserve Officer Training Corps
(ROTC)
mandatory universal service
in, 246
military academy closing
and investment in, 246
Miller, C., at Fort Bliss ADA,
16–17
Reserves, active-duty military
transfer to, 245–246
RIP/TOA. *See* Relief-in-Place/
Transfer-of-Authority
Rosen, Jeffrey, 215
ROTC. *See* Reserve Officer
Training Corps
Russia
al-Baghdadi raid and radar
of, 166, 167–168
expansion opposition, 230
nuclear arsenal and power
of, 239

sacrifice Army service
unresolved issues of,
150
Sadr City, in Iraq War, 91

satellite technology, for
    nuclear arsenal upgrade,
    240
Sayyd Alma Kalay village, in
    Afghanistan
    friendly fire incident at, 58
    Joint Direct Attack Munition
        at, 58
    unconventional warfare at,
        57–58
Schumer, Chuck, ix
Scowcroft, Brent, 21
SEAL. *See* Navy SEAL team
Second Infantry Division,
    Korea, 11
    assignments at, 14
    Be Ready to Fight Tonight
        motto of, 12
    Currahees of, 12
    one year tour at, 14–15
    Tactical Operations Center
        night watch officer, 12
2nd Battalion in Karbala Gap,
    in Iraq War, 92–93
Secretary of Defense, Office of
    civilian control importance
        in, 141
    Esper of, 159
    Miller, C., as Acting
        Secretary of Defense,
        184–188, 222
    Trump, D., removal of Esper
        from, 184–185
September 11, 2001 (9/11)
    attack
    COIN after, 144
    military spending reduction
        to pre-, 231

U.S. failure to change after,
    xii
Sessoms, Christian
    combat command gift,
        112–113
    missing SEALs recovery and,
        114, 118, 119, 120–121,
        125
SFG. *See* Special Forces Group
al-Shabaab Africa terrorist
    group, bin Laden ties
    with, 192
Shaffer, Earl, 149
Sherman, Tecumseh, 186
Sherman, William T., 238
Sherzai, Gul Agha "Lion of
    Kandahar"
    south of Kandahar warlord,
        74–75
    A Team Texas 17 Green
        Beret with, 74–75
Shia insurgent groups, 89
    Sunni persecution of, 91
shock and awe campaign, in
    Iraq War, 90
Shortal, John
    Eichelberger book by, 22
    Middle East assignment by, 22
SiLLS. *See* stops, looks, listens,
    and smells
Silver Star, for intense combat,
    13
Sinai Peninsula helicopter
    crash, 222–223
slogans, Army
    Mission first, men always,
        150, 153
    train how you fight, 61–62

Smith, Hank, 74–75
Socratic leadership style, of
  Paxton, 42
SOFs. *See* Special Operation
  Forces
Soleimani, Qasem, 198–199
Somalia
  CT task force in, 192–193
  troop withdrawal order in,
    194–195
Son Tay raid, in Vietnam War,
  165
South Korea DMZ, 10–11
Special Air Service in North
  Africa, during WWII, 30
Special Assistant to
  the President for
  Counterterrorism and
  Transnational Threats, of
  NSC, 157
Special Forces Group (SFG). *See
  also* A Teams, of SFGs
  A team at Asadabad, 111
  A Teams of 3rd Battalion
    Operations Officer, 87
  Iraq War challenge of
    getting ahead of armored
    columns, 92
  Karzai and early warning at
    health clinic, 61, 66
  opportunities in, 59
  PACE methods, 60
  tryout for, 58
  Wadi al Khirr as significant
    mission of, 92–97
Special Forces Group, 3rd (3rd
  SFG), A Team in Iraq War,
  112, 114

Special Forces Group, 5th (5th
  SFG). *See also* A Teams, of
  3rd Battalion, 5th SFG
  blue-collar, working class
    individuals in, 25
  borderline anti-authority
    of, 27
  CIB of team members of, 27
  competence and
    commitment importance
    in, 27
  E&E plan exercise of, 29–43
  Kuwaiti Army trained and
    advised by, 28
  manufactured crisis for, 29
  Middle East desert
    environment for, 25
  Miller, C., as Company
    Commander at, 51
Special Operation Forces
  (SOFs)
  Acting Secretary of Defense
    on influence elevation of,
    188
  Afghanistan daylight flight,
    56–57
  Africa ambush of team of,
    192
  CAPE and, 145–147
  Iraq War elements of, 92
  modern warfare realities of,
    146
  Mulholland as commander
    of, 139
Special Reconnaissance
  (SR) SEALs mission, in
  Korangal Valley, 114–134
  civilian compromise in, 116

civilian contact options, 115
contingency plans for
    compromise, 115
E&E protocol, 116
fated populated area
    insertion, 115
JSOTF on bad idea of,
    114–115
rescue helicopter shot down
    in, 116, 118, 130
Special Reconnaissance (SR)
    SEALs recovery team
Afghan commandos on, 119,
    120, 123, 125, 130–131
CONOP request, 120, 121
downed helicopter deaths,
    130
fire worm for, 122
flying column exhaustion,
    130
Green Berets exhaustion in,
    123–124
Navy SEALS on, 119, 123,
    127
pack mules for, 125–126
QRF on, 121
Ranger platoon fly in around
    helicopter crash site, 130
Ranger reconnaissance
    detachment on, 123, 127
Ranger rifle platoon on, 123
SEAL Luttrell rescue,
    131–134, 135
Sessoms on, 114, 118, 119,
    120–121, 125
SFG A and B teams on, 123
Star Wars. *See* Strategic
    Defense Initiative

statesmen, January 6 riot
    response from, xi
stops, looks, listens, and smells
    (SiLLS) stop, 32
Strategic Defense Initiative
    (Star Wars), 237
Strategic Reconnaissance
    teams, 30
Strickland, Dave, 88, 102
suicide vest detonation
    al-Baghdadi wearing of, 171,
        173–174
    results of, 171–172
Sunni Muslims
    al-Baghdadi as leader of, 168
    Shias persecution by, 91
surveillance, IC of citizens, 242
Swatek, Bruce, 96
Syria
    Baghdad mercenaries of,
        101–102
    al-Baghdadi raid and radar
        of, 166, 167–168
Syverson, Paul, 100, 223

tactical airlift, MC-130 Combat
    Talons in USAF, 93–94
Tactical Operations Center
    night watch officer, in
    Second Infantry Division,
    Korea, 12
Taliban
    Afghan Army and, 161
    allegiance switching by
        fighters, 68–70, 161
    defeat of, 161
    leadership escape from
        Kandahar, 75

tanks, Iraq War with, 90
TCPs. *See* traffic control points
Technological Revolution,
    nuclear arsenal support
    from, 240
technology
    Army War College on
        invincibility of, 138
    Operation RED WINGS and,
        134–135
    techno-warriors delusions,
        134–135
Tehran American Embassy
    failed rescue attempt, 2
    Iranian revolutionaries
        storming, 1–2
terrorism. *See also* September 11,
    2001 attack; *specific terrorist*
    border defense and, 232
Texas 17 Green Beret A Team
    with Sherzai guerilla army,
        74–75
    Smith as leader of, 74–75
Third Infantry Division,
    Baghdad capture by, 87,
        99
3rd SFG. *See* Special Forces
    Group, 3rd
3rd United States Infantry
    Regiment (The Old
    Guard), 52
    Alpha Company appearance,
        showmanship in, 18–19
    ceremonial unit of, 17
    Cordon Platoon of, 19–20
    Killed-In-Action burials by, 22
Thunder Run, into Baghdad,
    101, 103

Tomb of Unknown Soldier,
    at Arlington Cemetery, 17
Toyota Corollas, Fedayeen use
    of, 99
Traditional Warfare, of
    military, 142
TRADOC. *See* Training and
    Doctrine Command
traffic control points (TCPs),
    DC National Guard
    postings for January 6
    riot, 211–212
train how you fight slogan, of
    Army, 61–62
Training and Doctrine
    Command (TRADOC),
    Thurman of, 16
Truman, Harry, 247
Trump, Donald
    Africa hostage rescue
        mission and Esper, 184
    Africa military personnel
        removal order, 192–193
    America First worldview,
        181, 182
    al-Baghdadi raid Presidential
        address, 177–178
    Biden 2020 election victory
        question by, 205
    description of, 172–173,
        177–178
    efforts to end Afghanistan
        War, 158
    Esper and frustration of,
        181–182
    on January 6 riot DC
        National Guard numbers,
        213–214

Lafayette Square incident
and, 182
media on martial law
election conspiracy,
209–210
meeting on Iran attack on
American forces, 199–200
meeting on Iran uranium
enrichment purity,
196–197
military spending and,
230–231
neo-isolationism foreign
policy of, 189
NSC and senior advisor
for counterterrorism,
157
on penalties for joining ISIS,
178–179
Pentagon foreign policy fight
with, 203–204
SEAL raid into Yemen
approval, 166
Twitter diplomacy of, 200
U.S. service members as
suckers accusation,
183–184
White House Situation
Room for al-Baghdadi raid
and, 162, 165
Twitter diplomacy, of Trump,
D., 200

UN. *See* United Nations
unconventional warfare
at Sayyd Alma Kalay, 57–58
United Nations (UN), Bolton as
Ambassador to, 158

United States (U.S.). *See also*
America new way forward
proposals
Afghan Army necessary
support from, 160
empire of ideas collapse,
227
failure to change after 9/11,
xii
military overextension,
227
optimism about, 251–252
unprotected borders of,
227
universal service, in America
AmeriCorps service
requirement, 228
cost of, 228–229
mandatory ROTC at
federally funded
universities, 246
universities, mandatory ROTC
at federally funded, 246
unrestricted warfare, of China,
236, 237
uranium enrichment purity,
Trump, D., on Iran,
196–197
U.S. *See* United States
U.S. Air Force (USAF) Special
Operations Weather Team,
104
U.S. Air Force (USAF) Special
Tactics
MC-130 Combat Talons in
tactical airlift of, 93–94
Wadi al Khirr condition
survey by, 96

U.S. Air Force (*Continued*)
  year long training program,
    46–47
U.S. Central Command
  (USCENTCOM), on
  al-Baghdadi raid, 175,
  177
U.S. Interagency-Afghan
  Counterterrorism force, at
  Asadabad, 111
U.S. Marine Corps, Operation
  RED WINGS operation,
  114–134
USAF. *See* U.S. Air Force
USCENTCOM. *See* U.S. Central
  Command

veteran unresolved issues,
    148, 153
  betrayal, 149–150
  feeling of sacrifice, 150
  leadership guilt for
    casualties, 150
  Miller, C., marathon training
    for, 149, 154
  moral guilt, 149, 151–152,
    155
Vietnam War, 1, 10
  101st Airborne Division in,
    12–13
  Son Tay raid, 165
  Zais, Melvin, and Battle
    of Hamburger Hill,
    12–13
  Zais, Mick, in, 13
volunteer army in protracted
    war, mental health and,
    153–154

Wadi al Khirr Airfield, Iraq
  FLS at, 92
  incoming transport planes
    for, 96–97
  Predator reconnaissance
    flights over, 94–95
  Swatek as Ground Tactical
    Commander at, 96
  USAF Special Tactics survey
    of condition, 96
Wallace, George, 247
war. *See also specific war*
  digital, 62–63
  as horrible waste, 154
  Lee on, 152
  Majors planning of, 89
  military on solution of,
    109
  military technology-centric,
    135–136
  volunteer army mental
    health in protracted,
    153–154
warrant officer, 29
wave propagation theory,
  radio men and, 34
Weapons of Mass Destruction,
  Powell on, 88–89
West Point, Zais, Mick, as
  instructor at, 13–14
White House Situation Room
  Trump, D., and, 162, 165
  Trump, M., in al-Baghdadi
    raid meeting, 173,
    175–176
Williams, Tim, 88, 97, 102
Wilson, Woodrow, 190
Wolfe, Chad, 215

world map, for American
    forces locations, 200
World War II (WWII)
  British Long Range Desert
    Group in, 30
  CIB creation of, 10
  D-Day, 10
  Devil's Brigade in, 119
  Special Air Service in North
    Africa during, 30

Zais, Melvin, as four-star
  general in, 12

Zais, Melvin
  of 101st Airborne Division in
    Vietnam, 12–13
  as WWII four-star general, 12
Zais, Mitchell "Mick," 12
  in Vietnam War, 13
  as West Point instructor, 13–14

Christopher C. Miller served as Acting Secretary of Defense under President Donald Trump. A former Special Forces Commander and a proud Green Beret, Miller was the first of his generation—the generation that fought our nation's enemy's face-to-face in the streets of Baghdad and the mountains of Afghanistan—to serve as a Cabinet official responsible for America's security. Prior to his appointment as Acting Secretary of Defense, the Senate unanimously confirmed Miller on August 6, 2020, as the Director of the National Counterterrorism Center, where he was responsible for defending the nation from terrorist attacks.